Using Lacan, Reading Fiction

JAMES M. MELLARD

Using Lacan, Reading Fiction

UNIVERSITY OF ILLINOIS PRESS

URBANA AND CHICAGO

This book is printed on acid-free paper.

Library of Congress Cataloging-in-Publication Data

Mellard, James M.
  Using Lacan, reading fiction / James M. Mellard.
    p.   cm.
  Includes bibliographical reference (p.   ). Includes index.
  ISBN 0-252-01786-2 (alk. paper). — ISBN 0-252-06173-X (pbk. : alk.
paper)
    1. American fiction—History and criticism—Theory, etc.
  2. English fiction—History and criticism—Theory, etc.
  3. Lacan, Jacques, 1901-   —Contributions in criticism.   I. Title.
PS371.M46   1991
823'.009–dc20   90-11311

For Sue, whose being suggests, contra Lacan,
that *the* woman does exist

CONTENTS

PREFACE

While there are now many books on the psychoanalytic theories of the French-Freudian Jacques Lacan, most of those books focus on the theories as theories. They are on Lacan, not on the ways in which Lacanian principles might be used in the reading of literary works. That is as it should be. The fact is, Lacan's writings (literally, "writings"— *Ecrits*, as he called a large part of his life's work) are quite difficult, and the first task of any Lacanian criticism is to master the theoretical structures. Happily for those who prefer to "use" theoretical structures for the reading of specific, sometimes recalcitrant, always concrete pieces of literature, the critical exposition of Lacan has been accomplished to the point that one may more or less safely begin the use of the theories. Much of this interpretive work on Lacan has been accomplished by scholars such as Anthony Wilden, who virtually invented Lacan for Americans (but who no longer subscribes to Lacanianism—if he ever did), Anika Lemaire, who offered the first book-length explication, one that in the seventies became easily available to Anglo-American readers, and Eugen Bär, whose early, very long essay is probably not cited often enough. Since these there are many who have built on or worked around the early studies; among those whose work appears in English are Bice Benvenuto and Roger Kennedy, Christine van Boheemen, Catherine Clément, Robert Con Davis, Shoshana Felman, Jerry Aline Flieger, Jane Gallop, André Green, Julia Kristeva, Annette Lavers, Juliet Flower MacCannell, David Macey, Jeffrey Mehlman, John Muller, William Richardson, Stuart Schneiderman, and Antoine Vergote. There are many others, but I shall list one final name in this invocation of pioneering Lacanian scholars: Ellie Ragland-Sullivan. It is now her book *Jacques Lacan and the Philosophy of Psychoanalysis* (1986) that becomes the most complete synoptic overview of Lacan in English. After Ragland-Sullivan, the development of a book such as *Using Lacan, Reading Fiction* has become immeasurably easier—and, perhaps, particularly in the context of all the works of the others, more necessary.

Behind *Using Lacan, Reading Fiction,* as surely behind other books, is a story of sorts. I came upon Lacan's work largely because of my interest in tropes, figures of speech such as metaphor and metonymy, synecdoche and irony. Working in the early eighties on the essays that eventually became the chapters of *Doing Tropology* (1987), I began to study Lacanian theory because it focuses on language very intently, especially its uses of two of those four tropes—metaphor and metonymy—not only as the foundation of language use, but also of the functioning of the unconscious. Since my interest is mainly in the ways we may use any theory to understand features of specific works, when I found that I could use even a rudimentary knowledge of Lacan effectively to read rather difficult texts, I began to feel that learning Lacanian theory in more detail would be a fruitful project for me and others. While my story does not belong to that "genre" of "adventures of insight" I refer to in my conclusion, I suspect that it follows the pattern of all stories in which people identify a new realm of knowledge, attempt to learn it, and eventually arrive at the point of what—filled with trepidation—one might call "wise mastery," an understanding inmixed with irony, if not skepticism, and with humility in the face of the indeterminacy of ourselves as subjects and the subjects of our knowledge.

I have tried to organize *Using Lacan, Reading Fiction* as simply as practicable. The first chapter offers an introduction to the basic premises and organizing concepts within Lacanian thought, as well as an introduction to a Lacanian poetics and critical practice. For purposes of better explanation, the portions of the chapter devoted to the theory are marked by a deliberate redundancy. Though the two long sections in some ways repeat each other, they do so with a difference. The first long section is abstractly discursive. It stresses Lacan's premises regarding sign and subject, the crucial importance of language to the analytical process, and the interrelations of the Saussurean notions of signification Lacan assimilated to his own notions of human subjectivity. The second long section goes over much of the same material as the first, but the use of diagrammatic schemas offers a Lacan more accessible to the critical reader. Here, the essay lays out in steps the essential constitution of the subject and suggests the underlying narrative history that goes along with it. My use of diagrammatic schemas in this section may be troubling to many readers. Lacan's use of schemas is itself troubling to many who have studied his work. But I have

come to the conclusion that the essential unity of Lacan's thought may
be seen most clearly in the interrelationships of the various schemas.
I have not always been enthusiastic about some of his more complicated schemas (those of desire, for example), but, somewhat grudgingly,
I have come to see that even these have an integral relation to the
whole structure of Lacanian theory. I especially think that the schema
sometimes called L (and more descriptively ought to be called Z) and
the one called R are very useful. Not only can one see in them the
transformations of fundamental ideas emerging from simpler schemas
(the famous algorithm S/s, for example), but also one can see that the
almost mathematical symmetry of structural relations may be related
to the logical square employed by others such as A.-J. Greimas, for
example. I also happen to believe that simple schemas (as E. D. Hirsch
demonstrates in chapter 2 of *Cultural Literacy*) are helpful in visualizing
and then remembering and using concepts. The sequence of schemas
I offer as a synthesis of Lacan's fully articulated (but never fully conscious) subject represents my attempt, beginning with Lacan, to display
almost every important structuring concept (subject, other, ego, Other),
as well as some concepts that may best be called thematic (desire, law,
eros, thanatos). Moreover, on a topographic "model" of the Lacanian
subject that finally purports to be inclusive, I even try to designate the
most important "functions"—the mirror phase and the Oedipus complex, which are "in" the structure only in the way that energy is in a
body. It is certain, finally, that my incremental schematizations will
seem to oversimplify, perhaps even to trivialize, but that is a risk I
gladly take in exchange for an increased understanding of the order-
liness of Lacanian thought.

The remaining long section of the Introduction falls into several
related subparts. The focus of the entire section is the issue of a Lacanian critical practice. In looking at that issue, I have also addressed
the interrelations of text, reader, and current theories of intertextuality
as they relate to interpretation in literature and psychoanalysis itself.
Though frequently disagreeing with him, I use some remarks by Peter
Brooks from a recent essay to establish the parameters of my discourse.
More to my point, however, is the work of Ellie Ragland-Sullivan,
who has provided us with a densely argued case for a Lacanian poetics.
Ragland-Sullivan's notion of such a poetics is built on Lacan's concept
of the ego (*moi*) and the premise that one's identity is a text formed
mainly by language. Finally, addressing the matter of interpretation

itself, I look at several problems subsumed in the concept of "allegory." My position, shared with various theorists, is that all interpretation is essentially allegorical in the sense that interpretation "translates" one set of data into another set of terms. The structure of allegory or interpretation, I shall suggest, is built upon the Saussaurean algorithm— S/s—that underlies all Lacanian thought. But these—allegory and interpretation—are themselves subsumed in the relations defining language and, in turn, textuality. In a sequence in which I advert to important essays by Hans Kellner and Robert Con Davis, I conclude by suggesting that all interpretation is finally textual and is allied to what can only be called a textual unconscious. As interpreters, we are always in search of master codes, whether social, political, philosophical, or, yes, psychoanalytic. Ironically, given Lacan's perception of the Other as finally unknowable, one has to conclude that not even Lacanian analysis can be regarded as some infallible master code. It is simply one more code that we use in our ongoing hermeneutic activity.

The three chapters that comprise the body of this book address the "Reading Fiction" half of my title. These chapters, each rather long, with the third almost double either of the first two, may also increase the difficulties for readers, though I think not, for they are not "difficult" in the way that much modern interpretive practice may seem. These chapters depend heavily upon the theoretical material in the Introduction, for they assume a Lacanian epistemology instead of arguing for it or setting it out in detail. Chapter 1 depends on the topography of the subject given in the Introduction's theoretical sections. My earnest hope is that readers will have been sufficiently prepared for the intensive, concrete look here at some of the varied textual "inscriptions" of the subject found in Nathaniel Hawthorne's *The Scarlet Letter*. Those inscriptions are exemplified in a work canonical in American literature, to be sure, but also canonical as a text for rich psychoanalytic interpretation. The range of analysis it permits is extraordinary, and the relative purity in Lacanian terms of the discourses of particular subjects—Pearl, Hester, Dimmesdale, and Chillingworth— is especially useful in modeling those discourses. These characters, I think, provide exemplars for Lacanian analysis, just as, before, they had provided them for standard Freudian analysis.

If one feels that the later analysis (in chapter 2) of another character's seemingly anachronistic constitutive formation might be somewhat too metaphorical, *merely* metaphorical, a similar analysis of Pearl ought to seem only "natural" (though, for Lacan, nothing in the subject is *natural*), for she is the child seen to emerge as a mature subject out of the cocoon of her infancy. Hawthorne's language richly reveals the emergence of the mirror stage and the Oedipus encounter and resolution. Likewise, Hawthorne's language reveals, equally richly, in the creation of Hester Prynne some of the problems any subject encounters in the interrelations of the registers of the Imaginary and the Symbolic, particularly in connection with that concept Lacan has popularized called "the gaze." Lacanian theory also yields much in relation to the two other major characters in the tale. In Arthur Dimmesdale we see Hawthorne limning a character caught in a neurosis, but moving in the end toward a problematical cure. Finally, around Roger Chillingworth one may see the distortion of the subject associated with psychosis, but, ironically, at the same time the function Lacan associates with the analyst and the great Other (*le Grand Autre*). Thus a Lacanian reading of *The Scarlet Letter* not only provides an opening onto important analytic concepts, it also adduces important new insights into the interrelations of the work's major figures.

Chapter 2 addresses in a concrete way problems of the constitution of subjectivity as seen in Henry James's "Beast in the Jungle" and outlined in the Introduction and reviewed in the discussion of Pearl. But the chapter also attempts to go beyond that introductory outline by looking at the history of its fictional subject—John Marcher—in terms that Lacan calls a "countable unity." While consistent with the topographical structures seen earlier, the countable unity of the subject is likely to be less familiar to most readers than other Lacanian concepts. But there are three reasons to employ the notion: first, the enumeration of phases of the subject's history makes the telling of that history more comprehensible; second, it shows how Lacan consistently undermines any ordinary developmental theories of the subject by his insisting that the "unity of counting" is neither a totalizing nor a permanent unity; third, James's text has been studied fruitfully by various psychological and psychoanalytic critics. But analysis of this text through a Lacanian perspective helps to solve a persistent critical problem, for such analysis shows very clearly that Marcher, in constantly repeating the structures of the mirror stage (though not the actual stage itself), provides the figure of a subject never fully constituted in his resistance to the other registers that mark in a timely way the course of normative human life. Had his psyche learned, as it were, to count to four, he would have married May Bartram and taken his place in an adult world. The story James tells thus permits us to see how the apparent early stage called the mirror phase (in relation to which the register of the Imaginary emerges) is really a psychical "field" in the history of the subject that may dominate the subject into physiological adulthood in such a way as to appear to forestall the Oedipus function, which will appear to be delayed beyond the period regarded as normative in one's life. This tale suggests, therefore, that the Lacanian registers (Imaginary and Symbolic) and the functions (mirror stage and Oedipus complex) must be understood in both their synchronic and diachronic dimensions. Moreover, it suggests that the notion of even a countable unity must remain ontologically and epistemologically tenuous.

In chapter 3 I attempt the impossible—a Lacanian reading to end all Lacanian readings, at least in its "coverage" of the major concepts one associates with Lacan's post-Freudianism. Thus this part of the book presents my effort, through a detailed reading of a single, staggeringly important modernist work, to provide something of a review of the most important Lacanian concepts, namely, the registers Imaginary, Real, and Symbolic in their relations to both the mirror stage and the Oedipus complex. In the process, I discuss a number of other Lacanian concepts through Woolf's exemplifications, including *jouissance,* the *objet petit a,* mourning, and castration (both male and female). Obviously, most of the concepts will have been encountered in previous chapters, but here they are traversed in a much more synoptic way. Moreover, in the three major sections of this chapter, I try to show a little more explicitly how a literary text both has a textual unconscious and creates a textual unconscious in readers, whose unconsciousnesses, though much more vast, are texts much like those found in the richest novels and poems. This part of *Using Lacan, Reading Fiction* is meant, finally, to provide an explanation and illustration of the critical poetics on which all of the prior readings of novels have occurred.

The detailed reading of each of the major sections of *To the Lighthouse* is designed to show that Woolf's text, in its concrete "objects"—which is to say, its *language*—supports a Lacanian allegorical (Imaginary) reading. Thus the first major section focuses on some features of the register Lacan calls the Imaginary as those features—the Oedipus function and objects of desire (connecting to what Lacan calls *objets petit a*), and the four "drive" modes (oral, anal, scopic, and invocatory) of *jouissance*—are exemplified in the language of "The Window," part 1 of Woolf's novel. The second major section focuses on one of the most difficult of Lacan's concepts—the Real; early on Lacan called the Real "the impossible" because in itself it is not symbolizable, but later he came to regard it as an "order" that underlies the Imaginary and Symbolic registers. The section shows how time and the order of brute fact associated with the Real operate in the novel's middle section, "Time Passes," both as those concepts relate to the disappearance (metaphorical) of the subject or "subjectivity" itself in the section and to the problem of death and mourning as it revolves around Mrs. Ramsay. The final major section, in Lacanian terms, is the most comprehensive of the three, for it illustrates the process by which a fully constituted (though, of course, never fully conscious or totally stable) subjectivity emerges. This section addresses once again the problem of the Other, of the father, of the Name-of-the-Father, which, just for the sake of nonsexist consistency, I would call F(ather) to match Lacan's punning M(other). The section, moreover, addresses the problem of the Oedipus and castration, but it adds the perspective of the female to that of the male seen in chapter 2 in John Marcher. Finally, the section takes up the problem of mourning and the relation of the subject to the lost mother/M(other), a problem manifested in Lily Briscoe's grief over the death of Mrs. Ramsay and her reconciliation to it through the Symbolic agency of her art, the painting onto which she puts the last touch as the novel comes to an end. *To the Lighthouse* is a tremendously rich, variously therapeutic text, and my reading of fiction in *Using Lacan, Reading Fiction* appropriately concludes with it.

In my conclusion, I try to broaden the horizon of my interests by looking at issues surrounding Lacan addressed by other scholars. Since my perspective is inevitably gendered male, I have turned to another perspective, to readings by the Lacanian other identified in the female. I look first, for example, at varied explanations of Lacan's "originality" proposed and argued by Shoshana Felman. Next, I consider Catherine Clément's discussion of Lacan the man and his place in a particular intellectual climate, the France of the 1960s and after. Clément's reading is overtly feminist, and some of her conclusions lead me to a more fully articulated feminist study of Lacan, one by Juliet Flower MacCannell. While some of MacCannell's conclusions will surely be controversial to many Lacanians, her approach raises many important questions about patriarchy and any alternative in a matriarchal cultural orientation. Finally, then, I turn to Christine van Boheemen's rather feminist study *The Novel as Family Romance* (1987) to establish that not only can there be a Lacanian criticism, there can also be a Lacanian-based historical criticism. My final section perhaps ought to be regarded as a coda rather than a conclusion because I feel that, though turned over to my gender others in Felman, Clément, MacCannell, and Boheemen, it does not pretend to effect a conclusive statement from the position of the grand Other regarding Lacanian reading or any uses of Lacan in literary theory. For such ultimate statements, we are too much in the middle of what shall remain a contentious time where Lacan and psychoanalytic criticism are concerned, where, really, any theory and any approach to reading shall be subject to almost enervating forms of anxiety. We shall simply have to get on with the work of using Lacan for a time. Eventually, as it has happened with Freud, critics will come to accept a Lacanian hermeneutics as part of their critical culture.

ACKNOWLEDGMENTS

In writing a book such as this, one incurs debts to many people. It seems never possible to name them all. But I would like to name at least some, and I shall hope that those unnamed will neither take umbrage nor, worse, will decide that they would rather not be identified with the work anyway. To begin, I acknowledge *Critical Essays on "The Scarlet Letter,"* edited by David Kesterson (Boston: G. K. Hall, 1988), in which a portion of chapter 1 appeared as "Pearl and Hester: A Lacanian Reading." I also wish to thank two journals—*Style* and *The Newsletter of the Freudian Field*—for permission to reuse portions of reviews that appear, in revised forms, in my concluding essay. Further, I offer my gratitude to those who have read versions of different chapters and offered advice and encouragement. These include Marshall Alcorn, Mark Bracher, Robert Con Davis, Juliet Flower Mac-Cannell, J. Hillis Miller, Ellie Ragland-Sullivan, and Hayden V. White. It is by more than a convention that I consign all the book's defects to my ignorance or intransigence and any felicities of thought or form or style to their helpful interventions. Finally, I wish to recognize and say thanks to Cheryl Fuller and Caroline Critser, who made the writing and editing of the manuscript easier than I thought it could be and more enjoyable than it should be. All other indebtedness is subsumed in my dedication.

INTRODUCTION

But haven't we felt for some time now that, having followed
the ways of the letter in search of Freudian truth, we are getting
very warm indeed, that it is burning all about us?

—Jacques Lacan, *Ecrits: A Selection*

The post-Freudian reinterpretation of psychoanalysis by Jacques Lacan,
apart from any interests one may have in psychology or the social
sciences, has been one of the most stimulating areas of development
in European and Anglo-American literary studies in the last twenty
years. Though Lacan was an influential theorist in France as far back
as the 1930s, his Anglo-American impact did not really begin until
1966, the year of his monumental *Ecrits*.[1] But in that year, too, along
with several other important French thinkers generally regarded then
as structuralist, including Lucien Goldmann, Roland Barthes, and
Jacques Derrida, Lacan took part in a symposium at Johns Hopkins
University called "The Languages of Criticism and the Sciences of
Man." There, Lacan delivered a lecture (alternately in English and
French) entitled "Of Structure as an Inmixing of an Otherness Prerequisite to Any Subject Whatever." Useful in transmitting Lacan's controversial ideas, "Of Structure as an Inmixing" since has become most
notorious for the typically "Lacanian" metaphor describing his notion
of the unconscious as a lost object, an object barred from consciousness: "The best image to sum up the unconscious is Baltimore in the
early morning" (189). The metaphor caps a story Lacan tells his audience:

When I prepared this little talk for you, it was early in the
morning. I could see Baltimore through the window and it was a
very interesting moment because it was not quite daylight and a
neon sign indicated to me every minute the change of time, and
naturally there was heavy traffic, and I remarked to myself that

exactly all that I could see, except for some trees in the distance, was the result of thoughts, actively thinking thoughts, where the function played by the subjects was not completely obvious. In any case the so-called *Dasein,* as a definition of the subject, was there in this rather intermittent or fading spectator. The best image to sum up the unconscious is Baltimore in the early morning. (189)

In time, such remarks will become intelligible. But since the lecture was not published until 1970, perhaps more important in opening Lacanian thought to a wider audience was Anthony Wilden's *The Language of the Self* (1968). That work included a translation of Lacan's landmark "Function and Field of Speech and Language in Psychoanalysis," the report on his theory that Lacan delivered in Rome in 1953 at the first Congress of the newly founded Société Française de Psychanalyse. Wilden's book also included what is perhaps the first substantial piece in English on Lacan, his long essay "Lacan and the Discourse of the Other," and it included as well roughly seventy pages of Wilden's notes to intricacies in Lacan's text and his thought in general, and, to top it off, a bibliography—focusing on Lacan and structuralist thought—that much facilitated entry to those vexed areas of theory and practice.

Neither Wilden's book nor the "Inmixing" essay started a deluge of Lacanian studies, but the floodgates were at least opened. Anika Lemaire's introductory work *Jacques Lacan* appeared in Belgium in 1970 (though it did not appear in an English translation until 1977), and the American academic Stuart Schneiderman published the important "Afloat with Jacques Lacan" in *Diacritics* in 1971, then shortly after entered a training analysis with Lacan (in 1973), and thus became the only American ever trained by Lacan. Eugen Bär also published an essay in 1971, "The Language of the Unconscious according to Jacques Lacan," and followed it in 1974 with a nearly seventy-five-page introduction, "Understanding Lacan," to rival Wilden's lengthy essay. But as important as any single publication in opening up Lacanian thought was volume 48 of *Yale French Studies* called "French Freud: Structural Studies in Psychoanalysis" (1972). This volume became instrumental because it threw Lacan into a controversy that embroiled academic critics from several subdisciplines. It engaged psychoanalytic and deconstructive critics, to be sure, but perhaps more important it also engaged Americanists who previously were unlikely to have encountered Lacan. The volume's most controversial piece, one that forced Americanists to consider Lacan and Derrida, was Lacan's "Seminar on 'The Purloined Letter,' " translated by Jeffrey Mehlman. The essay (derived from Lacan's *Séminaire* II, of 1954–55) prompted Derrida to swell the gathering flood in 1975 and in turn to lure Barbara Johnson into the turmoil in 1977. Since then, many others have flailed in their wake (see *The Purloined Poe*). While it is impossible to say when the deluge really began, it would now appear that its beginning was at least signaled by the controversy over the Poe seminar. Thus when the English translation of a selection of Lacan's massive *Ecrits* appeared in 1977 as well, it seemed as if the tide of Lacanian thought had visibly risen, even if it had not crested yet. In the 1980s, since the thought itself was far from fully absorbed into the landscape of either Anglo-American psychoanalysis or literary criticism, we have been engaged in discovering precisely what Lacan has deposited on our shores. The 1990s no doubt will tell us.

What is certainly clear today is that many of Lacan's conceptions— of the unconscious, the ego and "the other" (in its two Lacanian forms, "other" and "Other"), the mirror stage and the cognitive "registers" (the Imaginary, the Symbolic, and the Real)—all have become increasingly important in structuralist and post-structuralist, deconstructionist and post-deconstructionist, as well as Marxist, feminist, and postmodernist, critical theories of English and American, not to mention French and other European, academics. Various theorists have embraced Lacan because his rereading of Freud has placed particular emphasis on several elements that constitute us as individuals and social beings. These include the material and structural relations of the subject's "I" to the social "other" and the "Other" of the unconscious, to be sure, but they also include the individual's relations within the family and the social matrix. Finally, and most important, they include the relation of the individual subject to the structure of language within its culture. Since these interests reflect current ideological orientations across several disciplines, Lacan, one must say, is nothing if not *au courant*. But, alas, for those who want to know more of Lacan's thought, he is also nothing if not difficult.

Thus, I shall attempt to outline in what follows some of Lacan's basic premises to prepare for my Lacanian readings of fiction to come in later chapters. By way of introduction of Lacanian theory I shall try to do two basic things. First off, I want to address Lacan's insistence on the agency of language in psychoanalysis and, it must follow, culture in general and literature in particular. It is Lacan's imperative to study language, I think, that makes Lacanian theory so amenable to the reading of works of literature, especially in the analysis of the subject and of human subjectivity in fiction. I begin my discussion with language (and related topics) because it is, from beginning to end, the most basic structural feature of Lacanian principles (in "Of Structure" he says, for instance, "I have never said that the unconscious was an assemblage of words, but that the unconscious is precisely structured" [187]). Second, I want to develop for the critical reader an understanding of Lacan's thematic *topoi* and, especially, the synchronic structure and diachronic narrative Lacan posits for the genesis of the subject. Addressing these essential matters, I believe, will also elucidate the structural and functioning economy existing within language and artistic discourse as seen from within Lacanian thought. Strange as it will seem to many who have begun the study of Lacan, there are in fact systematic regularities in his rereading of Freud. Indeed, the "Freudian truth" burning about us, Lacan demonstrates, is a truth of systemic economy that can be used to analyze any texts, whether literary or clinical.

But once I introduce Lacanian thought, I still must make the transfer to the reading of literature itself. To do that I shall look at the theory of psychoanalytic criticism, then at an outline of a Lacanian poetics, and finally at what Hans Kellner has called the "anxiety of allegory" in critical practice. In considering some of the problematics of psychoanalytic criticism in general, I shall examine an important essay by Peter Brooks. Though a well-known Freudian critic, in going over many of the objections to psychoanalytic criticism to frame his own brand of Freudian "reading," Brooks unwittingly ends up warranting a specifically Lacanian mode of interpretation that depends upon the reciprocity of text and reader's response through the phenomenon of intertextuality and the process known as transference. With various theoretical obstacles cleared away, then, I move on to an outline of a Lacanian poetics drafted by the foremost American Lacanian—Ellie Ragland-Sullivan. This poetics depends upon Lacan's conception of the ego or "self." Though Lacan is antipathetic to traditional notions of the self, the core of Ragland-Sullivan's poetics is the reciprocal process of ego definition emerging in the mirror phase. As between ego and other, so the "magnetism" that exists between text and reader, argues Ragland-Sullivan, functions because each is partial, each dependent on the other for its putative (never completed) completion. This poetics is both transferential and intertextual. The text constitutes the reading subject as the reading subject constitutes the text. The process, in short, is hermeneutic and allegorical: hermeneutic because of the reciprocity of the relations, wherein one position can never establish priority over the other, allegorical because of the structural relation—A is B—of the interpretation to the text.

In the concluding section I take up this issue of allegory and the critics' anxiety before it. That anxiety is a result of our very human need of secure foundations of knowledge. But since human knowledge, human understanding, cannot avoid the dichotomy of the Lacanian, structuralist algorithm—S/s—we are destined always to face that anxiety, for there is no crossing the bar, the gap, between the signifier and the signified, the text and its referential base, even the text and the very material that constitutes it as a text. Thus, as critics, as commentators on texts, we generate other texts. So interpretation or commentary is intertextual, a relation of texts to texts. The activity of critical commentary belongs to the register of the Imaginary, therefore. It is always dependent on an imagined—mirror stage—identity of one text or commentary with another text or commentary. But underlying this Imaginary relation of presumptive identity is another relation, that of the two to another register, the register of the Symbolic, the domain of the Name-of-the-Father, the Other, and the Unconscious. A psychoanalytic theory of interpretation finally rests on a theory of a textual unconscious, an unconscious that is shared by both text and critic, one mediated by language, of course, but one created between text and critic (as between analysand and analyst) in a process like the analytic transference. Peter Brooks speaks of the "human stakes" of reading literature, and it seems to me that precisely here—in the deeply transferential relation between text and reader, the relation effected in reading itself—lies the human value of any interpretation, but most particularly the psychoanalytic commentary. For what the reader finds in the text, the text has found in the reader as well, and what both reader and text find in each other are those "truths" of the human subject discovered by Freud and reinterpreted by Jacques Lacan. In life as in interpretation, these truths are perhaps nothing other than reconfigurations of the mirror stage and the Oedipal triangulation, the endless recapitulations of the dialectic of Desire and Law in human subjectivity.

The Insistence of Language

> The unconscious is neither primordial nor instinctual; what it knows
> about the elementary is no more than the elements of the signifier.
>
> —Jacques Lacan, *Ecrits: A Selection*

Jacques Lacan claims not to have replaced Freud but merely to have
rediscovered the essential Freud—the Freudian truth—that Lacan
claims most psychoanalysts since the 1930s have ignored. Though Lacan manages to review virtually every major text of Freud in the nearly
thirty years of the *Séminaires* (1953-80), he finds his most theoretically
essential Freud in the early writings, especially in *The Interpretation
of Dreams* (1900), *The Psychopathology of Everyday Life* (1901), and
Jokes and their Relation to the Unconscious (1905). He says of these
three, for example, that "one might call [them] canonical with regard
to the unconscious" (*Ecrits: A Selection* 170). In his "Function and
Field" essay, Lacan says in the same vein that *Jokes* "remains the most
unchallengeable of [Freud's] works" not only "because it is the most
transparent, a work in which the effect of the unconscious is demonstrated to us to its most subtle confines," but also and more important because "the face it reveals to us is that of the spirit in the
ambiguity conferred on it by language" (*Ecrits: A Selection* 60). Indeed,
the core of Lacan's reinterpretation of Freudian theory, suggested in
his comments on Freud's work, is its insistence in analysis not on the
primacy of events, but on the primacy of language. That insistence
focuses both on language as it operates on the axes of "connection"
and "substitution" (170) within the subject as a means of access from
the unconscious to consciousness and on language as it functions as
the agency of exchange between the subject and another subject, including, in the clinical situation, the analyst and, in the interpretation
of literature, the reader.

In this emphasis on language, Lacan may well speak for the dominant
ideology of our time, for ours is an epoch that valorizes the word even
as it denies *the* word, the *Logos* of metaphysical origins. The linguist
Emile Benveniste has made the sort of claim that typifies Lacan's position—in its logocentrism if not its implicit sexism. "We can never get
back to man separated from language," Benveniste says, "and we shall
never see him inventing it. We shall never get back to man reduced
to himself and exercising his wits to conceive of the existence of another. It is a speaking man whom we find in the world, a man speaking

to another man, and language provides the very definition of man" (224). Lacan's version of such a premise is simply that "whether it sees it as an instrument of healing, of training, or of exploration in depth, psychoanalysis has only a single medium: the patient's speech" (*Ecrits: A Selection* 40). Indeed, in another place Lacan adverts to the bromide that "psychoanalysis is a 'talking cure,' " and that "unless we are to deny the very essence of psychoanalysis, we must make use of language as our guide through the study [even] of the so-called pre-verbal structures" (Lacan and Granoff 266-67). It is not, of course, that Lacan's master, Freud, disregards language, for language, as John Forrester demonstrates in *Language and the Origins of Psychoanalysis* (1980), is very important to him. Lacan himself notes, for example, that "Freud has shown us and taught that symptoms speak in words, that, like dreams, they are constructed in phrases and sentences" (Lacan and Granoff 267). But, despite Lacan's emphasis on the Freudian truth, there is a difference between Freud and Lacan. Freud is always trying to go through language to something else—actual persons, events, or happenings, for example—that accounts for traumas in the subject. Lacan, by contrast, relegates those presumptive "original" sources to the same dustbin as, later on and under the influence of Lacan, Derrida relegates the *primum mobile* in the metaphysics of origins. Origins can never be available to us (even if they exist); what is available, Lacan would say, is a capacity for symbolization, expressed in language, that covers over the metaphysical or ontological gap where an origin might have been. Thus, Lacan would say, we must always forget primal scenes and recognize instead the primacy of the language of the subject, for it is in language that the subject, in the most philosophical sense of the word, subsists. What I want to demonstrate, then, is that the structuralist "formula" for language—the sign—underlies virtually all Lacanian thought regarding the subject—that is, human subjectivity.

Lacan's fundamental analytic principle is that the unconscious is like a language and can be understood only in the ways language itself is understood. In his essay "The Agency of the Letter in the Unconscious or Reason since Freud," Lacan makes the claim upon which his theory of psychoanalysis is based. There he says that "what the psychoanalytic experience discovers in the unconscious is the whole structure of language" (*Ecrits: A Selection* 147). By this statement Lacan does not mean to claim that the unconscious is a language, but only that it is structured like a language and functions in similar ways. These ways are akin to the Freudian concepts of condensation and displacement, mechanisms whose parallel linguistic concepts involve the tropes metaphor and metonymy. These tropes are represented in the symbolic "letter." For Lacan, the letter is the "material support that concrete discourse borrows from language" (147). But the letter is both metaphoric and metonymic, not merely one or the other. As metaphor, it substitutes itself for the thing it represents or, more properly, re-presents; as metonymy, it involves the displacement of meaning in a chain of significations that may be epitomized in the letter-by-letter formation of words or, on a higher level of diachronic organization, the word-by-word formation of sentences. Thus the letter stands, whether as metaphor or as metonymy, for the word or words upon which access to the unconscious depends.

In the beginning for Lacan, then, is the word, though it is not the classical *Logos* at all. It is not an Idealized word, either. "The word," Lacan says, "is a gift of language and language is not immaterial. It is subtle matter, but matter nonetheless. It can fecundate the hysterical woman, it can stand for the flow of urine or for excrement withheld. Words can also suffer symbolic wounds" (Lacan and Granoff 269). For Lacan, then, the agency of the letter is intertwined with acts of being in ways suggested by Lacan's playfulness with words: *lettre,* for Lacan, becomes *l'etre* (being) and, toward the end of the career, when language becomes *lalangue* and linguistics *linguisterie,* these both become *litiere* (litter). As he writes elsewhere, however, it is from the Freudian truth that Lacan draws the understanding that words "are the object through which one seeks for a way to handle the unconscious. Not even the meaning of words, but words in their flesh, in their material aspect." Lacan's summation of his view of the determinative place of language is very explicit: "words are the only material of the unconscious," and so it becomes easy to see why Lacan—perhaps, someday, even more than Freud—may be such a fruitful source of critical interpretation of the subject in literature ("Of Structure as an Inmixing" 187). For that subject is never anything but a construct of words to which only words may give us access.

Lacan generally is thought (a thought only partially accurate) to take his view of language from the structural anthropologist Claude Lévi-Strauss and the linguistic structuralists, particularly Ferdinand de Saussure and Roman Jakobson, but perhaps also Emile Benveniste.[2] The relationship between linguistics and psychoanalysis is very important for Lacan, though it is not the same relation for him as for others. For one thing, as Annette Lavers has noted, "if Lacan, like other structuralists, acknowledges linguistics as the scientific foundation of all other human sciences," Lacan reverses the priority and "views psychoanalysis as the psychological foundation of linguistics" (277). For another thing, Lacan—in a very real sense—simply invents his own view of language, his own linguistics, one that in *Séminaire* XX (*Encore*) he dubs as that mystifying *"linguisterie"* (*Feminine Sexuality* 20). Even so, Lacan shares some of the views of the structural linguists. For the structuralists—whose prime authority is Saussure—language is given to or imposed upon human beings from birth: it may be a human creation, but no single individual creates it. Moreover, though arbitrarily forced upon the individual, language has structure (itself arbitrary) that permits linguistics to claim the status of a science.

In his *Course in General Linguistics,* Saussure revolutionized for the structuralists the study of language when, in a statement surprising for its simplicity, he adduced for linguists the theorem "The bond between the signifier and the signified is arbitrary" (67). His theorem implies a formula (never actually given in *Course*) that is taken over by Lacan, but Lacan performs a crucial change on the relation of signifier and signified. He inverts the relation. Saussure shows the referential concept (signified) as taking precedence *over* the word (signifier), and thus he posits that the word is subordinate to what Saussure calls the "concept." In his closest approach to a formula-structure, Saussure pictures a tree above a line, and below the line writes a Latin word for tree: *arbor* (see *Course* 67). By contrast, Lacan places his symbol for signifier (uppercase *S*) over the symbol for signified (lowercase *s*). Thus, not only by the inversion, but also by the contrast of the upper- to the lowercase, Lacan connotes the subordination of signified to signifier, and, what is more, thus suggests that in the relation of the sign to some presumed "reality," the sign or what is usually called the signifier is epistemologically dominant. Lacan is blunt about the priority of language over "reality." He says in one way that "the concept . . . engenders the thing"; he says in another way that "the world of words . . . creates the world of things" (*Ecrits: A Selection* 65). Thus while Lacan—and we after him—may posit a primal real apart from words or signs or even perception itself, there is for Lacan another real, a symbolic Real that comes to have priority over the first because of its being available to apprehension by the subject. That apprehension occurs only through signs and symbols. So as Lacan writes S/s, we must also posit an R/r, a symbolized Real that veils—or is cut off from—a primordial unsymbolized and unsymbolizable real. In this respect, as I shall discuss shortly, Lacan appears to mediate between two polar philosophical positions, a naive materialism on the one hand and a naive idealism on the other. He has sometimes been regarded as both by different critics.

Ostensibly following Saussure, then, Lacan produces what he calls his "algorithm." That algorithm may be taken as the kernel, a monad or synecdoche, not only of all Lacanian thought, but, as we shall eventually observe, of the allegorical activity of reading or commentary itself. Virtually everything—indeed, everything that is structural—in Lacanian thought can be worked around the frame of this algorithm. In what follows I shall demonstrate a series of relations that can be adduced from Lacan's central symbol. The algorithm, in its basic structure, looks like a fraction: S/s (see *Ecrits: A Selection* 149). But it is never meant in a mathematical way, for there is no true commutability between the two levels. Instead, Lacan reads significance in each element. He finds significance not only in the letters but also in the line or bar. The line, indeed, is perhaps even more important for what it symbolizes than the letters in Lacan's epistemology. He makes as much of the virgule between the two letters as Saussure does of the notions of signifier and signified themselves. For Lacan, the line between the two letters points to an essential fact of human cognition. That fact emerges in Lacan's reading of his algorithm. It is read, Lacan tells us, as "the signifier over the signified, 'over' corresponding to the bar *separating* the two stages" (149; my emphasis).

For Lacan, the bar represents more than a mere separation of sign from meaning. Just as it divides signifier from signified, it represents a primordial barrier between subject and object, a barrier Lacan calls a *vel* of alienation. The *vel* of which Lacan speaks in *The Four Fundamental Concepts* (203–15) insists on the bar's separating instead of relating the epistemological subject and the ontological object (see also Bannet 12–48). Thus, in these disjunctions of either/or as opposed to both/and, the algorithm demonstrates not only the "arbitrariness of the sign" (*Ecrits: A Selection* 149) but also the arbitrariness of any notion in consciousness of a self (ego) unified with its world or—and this is most important—of a self (ego) unified in its relation to its Other, the unconscious. Saussure's implied algorithm becomes most useful to

Lacan, therefore, in large part because it symbolizes the alienation of the human subject not only from its world but also from itself, a condition of alienation Lacan posits even in the late 1930s in the essays on the mirror phase and on the family complexes, readdresses in "Aggressivity and Psychoanalysis" (1948), and a bit later (1955) describes as "the self's radical excentricity to itself" (*Ecrits: A Selection* 171).

But as important as these conceptualizations of "self" and "world" are to Lacan, perhaps more important are two aspects of another set of concepts the algorithm encapsulates. One aspect is Lacan's sense of the internal structural relations of subjectivity; the second is his sense of the ways in which subjectivity functions. While Lacan says that the topography of the unconscious is "defined by the algorithm: S/s" (163), in fact the algorithm is a monad or synecdoche of both the subject itself and the unconscious. That is, the algorithm displays in monadic form both the topographic organization (the "field") of the subject (consciousness versus the unconscious) and the topographic organization of the unconscious alone. Saussure's algorithm, most important, provides Lacan a means of showing the alienation of the subject from itself, for the bar—epistemological, if not metaphysical, in its implications—between signifier and signified can be seen as marking the gap between the conscious and the unconscious "regions" of human subjectivity (places wittily enfigured, we have seen, as "Baltimore in the early morning"). The sense of gap or lack or absence in this configuration of the subject is very important to Lacan and sets his theory apart from most American theories of the subject and their attendant interpretations of Freud. Where the Freud of the ego psychologists (mainly American) assumes that the individual's unconscious and, with it, the being of an autonomous ego or self exist a priori within a subject and are projected outward toward the individual's personal experiences, Lacan posits no such autonomy or mastery or unity of consciousness and the unconscious. Rather, he concludes that any conscious "self" and any unconscious "self" are taken from and are centered outside the subject (thus that neologism "excentric"). Each in fact comes into existence, Lacan says, in the subject's assumption of the power of symbolization effected by language and (eventually) transacted in speech. "Man"—meaning any human subject whatever—"speaks," Lacan has said, "but it is because the symbol has made him man" (*Ecrits: A Selection* 65).

Lacanian theory insists that the two most important functional "moments" undergone by the human subject are the mirror stage and the Oedipus complex. It is clear that both of these can be logically adduced, if not chronologically derived, from Lacan's algorithm as it symbolizes speech. To understand Lacan here, I must elaborate a bit on that split notion of the real (R/r) mentioned earlier. That notion has its foundation in philosophical realism (see Feibleman) rather than in Lacan's own explanations. Philosophical realism mediates between a pure idealism, such as the Platonic or the Kantian, and a pure naturalism, such as Berkeley's nominalism or solipsism. The idealist (Platonic or otherwise) posits ideas before things (*ante res*), but the naturalist posits no ideas at all. Mediating between these positions, philosophical realism posits ideas, but does so after things (*post res*). William Carlos Williams's famous refrain in *Paterson*, "No ideas but in things," is the claim of the philosophical realist, but the line also suggests why Williams, like Lacan, is so easily embraced by the materialists (naturalists, in philosophical terms) and the idealists both. Lacan could well have uttered Williams's words, for Lacan's "myth"—his story or "history"— of human subjectivity begins with that posited, unsymbolized real of existence that must become the object *of* a subject in order to become a Real of being. But Lacan here becomes subject to the assaults of the materialists, for this Real is no longer entirely dependent on that other real. Lacan's Real begins to appear an idealist's one, for, as Ellie Ragland-Sullivan says, "language produces a Real which does not have any *corresponding* reality" ("Lacan's Seminars on Joyce" 74). Even so, it would be wrong to make of Lacan either a materialist or an idealist. He is at bottom a philosophical realist, and his theory shows that mediation between the opposing views.

At the level of the human infant, the a priori real is an uncognized, material, somatic existence in which, Lacan theorizes, all objects appear to belong to the same object—the baby's or the mother's body. The move to the constituted Real happens in the moment of jubilation that occurs when the infant discovers otherness, and with it the potential— and the necessity—of signification: S/s. The structural foundation of speech—though speech is not actualized in it—emerges in that function Lacan calls the mirror stage. Lacan's favorite story from Freud occurs here. One of the most frequently discussed references to Freud occurs in Lacan's effort to explain the onset of the capability (the logical "moment") of speech in the infant. That enabling moment rests on the infant's assumption or introjection of a unified body image found not in itself, but in its other, the mother. We may say that the subject finds itself in the other, the mother who signifies for the child a totality introjected by the child, who before this moment was a congeries of parts that remained unsignified and perforce unthought as such. Thus for Lacan the *infans*-subject is brought into being precisely by a signifier, the other found in the mirror-phase identification. But at the same time as the subject comes into being (meaning that it becomes representable not *in* but *as* a signifier), the unconscious also comes into being in the suppression required by the *signified*'s passing under the bar entailed by representation in a signifier. Before this moment there is no unconscious, but, then, there is no true subject either.

In this moment we see the elements of the mirror stage reflected in the formation of the algorithm's double structure, for the algorithm S/s represents at once both the "field" of the subject and the "field" of the unconscious. The two taken together form the field of subjectivity itself. Thus, we may see why for Lacan there is no unconscious before the splitting manifested in the advent, in the first place, of the other, and, in the second place, of the sign or symbol; moreover, we may see why there is no subjectivity—no subject whatever—before symbolization. As Lacan is at pains to show in several ways (including the use of number and set theory in "Of Structure as an Inmixing"), the two come into existence for the subject simultaneously, not one after the other. The vicissitudes of subjectivity and symbolization are explained by Lacan in his discussion of one of Freud's most famous anecdotes—that of the *Fort! Da!* game. Freud's story of his grandson is important enough to quote at length:

> This good little boy ... had an occasional disturbing habit of taking small objects he could get hold of and throwing them away from him into a corner, under the bed, and so on, so that hunting for his toys and picking them up was often quite a business. As he did this he gave vent to a loud, long-drawn out "o-o-o-o," accompanied by an expression of interest and satisfaction. His mother and the writer of the present account were agreed in thinking that this was not a mere interjection but represented the German word "*fort.*" I eventually realized that it was a game and that the only use he made of any of his toys was to play "gone" with them. One day I made an observation which confirmed my

view. The child had a wooden reel with a piece of string tied
round it. It never occurred to him to pull it along the floor behind
him, for instance, and play at its being a carriage. What he did
was to hold the reel by the string and very skilfully throw it over
the edge of his curtained cot, so that it disappeared into it, at the
same time uttering his expressive "o-o-o-o." He then pulled the
reel out of the cot again by the string and hailed its reappearance
with a joyful "*da*." This then was the complete game—disappearance and return.[3]

Freud has his own purposes, but Lacan uses the tale of the grandson's
game with a sewing spool to suggest what happens in the mirror phase.
Lacan regards the child's behavior as at once an exhibition of symbolization and as a fantasy activity (fantasy, Lacan shows in *The Four
Fundamental Concepts,* has the same essential structure, one Lacan
signifies in $ \mathcal{S} \lozenge a $). The symbolization is exhibited in the spool that
stands for something else—the child's mother. The fantasy is exhibited
in the preverbal child's finding a momentary satisfaction in the activity.
Both symbolization and fantasy satisfaction, Lacan insists, are built on
a loss, a lack, a want of "being." In the gesture and vocal sounds it
repeats, Freud's grandchild unwittingly discovers its ability to symbolize
and thus, through a signifier, to make an *absence* present to itself. It
thereby is enabled to "cover" the departed mother (a signified, or s)
and thereafter—though only symbolically and in fantasy—to effect the
desired return of her. But there is yet another level of symbolization
here that Lacan points out. The "real" object employed as signifier
can be replaced by another type of signifier. Playfully tossing away and
reeling in the spool tied to a string and rhythmically vocalizing sounds
that Freud—perhaps needlessly—identifies with the German words *Fort*
(for *off, gone,* or *away*) and *Da* (*there* or *here,* both giving the sense
of a demonstrative to mean "here it is"), the child happens upon its
ability as a linguistic subject to "master" reality through symbols and
fantasy.

But for Lacan, of course, the important epistemological and linguistic
principle exemplified here, though as principle it is not yet internalized
by the child, is the principle of the bar, the barrier, the *vel* of alienation
so critical to Lacanian thought. While the signifier of difference (the
phallus) for the child will not actually appear until it learns sexual
difference around the age of five or six, there is nonetheless a sense

of difference that reveals itself in the implied relation of S to s: S/s. This important difference is not the one between the absence and presence of the spool as such; it is instead the principle of linguistic *differentia* represented in the contrasting sounds (see *Freud's Papers on Technique* 173). These inchoate words come to signify meanings in themselves. In the process, therefore, the real object (the spool) can be replaced by another "object"—the vocalizations themselves: "Thus the symbol," says Lacan, "manifests itself first of all as the murder of the thing" (*Ecrits: A Selection* 104). For Lacan, then, the child's most important discovery is that the mediation of the actual object—the spool—is not required in the future for satisfaction of a psychological desire (as opposed to a physiological need), though desire itself, in becoming "eternalized," is never really satisfied (104). But Lacan is careful to insist that thereby one has not simply moved into the universe of the Idealist. Words are material, and words remain rooted in the body and bodily affects, especially those associated with the body's openings onto the outside (the orifices of the head, the breasts, and the excretory functions). The child has learned that the actualities of departure and return, absence and presence, may be represented not merely by noises, but by material objects *of its own symbolic creation.* In the child's use of those contrastive sounds, says Lacan, lies "the point of insertion of a symbolic order that pre-exists the infantile subject and in accordance with which he will have to structure himself" (*Ecrits: A Selection* 234). The child, even if it really cannot yet speak, has learned the principle of language and the ambiguous power ("merely" symbolic, of course) that language gives the human subject.

It seems plain enough that the process Lacan describes here is narcissistic. But, basing his premise on Freud's texts, Lacan argues there are two narcissisms (see *Freud's Papers on Technique* 118-28), and both must be experienced by the subject in normative development. More clearly than we have so far seen it, Lacan's sense of the development of the subject begins to depend upon the formation of the cognitive registers—the Imaginary and the Symbolic. These two registers constitute cognition in the human subject. Perhaps the best way to explain them is to imagine those transparent overlays that one finds in textbooks and encyclopedias. In the subject, the one register—the Imaginary—is laid down first. It covers that primal, perceptual real of which we spoke earlier and thereby structures a Real of cognition. The "reality" structured by this register is characterized by bifurcations, by dialectical relations: doubles, paired affects, projective responses in which one object is obliterated by or within another. In cognition, the register of the Imaginary is fundamental, though it is not final. Anika Lemaire says of the Imaginary, for example, "The imaginary object will either repeat itself indefinitely, remaining identical to itself—in which case consciousness clouds over and sinks into the automatism of repetition—or it will submit to a discontinuity of aspect through continuous qualitative changes—in this sense imagination really is our faculty of creation." But that creativity does not mean a totally transparent function is made available to the subject. "Each image," says Lemaire, "is a blind alley in which subjective intention drowns in its own creation, collapsing into its object and failing to keep its distance from its own internal vision." The subject's Imaginary functions are not transparent to it because it is caught up in the play of the reflections themselves. Lemaire says in this connection that "Lacan defines the essence of the imaginary as a dual relationship, a reduplication in the mirror, an immediate opposition between consciousness and its other in which each term becomes its opposite and is lost in the play of reflections." The play here is the play of desire, the desire of the subject for itself in its mirror other. "In its quest for itself," says Lemaire, "consciousness thus believes that it has found itself in the mirror of its own creatures," though, instead, it in fact "loses itself in something which is not consciousness" (60).

Language and the Symbolic arrest the play of reflections in the register of the Imaginary, for the Imaginary is stabilized only by the accession in the subject of the Symbolic register. The Symbolic, to continue the illustration, overlays the Imaginary and restructures cognition along another dimension tantamount to the third dimension in space. Whereas the Imaginary is initiated in the mirror phase, the true register of the Symbolic is firmly laid in place by the cognitive changes that occur in the introjection of the law of Oedipus. The register of the Symbolic is characterized by mediation rather than immediacy. Here, in its mediating role, is where language becomes dominant, but here also is where human alienation becomes manifest. Language both constitutes and alienates the subject. We may say this is the moment, the moment of language, when the irrecuperable gap between signified and signifier becomes a feature of the subject's cognitive experience. In short, according to Lacan, the subject is constituted in the gap between signifier and signified, precisely the gap where language exists in the structure of the subject. Thus the subject, like language, subsists in a system of differences. It is finally neither idealist nor materialist, but realist, as we see in Lacan's explanation of thought in the register of the Symbolic. If Imaginary thought is concrete, "symbolic thought is a conceptual thought without any empirical intuition; it in fact releases the concept from all intuition of an object. Symbolism has only a formal signification; its signification, that is, depends upon the coherence of its relations. A symbol is only an operator in a structure, a means of effecting the distinctive oppositions necessary to the existence of a significant structure. It is essentially an indirect expression. Its condition is that of not being what it represents" (Lemaire 55).

In short, language and the register of the Symbolic introduce purely formal (that is, Idealist) values to material of the subject's cognition. The Symbolic, like language, is the order that functions through the mediation of the third term; it relies on the function of rules, laws, taboos, beliefs. Its effect is to provide the third point on the graph plotted along x and y axes that confirms or disconfirms the duality of the two points adduced by the Imaginary. In Freudian theory, which Lacan of course accepts even as he extends and clarifies, the symbol of all those mediating third terms is the Phallus whose power gives to the Oedipus its importance in defining normative subjectivity. Thus the Symbolic order, like language, permits human relations to occur on a plane of mediation that is exemplified in the figure of the judge, the ruler, the arbitrator, the authority, but even so it never eliminates the Imaginary, the plane of immediacy of lived experiences involving the body and affects. Thus, again, we may say that Lacanian theory remains realist, rather than materialist or idealist, because any realm of the merely ideal depends always on a basis of real, material facts. The two narcissisms point up this position.

The two narcissisms are implicated in the development of the two registers in the subject. As we might suppose, the first narcissism occurs in the mirror stage, wherein the infant assumes a sense of bodily unity cognized in the other and organized strictly within the register of the Imaginary. Onto this other the subject projects what Lacan, echoing Freud's "On Narcissism: An Introduction," calls the "ideal ego" (*Ideal-ich*). This first narcissism, which functions by venerating the ideal ego, is essential to the human being, to *being* a human subject. Dependent on the physical presence of the other, this first narcissism is connected with the subject's "corporeal image," says Lacan. "This image is identical for the entirety of the subject's mechanisms and gives his *Umwelt* its form, in as much as he is man and not horse. It makes up the unity of the subject, and we see it projecting itself in a thousand ways, up to and including what we can call the imaginary source of symbolism, which is what links symbolism to feeling, to the *Selbstgefühl,* which the human being, the *Mensch,* has of his own body" (*Freud's Papers on Technique* 125).

The second narcissism, that which gives the human subject its ego (Lacan's *moi*), is organized within the register of the Symbolic and generates a potential of knowing ("an original noetic possibility") not found in the mere animal. While Lacan suggests that even the animal has what he would also call the register of the Imaginary, since it rests upon "the real image," the register of the Imaginary, despite the name, does not function, he says, the same way in humans as in animals. "For the animal there is a limited number of pre-established correspondences between its imaginary structure and whatever interests it in its *Umwelt,* namely whatever is important for the perpetuation of individuals, themselves a function of the perpetuation of the type of the species" (125). But when the human subject accedes to the Symbolic register, it assumes a level of cognition not available to the animal subject. This level is perceived in the human subject's identification with the other. "For man," says Lacan, "the other has a captivating value, on account of the anticipation that is represented by the unitary image as it is perceived either in the mirror or in the entire reality of the fellow being." This sense of the other—as ego ideal (*Ichideal*)—is to be distinguished, Lacan says, from the Imaginary ideal ego or "alter ego," though "according to the stage in life" the one is often confused with the other.

This second narcissism, which Lacan insists is narcissistic identification, is that "identification with the other which, under normal circumstances, enables man to locate precisely his imaginary and libidinal relation to the world in general. That [identification] is what enables him to *see* in its place and to structure, as a function of this place and of his world, his being" (125). While Lacan mentions that he might accept Octave Mannoni's use of the word *ontological* to describe such being, he himself would prefer to express the notion as the subject's *"libidinal being.* The subject sees his being in a reflection in relation to the other, that is to say in relation to the *Ichideal* [ego ideal]" (126). Even though this second narcissism seems to move toward some sort of unified being, Lacan ends this discussion by insisting once more that just as one function of the ego lies "in the structuration of reality," another function is to insist upon the "fundamental alienation constituted by the reflected image of himself, which is the *Urich,* the original form of the *Ichideal* as well as that of the relation to the other" (126).

We may recap in brief, then, Lacan's story of the subject. In the first of those two logical moments—mirror stage and Oedipus—the infant who previously perceives itself as pieces or fragments is unified in the specular—mirror—image of its other, the mother. But just as quickly, in the later moment of the Oedipus, it is separated from that unifying image and may find its integration only in a Symbolic field, the field of language itself. Thus, in the first moment, a previously uncognizable being is suddenly, joyfully unified through its projection of a self into a totalizable other, thereby forming the possibility of a subject and an identificatory object. But this assumed, narcissistic unity is eventually (in the normative subject) to be split, not once but doubly (in the formation of a second narcissism), by the function called the Oedipus complex. This double splitting results in the quaternary form of the Lacanian subject. On one plane are an I and an ideal ego; results of the first narcissism, they exist on the plane of the Imaginary. On another plane are an ego ideal and the "great" Other, the *Autre* spelled with a capital letter; results of the second narcissism, they exist on the plane of the Symbolic and under the aegis of the unconscious that Lacan sometimes identifies with the great Other itself.

Thus, as a result of the two functions (the mirror phase and the Oedipus complex), the child-subject's lost and forever desired presumptive unity with the (m)other becomes identified with its images of the other (starting *with* the mother), but any sense of its "whole" identity is forever after only to be sought *in* others or those symbolic objects that symbolize the aim of desire, objects given a formulaic status that Lacan will call "*objets petit a.*"[4] The images of those substitutable persons and desired objects shall over time be replaced (metaphorically) by other persons and displaced (metonymically) by yet other images, by other objects/images chained together through associated meanings. Moreover, the subject itself shall "fade" or "disappear" into the register called the Symbolic, and any image of an "original" self thus shall be lost in the hole of the unconscious formed where the registers Real, Imaginary, and Symbolic all are knotted together by a signifier called the Name-of-the-Father.[5] We will learn more of this last concept in the next section.

The Structure of Lacanian Thought

> This schema [L] signifies that the condition of the S[ubject] (neurosis or psychosis) is dependent on what is being unfolded in [the great Other,] the Other O. What is being unfolded there is articulated like a discourse (the unconscious is the discourse of the Other).
>
> —Jacques Lacan, *Ecrits: A Selection*

In the preceding, I hope to have laid down a foundation for the more concrete discussion that follows. Here I want to present a Lacan for the reader, a way of getting at Lacanian thought that will make critical reading more practicable. Lacan's terms for subjective structure (subject, other, ego, Other), for the cognitive registers (Real, Imaginary, Symbolic), and for the developmental moments (mirror stage, Oedipus complex) all involve difficult (and, for the Freudian, because of Lacan's precise usages, perhaps confusing) concepts to master. Fortunately, Lacan has provided topographical schemas that illustrate the hypothesized relations among some of them, namely, the structural concepts and the cognitive registers. Why the subject—which Lacan calls the barred ($\mathcal{S}$) subject—must be seen as quaternary rather than merely dyadic (as linguistics, though not semiotics, might imply) can now be shown in a sequence of topographic transformations to fulfill my earlier claim that Lacan's algorithm can be seen as a monad or synecdoche of all Lacanian thought.

We must start with the basic algorithm. Its transformations have already been discursively (and, we may say, symbolically) presented above; now we may turn to what may be called an Imaginary representation of Lacan's theory since it is much more dependent upon merely concrete, dyadic representations. Since the Saussurean figure for "the sign" is in itself as arbitrary as the nature of all signs, there is no reason other than explanatory power for locating the signifier *over* the signified. Thus, for reasons of explanatory power in another direction (though one, I believe, consistent with Lacanian theory), I prefer to locate the signifier and the signified in a horizontal relation and divided by a vertical bar since what I want to stress are the two axes of language itself. In their simplest homologous forms (as I would revise them), "Saussurean" and "Lacanian" versions would look like this:

The Sign = s I S   The Subject = I I other
        Saussure   Lacan

Figure 1

This figuration, it seems clear, is more appropriate than the reading *signifier over signified* if we take into account the terms Jakobson establishes regarding the two axes on which language operates. The *x* axis is the horizontal one on which Jakobson positions the operations of displacement, metonymy, the syntagmatic. The *y* axis is the vertical one on which Jakobson positions the operations of substitution, metaphor, the paradigmatic in general.

Such a figuration is especially important for any Lacanian sense of the temporal inscriptions of the subject. There are two inscriptions; they occur in those two moments—the mirror stage and the Oedipus complex. The time of these moments involves in the second a repetition, a backward movement, a retracing of a groove already laid down in the first move. On the one hand, we must understand that if time for us as readers moves from left to right, any perception for us moves from the signified on the left to the signifier on the right. But, on the other hand, true cognition or *understanding* moves backward, from the signifier back toward the signified. While this double movement is schematized in Lacan's *Ecrits: A Selection* (chapter 9) in the "graphs of desire" and in *Séminaire* XX in the discussion of the four discourses, it is not my purpose here to consider either the graphs or the discourses (see, instead, Bracher; Ragland-Sullivan, "Plato's *Symposium*"). Rather, I want to set up a way to show graphically the critical stages in the logical development of the Lacanian subject. With that subject enfigured in this way—I I other—we have a clear sense of the division of the subject from its other even from the first moment of subjectivity that emerges in the mirror stage. Herein it is plain that the double movement (from signified to signifier, and back) of cognition indeed makes any notion of subjectivity dependent upon the other or otherness. In a logical, if not a temporal, sense, the other is always there first, for any opening onto subjectivity for the Lacanian subject begins in the other and moves backward to the subject. The subject only then becomes aware of itself—in the mirror stage—as a subject unified in its image of the other.

The use of the vertical bar, moreover, permits us to see the relation between this early symbolization of the emerging subject and the

schema Lacan uses in *The Four Fundamental Concepts* to explain
aphanisis, the "fading of the subject" at the point of the gap or bar
dividing signified from signifier, I from other. In his discussion of the
double operation by which the normative subject comes into subjectivity, Lacan implicates his notion of desire in a symbolization that, as
does my I | other figure, moves horizontally, but, like it, that figuration
comes with Lacan's admonition to "Be careful" (209). One must carefully note that there is in fact a double movement. The "anti-clockwise" "vectorial direction" is determined by the fact that "you read
things from left to right," but at some point that movement in turn
requires—again, anti-clockwise—a move from right to left. Lacan's
"algorithm" for desire operates around what Lacan calls a *losenge,* one
formed by normal and reversed Vs: $ ◇ a. On either side of this
losenge, forming what Lacan calls a *vel,* but what also is regarded as
a sort of *veil,* are located the barred subject ($) and the lowercase *a*
that sometimes stands for *autre* (other) in that locution Lacan sometimes enunciates as *l'objet petit autre.*

The critical issue for Lacan here is the "operation that we call *alienation.*" Lacan explains the double problem of the subject's either/
or this way: "Alienation consists in this *vel,*" for the *vel* "condemns
the subject to appearing only in that division which, it seems to me,
I have just articulated sufficiently by saying that, if it appears on one
side as meaning, produced by the signifier, it appears on the other as
aphanisis" or "fading" (*Four Fundamental Concepts,* hereafter *FFC,*
210). Here is the schematic way Lacan uses to illustrate the either/or
of being and meaning, concepts that evoke my distinction between
real and Real, perhaps even those between Imaginary and Symbolic:

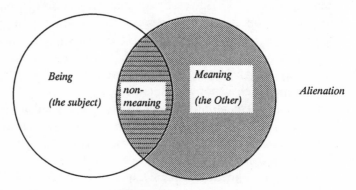

Figure 2

While it is important for my purposes to permit this schema to emphasize the *vel* of "being" and "meaning," it is equally important to use it to show the way in which Lacan conceptualizes the cognitive registers. For we may now see that on the side of being, in the place of the subject, is the register of the Imaginary, and that on the side of meaning, in the place of the Other, is the Symbolic. The gap of nonmeaning thus becomes a hole that eventually becomes very important to Lacan, for it is the opening onto the unsymbolized real of which I have already spoken. Moreover, this hole may well be the opening of subjectivity back into the body, the place where the *objet a* and its metonyms and the symptom-as-metaphor gain their entry to discourse. (Eventually, as I have noted above, Lacan will regard the Symptom itself as a register, on the order of the Real, the Imaginary, and the Symbolic.) In Lacan's figuration of subjectivity based on the Borromean knots (see *Scilicet*), we shall see the way in which each of the registers and the primal signifier known as the phallus interconnect—at least in the normative subject.

In the sequence of figures so far we have seen the original splitting of the subject that comes in the mirror stage. We have seen the separation of "I" from "other," but at the same instant the constitution of an "I" *in* the other. If this were all that were involved in the constitution of the Lacanian subject, the subject would be defined entirely by the register of the Imaginary, for that register operates through simple one-to-one relations in dualistic, negative or positive, identifications. But Lacan insists that each of the four corners of the quaternary subject is occupied by a psychoanalytic entity that functions as a node in a patterned discourse (see *Séminaires* XVII, XX; Bracher; Ragland-Sullivan, "Plato's *Symposium*"). For these nodal points to become functional, the basic structure—the one beginning with the algorithm S | s—must undergo not this single inscription, but a double inscription to complete the quaternary structure. This double inscription of the normative subject is illustrated by Lacan in his discussion in "The Agency of the Letter in the Unconscious" of the functions of metaphor and metonymy.

Metaphor and metonymy, for Lacan, are related, respectively, to knowledge and desire. Metaphor defines knowledge in the structure and functioning of the unconscious along the axis of "the vertical dependencies of the signified," while metonymy defines desire along the axis of the "horizontal signifying chain" (*Ecrits: A Selection* 164). Lacan schematizes the two tropes this way:

$$f(S \ldots S')S \cong S\ (-)\ s \qquad f\!\left(\frac{S'}{S}\right) \cong S\ (+)\ s$$

Metonymy   Metaphor

Figure 3

Because knowledge, desire, and the tropological functions are critical to Lacan, he takes some care in explaining that the formalized structures are not really read as mathematical formulae. Metaphor's structure represents two things for Lacan: first, it represents the "topography of the unconscious" as it is defined by the algorithm S/s (163), and, second, it is the structure of signification itself. That is to say, this schematization shows that metaphor (the original S'/S) constitutes the primal repression upon which the unconscious itself (S/S) is founded; the second is that metaphor constitutes what he calls the "emergence of signification" (164; see Davis, "Lacan, Poe, and Narrative Repression," 1004n.11; Thom 39–42).

The two together—repression and signification—thus embrace both the structure of the unconscious and the structure of its communication, for that which is repressed can emerge—can "cross the bar," as signified by the plus sign (164)—only by proxy, only through the substitution effected by the symptom. The unconscious "speaks" through the symptom, but the symptom, Lacan says, is a metaphor. The relation of the subject to knowledge is the same as that of the subject to the unconscious. The subject and knowledge, like the subject and the unconscious, exist on different levels, the one always barred from the other. "We accede to meaning," Lacan says, "only through the double twist of metaphor when we have the one and only key." That key, he says, is knowledge that "the S and the s of the Saussurian algorithm are not on the same level" (166). This double twist, which Lacan explains later in "On a Question Preliminary to Any Possible Treatment of Psychosis" (*Ecrits: A Selection* 200), can be shown in the form of a conventional mathematical conversion:

$$\frac{S}{\not{S}} \cdot \frac{\not{S}'}{x} \rightarrow S\!\left(\frac{I}{s}\right)$$

In that later explanation, Lacan suggests that metaphor-as-knowledge (the x) occurs in a first twist, the one in which a first signifier (S/S') is substituted for another set (S'/x), and this twist leaves the subject assuming that its knowledge (truth) exists in a relation to a signifier (S) and another signified (s). But that truth, Lacan says Freud taught us, lies at the axis where metaphor and metonymy cross. While that "place" is no longer a "nowhere" because of Freud, it remains beyond our grasp except through the "spark" of metaphor that jumps from the one to the other. One's being (the identity signified by I) thus eludes one in the play—the game—Lacan describes as "the active edge that splits my desire between a refusal of the signifier and a lack of being" (166), the language here describing once more the "fading of the subject" schematized in Figure 2 above. Knowledge is what one wants, but knowledge—of the ego, of the other, of the Other-as-the-unconscious—is precisely that which is always elsewhere, just as the subject is always elsewhere in Lacan's conception ("I think where I am not, therefore I am where I do not think" [166]). But, even if it were achieved, this knowledge would not satisfy desire; it would only reify its existence.

Perhaps more critical for Lacanian theory, therefore, is the structure of metonymy that represents desire. Since metonymy is structured along a string—S . . . S'—it maintains the bar between signifier and signified or between one signifier and another. The structure of metonymy, says Lacan, suggests the way in which the gap between being and meaning (see Figure 2) is installed in the human subject as a condition of subjectivity. The gap is expressed in the periods showing the ellipsis between one signifier and another; in grammatical terms, we may say there is a *para-* but not a *hypo*tactical relation; there is contiguity but no connection determined by a system. Lacan says that it is the metonymic structure that demonstrates it is "the connexion between signifier and signifier that permits the elision in which the signifier installs the lack-of-being in the object relation." This signifier installs such lack because the structure of metonymy always refers *back* to another signifier that is out of reach; it uses "the value of 'reference back' possessed by signification in order to invest it with the desire aimed at the very lack it supports" (164).

Thus, for Lacan, metonymy represents the irreparable gap in the subject that comes with consciousness ("knowledge") of oneself as a subject of a signifier, as a subject *for* another signifier. But metonymy also represents the structure of desire, the incessant movement of human subjectivity to fill the gap between signifier and signifier in that "reference back" to that always posited (but never grasped) original signifier of being. Lacan's riddling way of expressing this persistent human condition of self-alienation we have seen already: "I think where I am not." If metaphor introduces into the Lacanian subject the trauma of knowledge, then metonymy, in its effect, introduces the enigmas of desire. "And the enigmas that desire seems to pose for 'natural philosophy'—its frenzy mocking the abyss of the infinite, the secret collusion with which it envelops the pleasure of knowing and of dominating with *jouissance,* these amount to no other derangement of instinct than that of being caught in the rails—eternally stretching forth towards the *desire for something else*—of metonymy" (166-67).

But because Lacan eventually assimilated structuralism's valorization of linguistics (despite his late disclaimer in *Encore* of its being a mere *linguisterie*), it is necessary to understand that in the psychoanalytic subject, the barrier-cum-medium represented by the solid vertical line in Figure 1 is, in effect, none other than language itself. For Lacan, after the subject's accession to language, the subject (my "I" as a signifier standing before your "you," which is another signifier) is created by or within language. Or, put another way, "Language is thus the precondition for *the act of becoming aware of oneself as a distinct entity*" (Lemaire 54). Like the sign manifested within the construct formed by the signifier and the signified, the subject is completely enclosed within—or, philosophically and in Lacan's thought, "insists" or "subsists" in—the field of language, itself split phenomenologically between *la parole* and *la langue,* split, that is, between speech and the language one speaks. That subsistence Lacan sometimes expresses as *l'instance,* as "agency" or "insistence," terms that connote both "activity" and "constitution." The constitution of the subject between speech and language (*la parole* and *la langue*) can be shown in another transformation of the basic monadic structure.

Figure 4 suggests several points about Lacan's notion of the subject. First, it shows the way in which the subject is split into topographical regions of consciousness and unconsciousness. What is more, the way

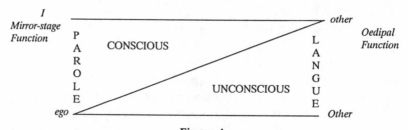

Figure 4

in which the two sides of such a figure reflect—or mirror—each other, but do so with a difference, also suggests the theory on which the subject rests and for which Lacan is probably most widely known. Essentially, this figuration adumbrates the splitting of the subject that comes in the mirror stage, but also, by showing the ego and the Other, it begins to show the effects of the Oedipal function and the second narcissism. With some omissions I shall fill in shortly, this figure shows most of what is essential in Lacan's thought about the structure of the normative subject.

I want now to move toward a modeling of a full synthesis of the terms of Lacan's thought as shown in Figure 5. As a preliminary, some narrative recapitulation is necessary. As far as the genesis of the subject goes, it can be outlined best in notions of a pre-mirror phase, a mirror phase, and a post-mirror phase. Since there is no subject as such in

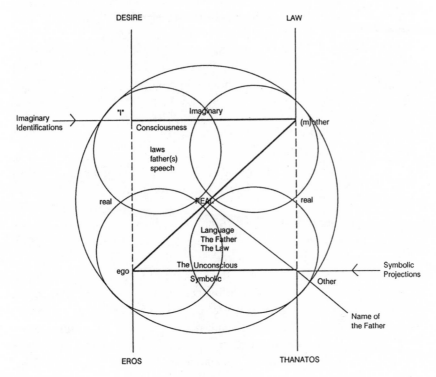

Figure 5

the beginning (that is, in the pre-mirror phase), the onset of a real subject occurs in the child's passage through the mirror phase, for from that pregnant moment both consciousness-as-consciousness and an unconscious built on repression are born. Even so, the mirror phase does not produce a fully realized subject. Although this moment initiates the subject into the *function* of the Symbolic order, the *rule* of the Symbolic is not yet formalized or internalized. Instead, for a time the subject's use of symbolism is marked by the dualities of the Imaginary order such as one finds in Lacan's conception of neurosis in later life. The Imaginary order is evidenced in the subject's awareness of "twoness," of others caught in either a narcissistic or an aggressive relation to the ego of the subject. The awareness of "threeness" comes with the subject's internalization of the Symbolic order. That moment first occurs when the infant cognizes the signifying possibility of speech, even if ordinary speech itself is not yet possible for it. In the Imaginary, the mother is the significant (signifying) other—the second person—of narcissistic duplication; in the Symbolic, the significant other—the third person—is the father as signifier, that is, as the intrusive *tertium quid* that incorporates in the child the potential for symbolic discourse, both within consciousness and within the unconscious. While it is true that for Lacan the orders of the Real, the Imaginary, and the Symbolic are always inmixed with each other (as Figure 5 suggests), it is also true that the normative subject must eventually move from dependency on the Imaginary to an acceptance of the function and power of the Symbolic, though without permitting the Symbolic alone to speak since in that direction lies pathology—as Freud's paradigmatic example of Judge Schreber attests (see Lacan's discussion in *Ecrits: A Selection* 226-80).

Passage through the Oedipus complex, with its attendant acceptance of castration, then, represents the final step in the process by which the normative subject is articulated and full symbolization is achieved. The Oedipal realization makes the subject capable of seeing itself in a formal or structural relation to others and to objects; moreover, the subject is now enabled to code and decode messages within a formal articulatory process. Such exchange is easily seen in economics. Symbolic exchange is not through mere "barter," where one object is traded for another; symbolic exchange is mediated through a third object, money, for example, that regulates value in objects within an articulated (however arbitrary) system. No longer is the subject or signification limited to mere counting—1 + 1 + 1 . . . —or to an A-is-B (or metaphoric) relation such as one finds in the Imaginary and mirror-phase narcissism; now the subject is capable of algebraic or economic equations. It can signify through the displacements (metonymies) of syntactical structures, as in A is to B as C is to D, or as in W is valued in relation to X as Y is valued in relation to Z, and so on. By introducing the primal signifier of this structural economy, the Oedipus complex therefore may be said "to mark the limits that our discipline assigns to subjectivity" (*Ecrits: A Selection* 66), just as "nothing can be interpreted except through the intermediary of the Oedipal realization" (Lacan and Granoff 274). These remarks suggest that the Oedipus complex concludes the constitution of Lacan's normative psychoanalytic subject by forming a signifying (mediating) triangulation within subjectivity. The subject is thereafter based on no more than the supposition of a symbolic value, and subjectivity is thus determined within a regulated exchange—as in an economics—of gain and loss.

This economy of gain and loss is involved in the traditional notions of castration and the phallus. Castration is one of the more difficult concepts in Freud and Lacan. Since Freudians have the habit—found in Freud himself—of taking concepts literally, one may be easily confused about the meaning of castration. It should not be taken to mean actual emasculation of the male nor should it imply that the female is somehow emasculated by nature since she does not possess the literal organ. In the same way, one must not conclude that the penis is the same thing as the Phallus in Lacanian theory. In Lacan, the Phallus is the first pure signifier for the emerging human subject, and castration is the symbolic function within the Oedipus complex that establishes the "position" of the father in the psychic structure. "Freud defined the Oedipus complex as the organized ensemble of loving and hostile desires felt by the child toward her or his parents," says Ragland-Sullivan. "This," she continues, "has been recast by Lacan to account for the evolution that, little by little, substitutes the father for the mother" (*Jacques Lacan and the Philosophy of Psychoanalysis*, hereafter *JLPP*, 278). The father—or the phallus, that which stands for the father—is seen by the child as the object of the mother's desire, since the mother's desire for the father comes to be regarded as more important to her than her desire for the child. Castration is delineated in this shift, for here the child realizes she or he is not the only object of desire to the mother. Breaking the dyadic, identificatory relation of child/mother, the father/Phallus introduces a third relation—thirdness itself, one might say (see my later chapter on James). Castration reifies lack in the emerging subject, and thus it reifies desire as well. It thereby opens the structure of subjectivity to otherness and the Symbolic—to, that is, "the Name-of-the-Father spelling prohibition, separation, and individuation" (JLPP 279). The theme of castration, then, is mediation, as the mother mediates the child's substitutive desire through the figure of the paternal metaphor that mediates law.

We might return for a moment to the metaphor of economics. At this more complicated, Oedipal stage where castration and the phallus are concerned, we discover much of Lacan's thought within the analogy of economics. That is an enfiguration traditional in Freudian thought, but in Lacan's discussions it is usually only implicit. There is loss in the child's passage from the mirror stage through the Oedipus complex, of course, but within this economy of regulated exchange there is compensatory or substitutory gain. The gain, at one level, is the subject's sense of a unified body found in the image of the other in the mirror. At another level, through the Oedipus complex, there is the gain found in the subject's ability to communicate as a social being. But these gains are at best Imaginary (that is, they surely are not real), and they lead us to the remaining key terms of Lacan's system. Lacan's terms for identifying the Symbolic system of substitutions here are Desire and Law. What the mirror-stage subject really gains, on the one hand, is Desire—Desire for those evanescent, totalizing images and objects it has lost, beginning with the mother; on the other hand, in the infinite repetitions of language, the post-Oedipal subject gains symbolic power to manipulate reality and so to appease—really, to fuel— Desire through metonymic, associative chains of signifiers comprised of metaphoric substitutions and metonymic displacements.

Thus we may say that the mirror stage opens up an endlessly fascinating world that comes to be regulated by the Oedipal function of the recognition of lack found in castration. That is, lest the Imaginary power to displace Desire seem limitless, the Oedipal realization brings a cognition of Law and thus of boundaries to the subject. That cognition occurs in the child's acceptance of its loss or lack of that signifier Lacan calls the Phallus. In its function as *the* signifier, the Phallus is central to Lacan's, as to Freud's, thought. "Freud," says Lacan, "revealed this imaginary function of the phallus . . . to be the pivot of the symbolic process that completes *in both sexes* the questioning of

the sex by the castration complex" (*Ecrits: A Selection* 198). The Phallus—called as well "the paternal metaphor"—is the symbol of the authority Lacan assigns to the concept of Law and localizes in the Name-
of-the-Father. That metaphor performs "the signifying function that
conditions paternity," for paternity can only be known or attributed
through a signifier (198–99). The Phallus and the Name-of-the-Father
symbolize that which comes between the mother and the child, separating the one from the other. Together, they also symbolize that
which the child comes to see the mother does not have—the phallus
or the Father's authority. Thus the child's acceptance of the mother's
loss is acceptance of a double loss: first, loss of the phallus in the
perception of anatomical difference, but, second, the loss of the mother
as Imaginary other. Loss—castration, in Freudian terms—not only entails in Lacan's terms acceptance of alienation into language (acceptance, in other words, that *the* Phallus indeed is lost and its loss is
irremediable except through a signifier), but it also entails submission
to the ultimate authority of Law. Desire may reside in the plane of
the (m)other, but Law resides in the *place* (though not necessarily the
person) of the other parent. Law resides in the *Name* of the Father
whose site on Lacan's schematic quadrangle is identified as Other and
is paralleled in the Symbolic with the place of the (m)other on the
plane of the Imaginary.

Thus, from the conflict within the subject between Desire and Law
are articulated the drives toward what Freud, if not Lacan, would call
Eros and Thanatos. Though these terms are Freud's rather than Lacan's,
it is possible, I believe, to synthesize Freudian and Lacanian thought
on these topics. The pivotal concept is *affect;* anxiety and guilt are the
two fundamental affects generated in the subject by Desire and Law.
Desire and Law establish polarities of anxiety and guilt within the
subject. These affects point to one of the most enigmatic features of
Freudian psychoanalysis—the paradox of the death-drive or death-wish
as a manifestation of the subject's desire for completion (see Kristeva,
Revolution in Poetic Language, 244; Laplanche 103–24). The aim of
the subject's Desire is to fuse once again with the Imaginary double
who is first the mother, but who then becomes (in images linking to
objets a) the displaced representation of the (m)other found in the
interaction between the ego and the other. The aim of Law is to refuse
the mother-as-other of the subject by introducing a third, more potent
symbol—one found in the place of the father-become-Father and ca-

pable of imposing a penalty of alienation and, ostensibly, even death on the subject who denies its authority. The paradox of Lacan's theory of the subject thus becomes this: one can be a subject-as-subject only by submitting to the greater power of the Symbolic, to the Oedipal law of alienation into language (Lacan's version of Freud's castration). But, alas, that Law exists on the side of Thanatos, not Eros. The drive toward subjectivity, therefore, is always toward death and the Symbolic; the contrary drive—toward loss of subjectivity—is always toward love and the Imaginary. The ego loses itself in the loved one; the ego regains itself in the loss ordained in submission to the Symbolic, the Law, the Father. This conflict between two drives—forming what one Lacanian analyst calls "a strange chiasmus" (Laplanche 124)—thus defines human life, for "between the imaginary and symbolic relationships," says Lacan, "there is the distance that separates anxiety and guilt"—the two emotions, Lacan suggests, that circumscribe human relationships to other(s) and to the Other (Lacan and Granoff 272). Thus, Lacan suggests, human subjectivity is finally driven by guilt and anxiety, Law and Desire, Oedipus and Narcissus.

The child's passages from the pre-mirror stage, through the mirror phase, and finally through the Oedipus conflict thus complete the thematic, narrative, and topographical outlines of Lacan's psychoanalytic subject. If we locate the terms of those further transformations imposed by the Oedipal realization within Lacan's topography, the results we see in Figure 5 begin to be fully comprehensive for our use in Lacanian analysis. Within the schema, spaces have been opened up for the perceptual real and for each of the cognitive registers (Imaginary, Real, and Symbolic), for consciousness and the unconscious, and for the "objects" that fill them—laws/Law, fathers/Father, speech/Language), as well as for those fields of force defined by the polarities of Desire and Law, Eros and Thanatos, that are transected by what Lacan calls Imaginary identifications and Symbolic projections. Radically condensed, the elements of the Lacanian topography and thematics of the subject, as I understand them, appear in Figure 5.

Despite the inclusiveness of Figure 5, however, it cannot "capture" the subject.[6] No static schema can capture the subject for the simple reason that the subject is not a thing; rather, it is a process. One thus has to imagine this schema as an organism in motion—not as a static object. Because the subject is in motion, is, in Lacan's words, "stretched over all four corners of the [topographic] Schema" (*Ecrits: A Selection*

194), no self or ego will ever be visible to the subject at any of the junctures except as a specular, merely illusory I-as-signifier in the register of the Imaginary. But the motility of the subject does not mean analysis can never know anything at all about it, for the mediations within the speech (*la parole*) of the subject will begin to illuminate on the side of language (*la langue*) the "hidden, but palpable, discourse which resides in unconscious networks of meaning" (Ragland-Sullivan, "Magnetism," 382) posited by the Other of the subject—by, that is, the unconscious. In psychoanalysis and in literature, it is this palpable discourse of the subject vis à vis the Other that must finally draw the attention of the literary critic who uses Lacan. We need now to consider some of the implications of a Lacanian theory and practice.

Toward a Lacanian Critical Practice

> It would not be difficult to imagine a Lacanian criticism—although I do not know that there has been one.
>
> —Fredric Jameson, "Imaginary and Symbolic in Lacan"

Despite all the evidence, it is not clear to everyone that psychoanalytic, much less Lacanian, criticism is viable, useful, or even possible. Thus I want to turn to others who have addressed the question of psychoanalytic criticism in ways that seem adequate to me and to my project. Perhaps because the work of Jacques Lacan has prompted a lively renewal of interest in psychoanalytic criticism, any number of books and essay collections have appeared during the last ten years or so that address the "problem" of literature and psychoanalysis. Many of these publications grew out of conferences or occurred as special issues of journals. Such phenomena are a sure sign that there is a burgeoning interest in a subject. Perhaps the most wide-ranging collection is that edited by Shoshana Felman called *Literature and Psychoanalysis,* published first as a double issue of *Yale French Studies* (1977) and then as a book (1982). A similar endeavor called *Psychoanalysis and the Question of the Text* (1978) was edited by Geoffrey Hartman; the essays in it grew out of papers delivered during 1976 and 1977 at conferences of the English Institute. The journal *Humanities in Society* (1981) devoted an issue to psychoanalysis and interpretation. And two journals, *Style* and *Poetics,* joined forces to publish a special issue, edited by Mieke Bal, on psychopoetics (1984).

Each of these collections addresses Freudian and Lacanian themes, as do recent books such as *The Psychoanalytic Study of Literature* (1985), edited by Joseph Reppen and Maurice Charney, and *Discourse in Psychoanalysis and Literature* (1987), edited by Shlomith Rimmon-Kenan. Since these titles are merely a few among perhaps dozens that have appeared since the mid-1970s, it seems clear that there is a spirited interest in psychoanalysis in general and literature and psychoanalysis in particular.

Rather than trying to survey all the work done recently, I want instead to focus mainly on just two critics—Peter Brooks and Ellie Ragland-Sullivan. I shall focus on these because each stresses an element or elements of what I would regard as absolutely essential to any theory of literary criticism. As I see theory, especially as it is implied in the practice of criticism and despite that, as E. D. Hirsch says, "No form of criticism is inherently privileged" (57), it must include three features: first, a working assumption of authority based on an awareness of a posited "origin" (or "singularity" in, say, the physicist Stephen Hawking's sense) from which any "reading" or "interpretation" may emanate; second, a concept of a privileged object of study coeval with or found "in" the literary work and, in all likelihood, reflecting the theory's posited origin and authority; and, third (heeding the plea of Frederick A. Pottle), a recognition of the relation between the synchronic and the diachronic, the potential of a work's being regarded at once as a unique act virtually outside time and as a function in a contextual field determined by history. All possible hypothetically "ultimate" orientations to authorities and objects—desiderata one and two—for literary criticism are located in a synchronic field always potentially subjected to history (as it is regarded, for example, by someone such as Fredric Jameson). The points of the compass of that field are identified, in the "orientation of critical theories" formulated by M. H. Abrams in the introduction to *The Mirror and the Lamp,* as the author, the work, the world, and the audience. Abrams's formulation of critical orientations (if not of objects of criticism) has seemed definitive to a generation of critics now (see Hernadi; Macksey), and it has seemed so for a good reason.[7] Regardless of the critic's theory or activity, it is not going to escape use of a posited or presumed authority or avoid focus on a privileged object, and the authority and object must be located in an orientation to one of the four fields Abrams names. As an activity, theorizing tends to focus on the justification of the authorities and objects, but the activities of critical readers tend to assume the already given authority of the paradigm and thus to mystify or veil from themselves the blind spot in it.

In this practical respect, as attests the charge leveled at Marxist criticism since the 1930s, New Criticism since the 1940s, archetypal criticism since the 1950s, structuralism since the 1960s, and psychoanalytic criticism since the beginnings, all theory and practice—to the extent that they are identified by an integrating model, metaphor, or paradigm (any of which is really a synecdoche)—will seem to be "monistic."[8] Though the real issue behind the apparent monism seems whether it is idealist or materialist, in fact there seems to be no modern critical theory that claims to be strictly idealist. Instead, even in those cases—as in structuralism and symbolism—that may appear idealist, the adherents insistently root the theory in the presumptively "real" world. The authority of any critical theory, in other words, will always be imputed to a concept that is posited to be "from" the real world (Abrams's "Universe") at the same time that the authorizing concept— myths, texts, desires, language, metaphor, symbols, structures, irony, history, archetypes, intentions, interpretive communities, modes of production—almost inevitably reifies one or another of the four possible objects of reading, analysis, or interpretation as natural, fundamental, or originary. While all practice of reading or analysis or interpretation, which I take to be the primary aim of most—though not all—contemporary critical theory (this aim itself a bias initiated by New Criticism, to be sure), is likely to valorize one or the other of the points of the compass Abrams has identified as mapping the field of literary theory, a valid theory must position itself in relation to each of the remaining points or orientations in some way. If it does not, a theory will be regarded as incomplete or invalid.

The whole history of critical theory, I suggest, is little more than the positing of one orientation and the critiquing of the failures of other theories to position themselves vis à vis that orientation in the context of the other three. I shall attempt to show in the following discussions that psychoanalytic criticism, unlike other types of literary theory, is most valuable—and most problematic—not so much because it valorizes just one orientation and one singulative origin or authority for analysis, but because its agency of authority—language, what Lacan calls the "agency of the letter"—potentializes almost equally all four possible analytic objects—work, world, author, audience. Freudianism frequently puzzles even its own adherents about the determining authority on which it is founded.[9] The clarity that Lacan has brought to both psychoanalysis and psychoanalytic criticism lies not in his style, which is regularly—and rightly—a target of opprobrium, but in his positing *language*—not myth or archetype or history—as the primal, originary, authoritative "scene" of any analysis or any speech act. But the effects of language create an unconscious discourse that is not understood "intellectually" by a speaker or even a writer. The lesson of structuralism and post-structuralism—from Saussure through Lévi-Strauss to Foucault and Derrida—is that language is the one agency that "contains" the author, reader, work, and world in the only ways available to the critic—that is, as results or effects of discursive practices. I shall first address Brooks and Ragland-Sullivan because they help delineate various aspects of the four objects on which psychoanalytic criticism may focus and the ways in which the mandating authority of such criticism may be enacted.

Text, Reader, Intertextuality

I shall begin with Brooks because, in "The Idea of a Psychoanalytical Literary Criticism," he has recently addressed the crucial questions raised by such criticism. Despite some specific disagreements with Brooks, I feel his essay is fundamental for any current understanding of the challenges to psychoanalytic literary criticism. A psychoanalytic critic himself, Brooks understands the ways others have attacked that critical understanding. He suggests at the outset that for many critics "psychoanalytic literary criticism has always been something of an embarrassment." He suggests, moreover, that though there has been a psychoanalytic literary criticism at least since Freud's essay "Creative Writers and Day-dreaming," these days, despite the renewal of interest in the mode because of "post-structuralist versions of reading, a malaise persists, a sense that whatever the promises of their union, literature and psychoanalysis remain mismatched bedfellows—or perhaps I should say playmates." Brooks goes on to say that the first and most basic problem in the "erotic" or "playful" union of literature and psychoanalysis is that this type of criticism has persistently mistaken its "*object* of analysis, with the result that whatever insights it has produced tells us precious little about the structure of literary texts." The objects criticism may take for analysis or the authorities it uses to orient values are determined by that set outlined by Abrams, though Brooks does not advert to him. The only possible objects—though the specific terms may not always be precisely these—are author, audience, work, and world. Brooks indicates that psychoanalytic criticism generally orients itself from within just three of the four. They are, Brooks says, "the author, the reader, or the fictive persons" (334), the latter being part of the text's relation to a "world" and thus a thrust in the direction of an imitated universe. As we shall see, Brooks, unwittingly though quite fruitfully, will eventually introduce the text itself as an orientation of the field of psychoanalytic criticism as well. Thus psychoanalytic understanding finally allows an orientation to each of the four points of Abrams's compass.

The first of these, the author, has become very problematical as an object of literary analysis in recent years, says Brooks, though he does not say why. It may well be from an inference that some famous examples such as Bonaparte's analysis of Poe have been undermined by more recent psychoanalytic theory, and have been called into question by critics such as Shoshana Felman in *Jacques Lacan and the Adventure of Insight*. Another possible reason for discrediting author analysis is related to Brooks's remarks about the third mentioned object, the character. "Like the author," Brooks says, "the fictive character has been deconstructed into an effect of textual codes, a kind of thematic mirage, and the psychoanalytic study of the putative unconscious of characters in fiction has also fallen into disrepute" ("Idea" 335). While Brooks admits that some of the feminist thematic readings of texts in terms of Oedipal triangles, of mothers and daughters, and of nurturing and bonding have been interesting, he avers (though without persuasive evidence) that they are "methodologically disquieting" in their use of the criticism in a "wholly thematic way, as if the identification and labeling of human relations in a psychoanalytic vocabulary were the task of criticism" ("Idea" 335). Finally, Brooks suggests that the third object of focus—the reader—has flourished in recent years "since the role of the reader in the creation of textual meaning is very much on our minds at present, and since the psychoanalytic study of readers' responses willingly brackets the impossible notion of author in favor of the acceptable and also verifiable notion of reader" ("Idea" 335). Despite the apparent claims of empiricism in the "verifiable," Brooks concludes here that the general problem of psychoanalytic criticism remains, for the analysis of reader response simply "displaces the object of analysis from the text to some person, some other psychodynamic structure." And that move, says Brooks, is "a displacement I wish to avoid"; he thinks, instead, that "psychoanalytic criticism can and should be textual and rhetorical" ("Idea" 335). Unfortunately, he does not explain how any criticism could be otherwise, including those methodologically "disquieting" modes of feminist and thematic criticism.

Ironically, because of his fear of a "sterile formalism" lacking any real relation to our existence (lacking, a Lacanian would say, any relation to *the* Real), Brooks does not always quite get the point of his own arguments. That blindness is a condition Lacan always acknowledges, for the Other of the unconscious always "knows" more than the subject who speaks or writes. "The unconscious," Lacan says, "is that part of the concrete discourse, in so far as it is transindividual, that is not at the disposal of the subject in re-establishing the continuity of his conscious discourse" (*Ecrits: A Selection* 49). Brooks's blindness lies in his reluctance to orient criticism from within the conventional fourth term in the configuration outlined by Abrams in *The Mirror and the Lamp*. Brooks simply does not want to turn to the text, the work itself. I do not think he ever realizes that what his various moves in his essay accomplish—through Jack Spector, Felman, Geoffrey Hartman, D. W. Winnicott, Terence Cave, and, above all, Freud and Jacques Lacan—is an explanation of the relation of literary text and psychoanalysis as the relations of nothing *other* than texts. Brooks himself surely would be surprised by my claim. Though it seems to me that the implications of his thesis directly lead one to the notion of the intertextual relations of literature and psychoanalysis, his overt comments about intertextuality are always negative. In the place, for example, where he explains the "forepleasure" literature holds out to the reader, he also explains that in the texts of literature lurk all sorts of "perversity," from fetishism, exhibitionism, and voyeurism all the way to the "polymorphous perverse," "the possibility of a text that would delay, displace, and deviate terminal discharge to an extent that it became nonexistent—as, perhaps, in the textual practice of the 'writable text' (*texte scriptible*) prized by Barthes, in Samuel Beckett, for instance, or Philippe Sollers." By this possibility of the perverse, worries Brooks, "the work of textuality may insure that all literature is, by its very nature, essentially perverse" ("Idea" 340).

Brooks continues to deny, however unconvincingly, the essential intertextuality of literary analysis. Just further along, for example, he speaks of the relation of literature and psychoanalytic criticism to the order of the Symbolic that Lacan posits as an ultimate, albeit veiled, authority. "The status of the *and* linking psychoanalysis and literary text may still remain at issue," Brooks says ("Idea" 340–41). Asking then what it means to claim that the structure of a metaphor in a specific literary work is equivalent to the structure of a symptom, Brooks directly challenges Lacan's well-known formula for metaphor and symptom, a formula that can be denoted by $S = S'/s$ (see, for example, *Ecrits: A Selection* 200). Brooks suggests that in the structure of the metaphor, itself the double of the structure of the symptom, lies the discovery of the "force of the occulted name of the father" within the Symbolic. But, he complains, one's invoking the name-of-the-father may be nothing more than a merely "ingenious piece of intertextuality" that subtly claims for psychoanalysis the authoritative place of an explanation for the interface between the critical mode and the literary work ("Idea" 341). It seems to me that in Brooks's unwillingness to grant intertextuality all that it might legitimately claim, he largely suppresses the role that it inevitably must play in any analysis, whether literary or psychoanalysis. What is at stake is in fact the relationship between several different "texts," and it may simply be moot to wonder which has authority over the other. The fact is, all that we "know" these days is regarded by structuralists, post-structuralists, and deconstructionists as some sort of text. Understanding and knowledge are textual, both generated by the relations among texts and textualities through the broadly defined medium of language. And for Lacan as well everything in understanding is textual, for understanding (knowledge of the truth of the subject, for instance) relies not on the real (which remains unsymbolizable), but on the Symbolic and the tropes of language (metaphor and metonymy) that make it function.

Paradoxically, Brooks's solution to his dilemma is ultimately Lacanian. Brooks valorizes one of what Lacan calls "the four fundamental concepts of psychoanalysis." Those concepts are the unconscious, repetition, transference, and the drive. Brooks uses the concept of transference to suppress that notion of intertextuality to which he hangs the idealist threats of mere formalism. He achieves the suppression through the notion of transference and his own concept of "reading." Brooks uses the traditional Freudian notion of transference because it allows him to mediate between psychoanalysis as a putative explanation and the apparent authority of the explanation as a piece of ingenious intertextuality. Ironically, the impetus behind Brooks's entire essay seems intertextual; that impetus lies in the challenge by Terence Cave to Brooks's *Reading for the Plot*. Brooks feels forced to address Cave's two-pronged remark that Brooks had valorized the Freudian model of the way human desire operates without at the same time becoming "imperialistic" about a psychoanalysis released from its "claim to tell the truth" (Cave 14). Brooks concedes both points to Cave. He says, "I am happy to be exonerated from the charge of imperialism in the reverse—the imperialism that would come from the incursion of literary criticism into psychoanalysis in search of mere metaphors, which has sometimes been the case with post-structuralist annexations of psychoanalytic concepts." He adds, moreover, that he certainly would "grant at least a temporary privilege to psychoanalysis in literary study, in that the trajectory through psychoanalysis forces us to confront the human stakes of literary form, while," he says, "I think also that these stakes need to be considered *in* the text, as activated by reading" ("Idea" 341).

The "human stakes" of reading hinge on transference. The reader's activation of the text through reading occurs through the transference. Thus *reading* becomes the trope for Brooks of transference in action. The activity of reading permits Brooks to elide the distinction between or among texts, for the verbal act ("reading") veils both the reader and the text read, the reader-as-text and the text-read-as-text. A transferential model, says Brooks, "allows us to take as the object of analysis not author or reader, but *reading,* including, of course, the transferential-interpretive operations that belong to reading. Meaning in this view is not simply 'in the text' nor wholly the fabrication of a reader (or a community of readers) but comes into being in the dialogic struggle and collaboration of the two, in the activation of textual possibilities in the process of reading. Such a view ultimately destabilizes the authority of reader/critic in relation to the text, since, caught up in the transference, he becomes analysand as well as analyst" ("Idea" 345; my emphasis). But Brooks realizes that this transferential model will not permit him automatically to escape Cave's complaint about psychoanalysis-as-mere-metaphor. Brooks's problem comes not in the movement from reader to text, but in that from text to reader. By what authority can the text speak not merely to, but also *for* the reader?

"How can there be a transference," asks Cave, "where there is no means by which the reader's language may be rephrased in coherent and manageable form by the text-as-analyst?" (14).

Brooks's argument, though he does not say it, is essentially hermeneutic. His construal of intertextuality relies on metaphors of dialogue, but his sense of dialogue always involves the reciprocity of hermeneutics. Meaning in reading is constituted through a reciprocal relation between specific and general, textual details and generic structures that come from the principles of any analytic method (whether psychoanalytic or otherwise). The hermeneutic circle emerges in Brooks's comments about analyst and analysand. Suggesting that though Cave reverses the usual model that sees the text as analysand and the reader as analyst, Brooks is nonetheless willing to concede that his transferential model permits such a reversal. That reversal amounts, I would suggest, to a "troping," to a change of metaphor, if not to "mere" metaphor—to a concept of the text as a trope or figure of the reader's experience. Still, he prefers to suppress a notion of intertextuality, "mere" intertextuality, that he deprecates about as much as he does "mere metaphor," and about as blindly, since all we have in understanding *is* tropes such as metaphor and metonymy, synecdoche and irony. Brooks's own move is metonymical, a turn to the authority of associations contained in a name. Brooks closes the hermeneutic circle by a return to Freud. In Freud's "Constructions in Analysis" Brooks finds his apparent answer to Cave's challenge. Freud's essay, as Brooks reads it, covers the roles of both analyst and analysand, reader and text, but these are seen as wholly interchangeable with one another. The analyst may start with the "traces" found in the analysand's story, but in the end the analyst's activity is "creative," constructive, or constitutive. Says Brooks, "Freud notes that since the analyst has neither experienced nor repressed any of the story in question, he cannot be called upon to remember it" ("Idea" 345). But the analyst can "construct"—trope or enfigure—it from or around what she or he is given, given, one assumes, both by the analysand and by the inner (typal) resources of the analyst.

The process, if clearly dialogic in Bakhtin's and interactive in Norman Holland's terms, is also fundamentally intertextual. "As in reading," says Brooks, "hypotheses of construal prove to be strong and valuable when they produce more text, when they create in the text previously unperceived networks of relation and significance, finding confirmation in the extension of the narrative and semantic web. The analytic work, the process of finding and making meaning, is necessarily a factor of listening and reading as well as telling" ("Idea" 346). The process of textual interaction may be profoundly creative, moreover, for though it may result that the analyst's construction "does not lead to the analysand's recollection of repressed elements of his story," the tropological construction may nevertheless have a positive rhetorical effect in causing the analysand to accept it with "an assured conviction of the truth of the construction which achieves the same therapeutic result as a recaptured memory" ("Idea" 346; Freud, *Standard Edition,* hereafter *SE,* 23:266). Thus, concludes Brooks, "Constructions in Analysis" provides us with a "view of psychoanalytic interpretation and construction that notably resembles the active role of the reader in making sense of a text, finding hypotheses of interpretation that open up ever wider and more forceful semantic patterns, attempting always to reach the totality of the supreme because necessary fiction" ("Idea" 346). The textual interaction, moreover, is two-way, from analysand to analyst, analyst to analysand, as it is from text to critic, from critic to text. "The reader may not have written the text," says Brooks, "yet it does change and evolve as he works on it—as he rewrites it, as those readers we call literary critics necessarily do. And as the reader works on the text, it does 'rephrase' his perceptions. I think any of us could find confirmation of such a truly transferential and dialogic relation of text and analysis in our own experience" ("Idea" 347).

Though I agree with Brooks's notion of reading as involving transference, and I especially like the notion because it explains the dual movement of the reader/text relationship, it seems to me that Brooks still fails to answer the question Cave raised regarding the interpretive authority of psychoanalysis. It seems to me, moreover, that the move Brooks makes to answer Cave is symptomatic of the problem that any of us has in searching for the authoritative foundation of the models by which we assess "the Real." We cannot ever truly find those answers *in* the *real* Real (though in the late seminars Lacan suggested otherwise). For the Real is precisely that which, according to Lacan, is "the impossible" since it remains unsymbolized. Unsymbolized, it is precisely that which cannot be absorbed into our discourse, though we infer its existence from the empty space around which our speech, our rhetoric functions, or, as Lacan says, by deciphering the material around the *objet a.* The *real* Real remains itself. Thus, in the face of its intractability, we are thrown back upon the notion of the Symbolic, the notion of the authority of the signifier. And that means we are thrown back upon the authority of the patriarchal, the system of discourse by which we attain ourselves in our subjectivity, the system within which we constitute meaning, and the system within which we create the other of understanding and knowledge—what Lacan calls "the *effects of truth*" (*Ecrits: A Selection* 158). As Alan Sheridan, the translator of *The Four Fundamental Concepts of Psycho-Analysis,* tells us, the symbols referred to in Lacan's concept of the Symbolic "are not icons," mere "stylized figurations"; rather, they are "signifiers, in the sense developed by Saussure and Jakobson," by, that is, the structuralists. This structuralist sense of the signifier is "extended into a generalized definition." Signifiers are "differential elements, in themselves without meaning," and as differential elements they "acquire value only in their mutual relations" and within the "closed order" they form. It is thus moot to wonder whether this closed order is complete or incomplete; it is consequential only that this order—the order of the Symbolic— "is seen to be the determining order of the [perceiving or cognizing] subject." Thus the effects of the Symbolic, says Sheridan, "are radical: the subject, in Lacan's sense, is . . . an effect" of the Symbolic (*FFC* 279).

Brooks's rhetorical turn is consistent with Lacanian theory. His apparent move, in locating an epistemological authority, is to name the father of psychoanalysis, Freud, but the real move is simply to invoke the Name-of-the-Father. Brooks's move permits me in turn to get back to Lacan, a Lacanian view of interpretation, subjectivity, knowledge. The basis for that view, which goes beyond Brooks's argument and subsumes Freud's concept of transference, is language, really the relation between language-as-language and language-enacted-as-speech in the phenomenological (and therefore spatial and historical) expression of language within our experience. As Marshall Alcorn has commented to me, "What comes to be in the rhetoric of the transference is a fiction of the subject that *moves* the subject in an essential way" (personal communication). Though Brooks tends (or pretends) to valorize Freud over Lacan, he nonetheless expresses Lacanian premises from time to time. And there is in the essay a deep sense that Lacan, more than Freud, provides his more important ideological base, for Brooks concedes that "we constitute ourselves as human subjects in part through our fictions." He therefore concedes "that the study of human fiction-making and the study of psychic process are convergent activities and superimposable forms of analysis" ("Idea" 341). With these claims we are enabled to see clearly how the text of the subject and the subject of the text—that is, ourselves and the contents of our verbal creations—come together in the reader or analyst through a concept of intertextuality. The stage, finally, is set for a move to a more definitively articulated Lacanian poetics, one that explains how and why the structure—especially one aspect of the structure—of the Lacanian subject gets into the act.

A Lacanian Poetics

Because language—seen as both *la langue* and *la parole*—is the key to the interface between the reader-as-text and the text-as-textual other/Other, Ragland-Sullivan's essay "The Magnetism between Reader and Text: Prolegomena to a Lacanian Poetics" is especially important to my project in *Using Lacan, Reading Fiction*. Ragland-Sullivan's sense of a Lacanian poetics is as intertextual as Brooks's. In her abstract introducing the essay, Ragland-Sullivan states that "Lacan viewed language as playing a profound and multivalent role in the structuring of human perception" (381). Thus, in the body of the essay, she takes up in detail the way in which the perceiving subject—both the subject of speech and that which Lacan calls the ego—is represented by and in language. The ego is the identificatory construct the reader exchanges with the literary text; the medium of exchange is language. The literary text exerts, she suggests in her controlling metaphor, "a magnetic pull on the reader because it is an allegory of the psyche's fundamental structure" (381). As a consequence of this allegorical—or metaphorical—relation of text and reader, she says, a "Lacanian poetics would not aim to psychoanalyze a text, then, but would study the paralinguistic points of join between visible language and invisible effect" (382). In the course of the essay, therefore, Ragland-Sullivan discusses in succession her assessment of the ego, the "analogous laws of cognitive function between text and reader," repression and representation in the unconscious mind, and, synthesizing everything, some "prolegomena to a Lacanian poetics" (382).

To see how the intertextual or magnetic relation between reader and literary text operates, we must look at the way Ragland-Sullivan describes the ego as seen by Lacan. To begin with, she insists, Lacan does not posit an a priori self, a self that can exist prior to any perception. Rather, the ego comes from the system that individual human perception puts into place from birth; it "is itself created by the perception of objects—redefined by Lacan as 'symbols'—which are recorded as unconscious representations" (383). The crux of Ragland-Sullivan's explanation of the ego includes several major points. First, she says, "These representations are 'in play' throughout life, carrying the energy needed to translate them from one meaning system to another—unconscious to conscious—by means of substitution, displacement, condensation and contiguous referentiality." Second, she insists that, "through the identificatory and mimetic processes of introjection and projection, the ego is constituted from the Other" and others. Third, she makes it plain that the ego is a text, a fiction. "Although it continually builds up identificatory layers through interacting with others," she says, "the *moi* [ego] is fixed early in life by a few narcissistic fictions that provide a unity to perception." But, fourth, she also makes it plain that the self Lacan posits is unavailable to any totalizing knowledge in consciousness. "As an inherently limited principle of identificatory conservation, the *moi* [ego] occupies a space in consciousness, but is unaware that its individuality derives from the Other." Finally, she insists upon the intersubjective and, therefore, intertextual nature of our "selves." "Throughout life," she says, "social and verbal situations push people *to exchange* [my emphasis] their *moi* as symbols ([as] substitutes for an ideal 'self') within the vibrant arena of ego ideals ([within the context of] others)." In sum, she says, "The *moi*, thus, serves as the essence of being and personal uniqueness" (383), but, Lacan always insists, this being and uniqueness are never fully known and in control in the way suggested of the ego in American ego psychology.

Once she has put the essentially textual ego into place, Ragland-Sullivan can go on to the relationship between it and the literary text. What she suggests, it seems to me, is that the literary text is a projection from the locus of the subject's ego, whether that ego is the author's or the reader's, *toward* the locus of the Other, the unconscious structure of the subject. The literary text, that is, offers itself as a structuration for the one position—the ego—of the author or the reader as subject, but it does so precisely through the locus of the Other. There are thus several points one must bear in mind when thinking a Lacanian poetics. To begin, it is important to understand that though a projection from the authorial/readerly ego, the literary text for its part may represent all four of the positions of the quadrangular subject, as one may see, for example, in Lacan's reading of Poe's "Purloined Letter." What's more, the ego thus has a metaphorical relation to the literary text, since the text stands in for—or substitutes for—the projected ego of author or reader. In itself, the ego is metaphorical, but in relation to desire it is metonymical since it is merely a part, not a whole. The ego is thus a partial or—in Lacan's terms—a fragmented text that, in the case of the author, "writes" itself and, in the case of the reader, "reads" itself *as if completed* in the text. Finally, functioning in writing and reading in the domain of the Symbolic, then, the ego meets itself more than narcissistically in the literary text, its Symbolic, rather than merely Imaginary, textual double. It does so in the way that a figure of the metonym (a part or part-object) fulfills itself in the figure of the whole in the rhetorical function of the synecdoche.[10]

Since a Lacanian poetics, Ragland-Sullivan suggests, "would reveal the *moi* [ego] as the true subject of being, and at the same time a compilation of myths, fantasies, and desires taken on from others," those texts, in her words, "become a repressed Other," an unconscious that knows the self in ways the self cannot fully know. Thus, since it is signified in the register of the Symbolic, the reader's ego may not gain mastery over those identificatory texts any more, finally, than may the author's ego, although, to paraphrase Jake Barnes to Lady Brett Ashley, it would be nice to think so. As Ragland-Sullivan says, because "the *moi* is a mystery to itself, it is ever dependent on others [including literary-textual others] to place value" on it, to give it the recognition the self requires. It is that recognition, among other things, that the literary text provides the subject who writes and the subject who reads, whether that reader is the fabled "general reader" or the more self-conscious literary critic. In itself the ego, however much it represents the uniqueness of human personality, simply "becomes one more proof of an unconscious ([and therefore] absent) space in being." The literary text, albeit only figuratively, as a metonym to a synecdoche, helps the reading subject "fill" that space. To that end, Ragland-Sullivan suggests, the strategies of the ego for effecting its rhetorical, communicative exchange in all discursive relations are irony, humor, fiction, drama, poetry, and the like. The aspect of these strategies, says Ragland-Sullivan, that makes them useful in the intertextual relation of textual ego to literary text is that all are uses of language that "point to a 'logic' beyond conventional meaning" (387), to a logic in an absent space, to, that is, the logic of the unconscious. In effect, Ragland-Sullivan suggests, since the ego is nothing other than the texts of which it is made, like the literary fiction, it is a fiction maintained by the position of the speaking subject in the Lacanian quadrangle, the "I," the *je*, the shifting function that carries the ego in speech and interprets it, though only Imaginarily, to the external world. In this context, she says, the I is the *porte-parole*, the bearer of the "letter" of identity, as it were, but it is not the identity itself. In a nice turn of phrase, then, Ragland-Sullivan suggests that within the individual's subject text, "the *moi* reveals the *je* as an unreliable narrator" (387). We are always unreliable when—as an "I"—we try consciously to explain or narrate our "true" selves.

The exchange of the ego and the literary text occurs through the medium of language. Language is always the Other that "knows"; as Lacan frequently calls it, it is *"Le sujet supposé savoir,"* the subject that knows everything in both ego and text. In that exchange, the enriching intertextuality of writing and reading comes into play in a Lacanian poetics. Such a poetics begins to "explain" for writers and readers our attraction to literature. Ragland-Sullivan's summary is precise. First, "If the *moi* operates perception, both the author's and reader's, through a kind of representational dispersion within language, then literary texts unveil the Real fictionality of 'self.' " Second, "Such a connection between language, identity, and mind would go a long way toward solving the riddle of the 'truth-value' of literature." Third, "Like Lacan's vision of psychic experience, literary discourse would operate by sliding from one perceptual register to another: the Imaginary (identificatory fusions), the Symbolic (language, cultural codes and conventions), the Real (what *is*), and the Symptom (knots in the unconscious signifying chains which show up in conscious life as missing—repressed—words, or in ascertainable behavior patterns, or in organic disturbances)." Finally, "These four registers prescribe protean waltzes around a void: what one knows (but misrecognizes and denies) about one's unconscious" (387).

Here we come to what Brooks has called the "human stakes" of reading. By passing from the ego-as-text to the way in which the writer's or reader's ego is necessarily found *in* texts, Ragland-Sullivan is enabled to begin to explain some of the specific values of literature and its genres. She says, for example, that a "Lacanian poetics would argue that the genres and rhetorical devices of literature formalize the human drama by organizing themselves around universal key signifiers: the mysteries of love, the tragedies of misunderstanding, the horrors of death, the enigmas of affect and rhetoric (humor, irony, and so on)" (392). We shall see these in the examples studied in *Using Lacan, Reading Fiction*: the mysteries of love in *The Scarlet Letter*, the tragedies of misunderstanding in "The Beast in the Jungle," and the horrors of death in *To the Lighthouse*. Moreover, because she feels that a Lacanian view of literature must show how it points to a "representational underside of consciousness," at the same time that it gives "voice to a hidden dialectic," Ragland-Sullivan can claim that "neither the 'truth value' of fiction, nor the power of literature" can be "explained by reference to the rules and conventions of language." Literary forms thus become "privileged" uses of language because they display in a higher ratio than "ordinary" language the "power of Imaginary resonances and dramas in life" and their references "to their source in the Real of unconscious experience."

It is in this context that she is able to speak directly of poetry, drama, and prose narrative. She indicates that lyric poetry, such as, we might suggest, Dylan Thomas's "Fern Hill," permits authors, texts, and readers to get at primordial ego sources in the lyric's "evoking primary repressions that reverberate back to the earliest representations." She suggests as well that distinctions can be seen between conventional drama and modernist drama. "In traditional drama," she says, "the *moi* simulates verbal debate with the forces of Desire and Law," seen, we might point out, in Lacan's analysis of desire and mourning in *Hamlet*. By contrast, modernist drama "dispenses with a unified (or substantive *moi*) discourse in favor of revealing the tricks of primary-process laws (irony, the comic, and so on)." A modern play such as Samuel Beckett's *Waiting for Godot* or Edward Albee's *American Dream*, we might suggest, thus "unravels *moi* unity, and subverts linguistic conventions," though we may also point out that a modernist novel such as Faulkner's *The Sound and the Fury* does the same things. Finally, touching on the area of literature that attracts me most in *Using Lacan, Reading Fiction*, she says of narrative: "A Lacanian poetics would say that narrative focuses on the *moi*'s identity quest, and thus uses language in a variety of discursive modes. By setting characters in opposition, the author can dramatize the diversity of his own *moi* voices, and their dialectical disharmony in relation to an Other's Desire" (392). In a variety of ways, we will see all these phenomena in the analyses of *The Scarlet Letter*, "The Beast in the Jungle," and *To the Lighthouse*.

Lacan and Interpretation

Before concluding an already very long introduction, I need to consider one other matter—what happens when we do interpretation. I started with Lacan's focus on language and the algorithm used to suggest its basic structure: S/s. I think I can end with that same essential enfiguration, for doing interpretation of any sort puts into action on a larger scale the same structure upon which Lacan builds his entire system. We may feel we inhabit a hall of mirrors, a place where the same structure repeats itself into a vanishing point. Lacan's own translation of linguistic into psychoanalytic terms reveals the same pattern. Though Fredric Jameson has said that "on the level of interpretive codes Lacan's position is not one of substituting linguistic for classical psychoanalytic concepts but rather of mediating between them" ("Imaginary and Symbolic" 372), mediation, in Jameson's sense, still means substitution. For in any case—whether one interprets linguistically or psychoanalytically—the interpretation functions through a representation, a stand-in, one thing standing for something else—a signifier standing in for a signified. But the reason for the repetition of these structures is that all commentary or interpretation works the way Jameson describes, that is, by a mediation between or among "interpretive codes." The implications of that mediation have been troubling to many modern critics, for it suggests that all interpretation is "merely" metaphorical or otherwise tropological and thus perhaps allegorical. Ragland-Sullivan herself broaches the subject when she calls her Lacanian poetics—the magnetic pull of texts on readers—allegorical ("Magnetism" 381). Indeed, that term—*allegorical*—has become the subject of one of the epoch's major "anxieties."

In a very illuminating essay on trends in intellectual history, Hans Kellner has recently argued that there are several basic anxieties troubling historians and, by extension, others who engage in interpretive discourse. Kellner suggests that at this moment in the writing of intellectual history, there are three radically distinct modes of inquiry that create a triangular field of forces acting upon historical and analytic discourse. These three are Marxism, structuralism, and psychoanalysis. Each of these exerts a powerful influence on the other two, and frequently, because of the attractiveness of what a practitioner in one can comprehend in another's methodology, one modality is drawn toward another. Kellner notes, for example, "that anxieties arise in historical thought when something is perceived to be lost or excluded" because "the triangle of hermeneutic camps divides the analytic field—context, intention, and textuality"—among the three (126). This anxiety will not mean that practitioners in the different modalities will cease to practice. In the writing of history, for example, "Freudians will, to be sure, continue to write their form of psychohistory; Marxists, their form of contextual history, and so forth." Kellner's point is that when the "desired" object belongs to one of the other modes, then the desiring practitioner will begin to reach toward it, but only through a mediating third party or object. What the critic desires is not the modality of the "other"; rather, it is the "content" that the mode of the "other" can encompass or inscribe. Kellner describes how the triangular process works when he says, "the Marxist, for instance, can grasp at the desired psychological richness of the Freudian only by imitating or adapting in some way to the problematic or terminology of the other." Thus, says Kellner, our intellectual discourse is now marked by such triangular amalgams as "structuralist Marxism, linguistic psychoanalysis, universal structural strategies of desire, and a deconstructive technique that calls into question the basis of meaning itself" (127).

The critical point that Kellner makes, however, is more far-reaching than the presence of such triangular anxieties might portend. That point—essentially deconstructive—has to do with the possibility of analytic discourse at all. Kellner has a name for it. The even graver problem that faces any critic when he or she interprets a literary work these days is what Kellner calls the "anxiety of allegory." Referring to the words of Northrop Frye, Kellner notes that "all commentary is allegorical interpretation." Like Frye, Kellner means to say that allegory "is the essential genre of interpretation" (29). Thus, we are destined to suffer this anxiety, for there is no way around allegory, in a broad sense, if we mean to interpret events or development of ideas through history or if we intend to interpret literary works, of whatever scale or magnitude—poem, story, novel, drama. The dream of analysis, hermeneutics, interpretation is to incorporate the object without mediation, but that is precisely what one cannot do and engage in *represen-*

tation at the same time. This recognition thus leads to a further problem, one more generally deconstructive, even apparently nihilistic. "The *anxiety* before allegory," says Kellner, "comes from the heightened awareness of the distance between what we mean and the texts we produce, or whether we *can* mean without producing a text, the existence of which always already undercuts the grounds of meaning" (130).

Kellner brings us back to the structure of the Lacanian algorithm: S/s. Allegory is nothing more than the transfer from one way of saying something to another way of saying that "same" thing. In this respect, allegory is perhaps merely the function writ large of the linguistic trope, whether, as is usually the case, epitomized by metaphor, a word whose Greek root means "to bear" or "to transfer," or whether including a system of tropes within a "tropology," and thus including the other figures of metonymy, synecdoche, and irony as in the "tropologies" of Kenneth Burke or Hayden White, whose sense of tropology I have employed in *Doing Tropology*. But by seeing that allegory as a means of interpretation is related to tropes and tropology, we also see that allegory has a more basic dimension. That dimension is repression. Robert Con Davis has discussed the main issues of narration, interpretation, and repression in a very important essay called "Lacan, Poe, and Narrative Repression." Davis suggests that repression is a trope (983), but in fact the trope is a metaphor. He suggests, for example, that an essential Freudian text on which to base a Lacanian theory of narrative repression is "Instincts and Their Vicissitudes." In that text, Davis suggests, "Freud shows a metaphoric operation at work" (988). The operation is metaphoric because "the text at one moment inscribes the exhibitionist and suppresses, but in this sense also 'writes,' a voyeur; at another it inscribes passivity and suppresses, but also 'writes,' activity. In each case the text marks the changes controlled by metaphor in a process of linguistic substitutions among structural positions" (988–89).

On this argument Davis makes his claim about Lacan: "Lacan's primary contribution to psychoanalysis—and, by extension, to narrative theory—has been to elaborate this notion of the text: an economy of conscious and unconscious systems in various stages of disunity—a text/system governed, as Lacan shows, by metaphor. A primary assumption underlying Lacan's reading of the Freudian text is that in it words as such exist in a 'conscious' system where signifiers in one constellation (or chain) of association continually stand in for signifiers in another" (989). In developing this thesis, as well as in providing a very enlightening set of illustrative examples, Davis resorts to Lacan's "little letters"—to that algorithm, the S/s, the structure that Lacan himself (as Davis shows) transforms into the "formula" of repression and metaphor itself—at least the one found in *The Four Fundamental Concepts of Psycho-Analysis* (248):

$$\frac{S'}{S} \cdot \frac{S}{s} = \frac{\dfrac{S'}{s}}{\dfrac{S}{S}}$$

On the side of the quotient, explains Davis, the S' stands for the manifest or conscious system, the s for the preconscious system capable of becoming conscious, the $\dfrac{S}{S}$ for the unconscious. But the major point for Davis is the way the bars of repression support signification and—ultimately—narration itself. In short, Davis suggests, "the metaphoric system functions as an unconscious writing agency, inscribing differences in two texts at once. Metaphor, therein, creates systems of discourse and in so doing governs textuality" (992).

Even more basic than the relation of allegory to the trope of metaphor and Lacan's algorithm is the relation of allegory to language and textuality themselves. Language is founded on the necessity of making a transfer or translation from one system to another. In a structuralist conception of language built on the function of the sign, the one thing that language and its system of signs cannot do is capture and convey the original signified. Thus it seems true, however sad or frustrated it may make us, that any interpretation, whether Freudian, Marxist, structuralist, or otherwise—Lacanian, for instance—must rely upon a "transfer" of the object analyzed into another set of terms. One may argue that this transfer is "merely" allegory. But in our lived, phenomenological relation to our objects, our allegories are never "merely" allegorical. For whatever the case, there is no interpretation apart from "mere allegory," no more than there is interpretation apart from our desire. One chooses, though seldom because of desire "simply" chooses, the terms of one's allegorical figure. Though mine is not the Lacan of the "final state," as David Macey calls the Lacan seen in *Encore* and after (see Macey, *Lacan in Contexts*), my allegorical figure *is* Lacan as his work is generally understood at this time. Thus, in looking at characters in fiction, I shall constantly look for points of translation, moments of possible allegorization.

If, as I think, all interpretation is allegorical (or tropological), it is predicated, too, on another fundamental principle. All interpretation, as Davis suggests in his reading of Poe's "The Tell-Tale Heart" ("Lacan, Poe, and Narrative Repression" 992–1000), is textual. But the textuality of interpretation is based on an understanding that our experience— as experience, as an "object" of study or analysis—is also textual. We must "read" our experience as a text, whether it is experience of life's events or of an actual verbal text such as a novel or a history. In the process of that reading, consequently, we engage, whether we like it or admit it, in an act of intertextuality. That is precisely the point of my analysis of Peter Brooks's "The Idea of a Psychoanalytic Criticism" and of Ragland-Sullivan's essay on a Lacanian poetics. Thus it is the case that my "readings" of texts such as *The Scarlet Letter,* "The Beast in the Jungle," and *To the Lighthouse* are intertextual. Each involves the process of placing side by side, as it were, some aspect of my Lacanian model and the text of novel or story. But it seems to me that there is yet another, a Lacanian, dimension to this intertextuality. The model just enunciated is essentially binary; it implies a deceptively simple, one-to-one relation between a subject text (that is, the novel that is the object of analysis) and an "other" text, the model on which the subject text is to be analyzed, in what, in Lacanian terms, can only be an Imaginary relation. In that respect, all interpretation is Imaginary. Various critics have offered that insight, but there is as well a Symbolic dimension to the intertextual relation. That is the relation between an unconscious ego and the unconscious subject itself, the domain that Lacan identifies as the Other, the Symbolic. In this relation, there is an inevitable two-way interaction. We cannot simply say that the subject text (say, the novel analyzed) is the ego, nor can we say either that the dominating unconscious is the analyst or the reader. The relation becomes rather undecidable, just as the relation of the signifier to the signified in a hermeneutic, if not deconstructive, linguistics becomes undecidable.

What we have reached here is a concept of a "textual unconscious." Davis uses this concept in his essay on Poe. Speaking of Freud's "Instincts and Their Vicissitudes," Davis says that Freud's insistence on "the existence of a nonmanifest text" with "no positive terms" reveals a textual unconscious "in which positions exist in a decentered system by virtue of differing from each other" (989). The idea of a textual unconscious has also been broached by, among others, Fredric Jameson, in what he calls "the political unconscious," and by Jonathan Culler, in a conceptualization much closer to what I speak of above (see also Bellemin-Nöel; de Man; and Flieger). Culler writes of the textual unconscious in the context of Jameson's notion. For Jameson, the political unconscious is the hidden story or narrative that every literary work, perhaps every verbal expression, will carry. "Jameson's political unconscious," says Culler, "is an underlying narrative within literary works," and that narrative "surfaces only in disguised and symbolic forms" (Culler 370). Culler is not willing to limit the unconscious of texts to the political alone. He quotes Jameson himself in a place where he remarks that interpretation is "construed as an essentially allegorical act," one that "consists in rewriting a given text in terms of a particular interpretive master code" (Jameson, *Political Unconscious*, 10; Culler 370). It is simply that Jameson takes the code of Marxism as a master code, the code that includes, but subsumes all other codes, including of course the psychoanalytic.

Jameson's fault in his assumption of Marxism as an authority for his allegory lies not in the authority itself. Rather, it lies in the assumption of an ultimate authority. Jameson must be as aware as I am of the indeterminacy of our thought, intentions, and messages; I am particularly well aware that a Lacanian—no more than a Marxist— critic can hardly claim to be the Other of interpretation, the one who not only is supposed to know, but actually *knows*. It seems to me, however, that all who write criticism or commentary do so with the at least provisional notion they have something to say that is worthwhile, even if not possessed of a totally godlike authority. Any use of language involves a presumption of mastery. Now that every literary critic understands the instability of meaning and interpretation, it seems to me a mere redundancy to frame our interpretations in repeated assertions of our lack of signifying authority, our indeterminacy as subjects, the instability of the text as a subject. In Lacanian terms, our critical endeavors are always exchanges in the Imaginary and Symbolic, even as they invoke the primality of the Real. If we were to speak in our criticism as if we believed absolutely in our posited meanings, as if, that is, the Symbolic spoke through us, we would place ourselves quite clearly in the position of the psychotic as defined by Lacan. Thus it seems to me that as critics we operate largely—though one hopes not unconsciously—in the Imaginary, and, given our awareness that the only authority we have is the Symbolic and therefore the unconscious, we must make our interpretive claims of master codes in all humility.

Whether our master code is socioeconomic life or the structure of the unconscious, reading must involve, as Brooks suggests, fundamentally human stakes. Thus, since I assume that all interpretation is allegorical, though not "merely" allegorical, it is not crucial to agree or disagree with Jameson on the point of his master code. What is crucial is to recognize that the textual unconscious exists in the relation between the analyst (social, literary, or psychoanalytic) and the "text" under scrutiny. It is involved, as we saw in the discussions of Brooks and Ragland-Sullivan, in what Freudian psychoanalysis calls "the transference." Culler can add to our understanding of that process. Lacan has reformulated the concept in a way Culler—as literary critic—has found instructive. "The unconscious here," writes Culler, "is not an underlying narrative the analyst discerns in this discourse but rather what is at work in the drama of the analyst's involvement." Says Culler, "In taking my cue from Lacan's formulation of the Freudian discovery—that transference is the enactment of the reality of the unconscious—I am joining Jameson in assuming that a literary work can have an unconscious." But Culler does not join Jameson in accepting Marxism as a master interpretive code. Instead, he suggests "that his notion of that unconscious . . . is not what is unveiled by the masterful hermeneutic of Marxism but is rather, in my definition, what is at work in the analyst's transferential relation to the text" (Culler 371). That transferential relation means, then, as both Shoshana Felman and Barbara Johnson have shown in different ways, that what the analyst "finds in" the text is also "found" by the text "in" the analyst. It is this "deeper," more unconscious relation, I believe, that makes our reading of literature so vibrantly meaningful for us, and explains why we cannot always say why a work will touch us so powerfully. That power of affect is the one that comes from the unconscious, whether it lies in us or in the texts that seem to bring it up or from which we bring it up.

Conclusion

As a way of concluding this discussion, I would like to suggest the advantages Lacanian analysis offers to literary criticism. First, regardless of the close historical relation between the development of Freud's concepts and his literary examples, Lacanian analysis is immediately more "literary" than Freudian analysis. As I have tried to suggest in the first major section of this introduction, Lacan insists upon the absolute primacy of language and tropes or figures of speech in psychoanalysis. One does not need to search out traumatic events, actual happenings, to locate the psychological cruxes of character or subjectivity. By focusing on language, on the mechanisms of language found in tropes, Lacan brings his analysis immediately into the domain of literary analysis (or vice versa, Lacan might say), and whatever the consequences for psychoanalysis, that congruence between psychoanalysis and literary analysis makes the work of the Lacanian critic much more compatible with ordinary habits of literary attention. The attention to language, moreover, brings a tact and subtlety to interpretation not always found in old-style Freudian criticism. The Freudian seems to literalize such metaphors as the phallus, the Family Romance, the murder of the father, the desire for incest with father or mother, and the like. Lacan asks the critic, instead, to work within the figurative, the Symbolic domain. He suggests that in the "normal" subject, the events and roles played in psychoanalysis are functions of structured positions within a symbolic field. When those symbolic figures become literal for the subject, Lacan suggests, we may indeed be outside the normative and into the realm of the psychotic (See Rosenbaum and Sonne), though one must not suggest that the Freudian *critic* suffers from psychosis.

The second major advantage of Lacanian over Freudian analysis is indeed its ability to deal with the "normal" subject. While to analysis there is never a purely normal subject (and when there seems to be one it is probably pathologically so), there is a case to be made for the ordinary subject who does what most subjects do in the course of their lives. We do not have to look for narcissism's pathologies or the pathologies of Oedipus. We may, instead, simply look for manifestations of the subject's passages into or through the mirror stage and the Oedipus complex. In the chapter that follows, for example, we find that the "normative" mother—Hester Prynne—and her daughter, Pearl, are as interesting from a Lacanian perspective as the more pathological Dimmesdale and Chillingworth. Though Pearl and Hester are hardly "ordinary people," the Lacanian reading does illustrate that nonpathological subjects can be analyzed in fruitful and interesting ways. Although Freudian literary analysis is not limited to the neurotic and the psychotic, it appears that it is so limited in the critical praxis, despite the excellent analysis of the nonpathological that Freud himself performs in his essay on Jensen's *Gradiva*. This limitation in the praxis, if not in the actual theory, can be observed in Frederick Crews's classic Freudian interpretation of *The Scarlet Letter*. Crews seems solely interested—perhaps only capable of interest—in one character: the very troubled Reverend Arthur Dimmesdale. Crews occasionally refers to Hester and Chillingworth as potential subjects in his interpretation, but never to Pearl. Despite his insight that Chillingworth is "the psychoanalyst *manqué*" (141), virtually all his attention is devoted to Dimmesdale as the pathological subject in whom is manifest the combination of guilt and repression Crews's (though not all) Freudianism must assess. While Crews's essay will remain a landmark in psychoanalytic interpretation of fiction (despite Crews's disaffection from this mode of interpretation), it may well remain as a representation of the particular blindness of Freudian analysis as well. I would hope that as Lacan rereads Freud, so my Lacanian rereadings of *The Scarlet Letter*, "The Beast in the Jungle," and *To the Lighthouse* may illustrate the critical openness of the philosophy of psychoanalysis found in Lacan.

Despite the length of my introduction, readers must feel that not enough space has been devoted to concrete illustrations of Lacan's revisions of Freudian theory. Beginning with the following reading of Nathaniel Hawthorne's *The Scarlet Letter*, one may get the opposite impression—that there is relatively little abstract theory amidst the concreteness of textual illustration. What I hope to do in this—and the next two chapters—is exhibit that allegorizing tendency of interpretation that pivots on the exigencies of the Lacanian and structuralist algorithm—S/s. Where a critic such as Robert Con Davis in an exemplary essay such as "Lacan, Poe, and Narrative Repression" admirably displays the complexity of the interpretive transaction, I shall exhibit it at its simplest level—that of the basic algorithm rather than that of the more complex formulation of metaphor and repression. Ostensibly ignoring the bar (the virgule representing the gap between signifier and signified), I shall place side by side just two sets of terms— textual evidence and Lacanian theory—rather than the four terms of the formal analysis manipulated in the formula of repression. Since my aim is a simpler one, namely, to introduce Lacanian reading, I feel the simpler approach is likely to be more amenable to most readers at this time. More complex readings—many of which are already in print, written by critics such as Davis, Jameson, MacCannell, Ragland-Sullivan, and others—have their place in Lacanian studies. The beginning Lacanian will see that their place is not in *Using Lacan, Reading Fiction*.

Notes

1. In the text's next several paragraphs I will give a rough historical synopsis of the introduction of Lacanian thought to Anglo-American scholars. Here, I shall offer a more descriptive synopsis of the scholarship. Lacan's work, much of which exists only in notes taken by others at his famed *séminaires*, is now being translated into English on a large scale under the direction of Jacques-Alain Miller. The most important translations so far are *Ecrits: A Selection, Feminine Sexuality, The Four Fundamental Concepts of Psycho-Analysis*, and the first three of the seminars: *Freud's Papers on Technique 1953–54, The Ego in Freud's Theory and in the Technique of Psychoanalysis 1954–55*, and *The Psychoses 1955–56* (scheduled for 1992). I should add that two of the twelve chapters of *Séminaire XX*, called *Encore*, are included in *Feminine Sexuality*, and that the work called *Television*, based on a television broadcast of 1973, was translated and published in 1990, along with documents related to Lacan's many battles with the International Psychoanalytic Association. The longest of the essays in *Ecrits*, "The Function and Field of Speech and Language in Psychoanalysis," was translated early on by Anthony Wilden in *Speech and Language in Psychoanalysis*, originally published (1968) as *The Language of the Self*. Critiques of Lacan are becoming rather numerous; one "authorized" by Lacan is Anika Lemaire's *Jacques Lacan*; for a lengthy exposition (yet shorter than Lemaire), see Eugen Bär's "Understanding Lacan." For a rather lucid brief account of the main premises from a semiotic perspective, see Kaja Silverman's *The Subject of Semiotics*. Juliet Mitchell and Jacqueline Rose, in their two introductions to *Feminine Sexuality*, offer an excellent assessment of Lacan's views of gender assumption. For a variety of discussions on issues related to Lacanian theory and language, see two books: *The Talking Cure: Essays in Psychoanalysis and Language*, ed. Colin MacCabe, and David Macey's *Lacan in Contexts*. Macey is rather negative on Lacan and will annoy many Lacanians, but the book nonetheless contains much useful objective information. Detailed, line-by-line, essay-by-essay "explication" of Lacan's *Ecrits: A Selection* appears in *Lacan and Language: A Reader's Guide to "Ecrits,"* by John P. Muller and William J. Richardson; Bice Benvenuto and Roger Kennedy, in *The Works of Jacques Lacan: An Introduction*, offer a similar, but not quite as extensive, reading of Lacan. The most comprehensive synthesis of Lacan is Ragland-Sullivan, *Jacques Lacan and the Philosophy of Psychoanalysis*; her essay "The Magnetism between Reader and Text: Prolegomena to a Lacanian Poetics" is also useful to any

reading of a literary text. A diverse collection of essays very important in the early transmission of Lacan's ideas is *Interpreting Lacan*, ed. Joseph H. Smith and William Kerrigan. Ground-breaking Lacanian interpretation of literature may be found collected in two books edited by Robert Con Davis: *The Fictional Father: Lacanian Readings of the Text* and *Lacan and Narration: The Psychoanalytic Difference in Narrative Theory*. A series of volumes generated by presentations at the Lacan Conferences held at Kent State University is planned; the first volume from these, *Compromise Formations: Current Directions in Psychoanalytic Criticism* (Vera Camden, ed., 1989), though not devoted entirely to Lacan, includes several enlightening essays. The best bibliography of works by and about Lacan is Michael Clark's *Jacques Lacan: An Annotated Bibliography*.

2. For reasons I cannot entirely explain, Lacan almost never cites Benveniste when he speaks of the relation between linguistic theories and psychoanalysis. There is at least circumstantial evidence that Benveniste was more important in forming Lacan's linguistic bias than either Saussure or Jakobson—or, for that matter, Lévi-Strauss. For example, Benveniste reviewed the work of Karl von Frisch on communication among honey bees in an essay published in *Diogenes* in 1952; later, Lacan also spoke of von Frisch's work on bees—in his "Function and Field" address of September 1953. More to the point, Benveniste wrote of the importance in psychoanalysis of rhetoric and tropes (such as metaphor and metonymy) in an essay called "Remarks on the Function of Language in Freudian Theory," published in Lacan's journal *La psychanalyse* (vol. 1) in 1956; Lacan's "Function and Field" address of 1953 was published in the same issue. Only after that, in May of 1957, did Lacan make his first explicit remarks on the function of language per se; these came in "The Agency of the Letter in the Unconscious or Reason since Freud." It was in this essay that Lacan delineated the function of metaphor and metonymy (as well as the contributions of Saussure on the theory of the sign). Benveniste quotes Lacan's "Function and Field" essay in his essay on Freud; Lacan does not refer to Benveniste in "The Agency of the Letter," though he does pay homage to Jakobson (see *Ecrits: A Selection* 177n.20). In this context, it is to be remarked that he makes a querulous comment in the same note about R. M. Loewenstein; Lacan claims that Loewenstein, who was Lacan's own analyst for seven years, ignores work on the role of speech in psychoanalysis published after 1952, Lacan apparently meaning to imply that Loewenstein should have referred to his 1953 "Function and Field" address. In Loewenstein's defense, one may point out that "Function and Field" was not published until 1956, the same year as Loewenstein's essay. Where language and psychoanalysis are concerned, Lacan thus seems to express a more than usual concern about primacy of authority. Likewise, Elizabeth Roudinesco remarks in *La bataille de cent ans* (149–56) that Lacan was quite jealous of the reputation and influence of Alexandre Kojève, whose virtuoso lectures on Hegel seem to have been a model for Lacan's own lectures.

3. Freud's discussion of the *Fort! Da!* game occurs in *Beyond the Pleasure Principle*, SE 18:14–17. Lacan discusses the consequences of the *Fort! Da!*

game in the formation of the register of the Symbolic in the essay in *Ecrits: A Selection* called "Function and Field of Speech and Language in Psychoanalysis," 30–113, esp. 103–4; see also 215. Brenkman (141–83) provides an excellent discussion of the relationship of the child's game to language, social structures, and the development of the subject.

4. The concept of the *objet a* or *le petit objet a* is not a simple one in Lacan. In his translator's note to *Ecrits: A Selection,* Sheridan tells this much: "The '*a*' in question stands for '*autre*' (other), the concept having been developed out of the Freudian 'object' and Lacan's own exploitation of 'otherness.' The '*petit a*' (small '*a*') differentiates the object from (while relating it to) the '*Autre*' or '*grand Autre*' (the capitalized 'Other'). However, Lacan refuses to comment on either term here, leaving the reader to develop an appreciation of the concepts in the course of their use. Furthermore, Lacan insists that '*objet petit a*' should remain untranslated, thus acquiring, as it were, the status of an algebraic sign" (xi). But we also learn in Lacan that the *objets a* are identified with bodily parts that, at least Imaginarily, may be separated from the body; these are, for Lacan, the breast, the penis, feces, and the urinary flow, as well as the phoneme, the gaze, the voice, and "the nothing" (see *Ecrits: A Selection* 315). These so-called objects are the "aims" of the four basic drives—oral, scopic, invocatory, and anal. Objects of all sorts that have meaning in human life, Lacan suggests, link up to one or the other of these drives and the drives *drive backward* to the *objets petit a* for which the objects come to stand, though the objects themselves are *not* the *objets petit a* themselves, a confusion that many interpreters have made and will continue to make. See *Four Fundamental Concepts* for discussion of drives, partial drives, and *objets petit a.*

5. Though in the late work Lacan came to regard the symptom as a register too, I am not so regarding it. In some of her most recent work, Ellie Ragland-Sullivan has begun to assimilate the symptoms into the system Lacan worked out first (see "Plato's *Symposium*").

6. I must make further comment on Lacan and the use of schemas: since Lacan habitually used graphs and schemas to explain difficult points in his theory, others have been inclined to do so as well. I should point out that my schema in Figure 5 benefits from one by Jean Laplanche found in *Life and Death in Psychoanalysis* (124). My locating Eros and Thanatos on the axes of Desire and Law, respectively, is a result of Laplanche's somewhat hourglass-shaped schematization (the "strange chiasmus" [124] of which he speaks) of the "death drive" and the lure of eros. Laplanche's schema appears to be based on Lacan's quadrature of the subject, but with this difference: Laplanche reverses the sides, placing the subject on the right-hand side of the quadrangle, the "other" on the left. Essentially, what results, ironically, is Lacan's basic quadrangle (schemas L and R) reflected in a mirror. In short, Laplanche's schema seems convertible directly into Lacan's. There is much more in Laplanche's discussion than I am suggesting here, but suffice it to say that his insights do permit me to locate Eros and Thanatos in ways, I believe, consistent with Freudian and Lacanian theory. Moreover, since there is the possibility of our seeing Lacan's schematization in relation to A.-J. Greimas's

semiotic square, we may begin to be able to use the schema as an analytic heuristic device. I do not want to suggest that any analyst or critic can mechanically apply the inductions presupposed by the square as it might be superimposed on Figure 5. But the likelihood of words or images clustering around the points of the square where the *topoi* of the subject are located makes the analytic chore somewhat more practicable. As in psychoanalysis, literary analysis requires knowledge and judgment.

7. I should explain that the diagram Abrams provides in the introduction is shaped more or less like a Y and shows the work at the intersection of the three vectors, while world (universe), author, and audience are ranged around the outside at the points of the vectors. One should not misread Abrams's claims regarding this schema, for it is essentially designed to indicate the "content" of the work itself as determined by the critical orientations—mimetic, expressive, and pragmatic—ranged around it (the orientation toward the work itself is called "objective"). Other critics such as Hernadi and Macksey have opened up the Y, turning it into a quadrangle with what amount to *x* and *y* axes, so that the four terms all are ranged "outside" the points of the vectors. This way of schematizing the four orientations stresses authorizing agencies more than Abrams's way. Structuralism as a critical method, on the one hand, has made it easier for us to see that the four orienting points of the quadrangular schema are essentially "positions" that anyone may take in thinking about the objects and authorities of literature or literary criticism in the same way that one sees the positions of Lacan's Schéma L as potential subject positions from which, at least in thought, one might regard the others. Lacan himself has proposed such an extrapolation in his formulation of the four discourses—those of the analyst, hysteric, the university, and the Other. The lesson of deconstruction, on the other hand, is to show that any centering of theory or consciousness in one of the positions entails mystification of that position, rather in the way the subject—says Lacan in *Four Fundamental Concepts*—loses "being" when focusing on "sense," and loses "sense" when focusing on "being," all in the phenomenon he calls "aphanisis" in relation to the concepts of "alienation" and "separation" (*FFC* 208–11). Yet one more reason Lacan seems so seminal to contemporary thought lies here, in the ability of his theories to subsume powerful methodologies such as structuralism and deconstruction or post-structuralism.

8. Just one example of such a charge of monism can be seen in the essay by the Chicago Aristotelian R. S. Crane called "The Critical Monism of Cleanth Brooks." Crane focuses on Brooks's *The Well Wrought Urn*. "It is not so much the particular theses advanced by Brooks," says Crane, "as the tacit assumptions about critical theory and method which have made the questions debated in this essay seem of such crucial importance to him" (83). Brooks's crime is to assume that irony, or paradox, is the only principle of composition or interpretation. "Irony, or paradox, is poetry, *tout simplement*, its form no less than its matter; or rather, in the critical system which he has constructed, there is no principle save that denoted by the words 'irony' or 'paradox' from which significant propositions concerning poems can be derived. It is the One

in which the Many in his theory—and there are but few of these—are included as parts, the single source of all his predicates, the unique cause from which he generates all effects" (84). I dare say we can find similar complaints about any critical ideology; if it is not objecting to positing irony as the One authority for critical practice, then it is objecting to positing structure or modes of production or whatever as the One. It is my view, in any case, that when we *do* literary criticism we inevitably proceed as if our authorizing agency were ontologically and epistemologically secure, though we may realize full well that we are acting in what Lacan calls the register of the Imaginary and that the register of the Symbolic—where resides the "subject supposed to know"— is beyond our consciousness. To be aware of the provisionality of any authority ought to make us—including theorists—more tolerant of the Imaginary answers critics choose.

9. Marshall W. Alcorn, Jr., and Mark Bracher, focusing on an interactive theory modified from Norman Holland and augmented by recent object-relations theory (Meissner, for example), discuss some of the ways in which psychoanalytic critics relate the text and the reader. In *The Literary Use of the Psychoanalytic Process*, Meredith Anne Skura takes a more pluralistic approach to the issues underlying ways in which literary texts and psychoanalytic theory relate. Her eclecticism is observable in her topics: "Literature as Case History," "Literature as Fantasy," "Literature as Dream," "Literature as Transference," and "Literature as Psychoanalytic Process" (chaps. 2-6). While it is plain that even from a Lacanian perspective literature may serve in all these functions, the one point Skura and Alcorn and Bracher fail to make regards the originary or determining role of language. It is the working of language—between the analyst and analysand, the author and the text, the reader and the text—through all those verbalizations (case history, fantasy, dream, transference) that permits the final possibility of literature's being an allegory—in, as we shall see, Ragland-Sullivan's terms—of the psychoanalytic process. For another view of psychoanalytic literary criticism, see Elizabeth Wright's essay, which valories the ostensibly post-Lacanian methodology of Deleuze and Guattari's *Anti-Oedipus: Capitalism and Schizophrenia*.

10. Regarding the way in which tropes may be used to "explain" or frame differently some of the Lacanian concepts, I say this in an essay on Joseph Heller's *Something Happened:*

> Lacan's dyadic theory conceivably would be more intelligible as a tetradic system. The addition of synecdoche and irony would provide more adequate conceptual space for the four-stage narrative the discourse of the family outlines in the move from Imaginary to Symbolic levels [or registers]. In this view, which would be consistent with Todorov's analysis of the tropic basis of Freud's dream-work and Hayden White's accounts of both Freud and Piaget, the onset of the mirror stage would be metaphoric, a stage of simple, one-for-one correspondence or total identity. The onset of language would initiate a metonymic stage, one partaking of features of the mirror phase in the constant reduplication in language

of the objects of desire. The entry into the Symbolic would involve the trope of synecdoche (in White's terms) at the point where the individual arrives at an identification (*pars pro toto*) with the law or the father in the Oedipal complex. When the identification is secure, the fitting of the part into the whole will be entirely synecdochic, but when the sense of unity or completion or satisfaction wanes, then the Oedipus stage will bring with it the ambivalences assigned to the trope of irony. (*Doing Tropology* 57)

Works Cited

Abrams, M. H. *The Mirror and the Lamp*. New York: Norton, 1958.

Alcorn, Marshall W., Jr., Mark Bracher, and Ronald Corthell, eds. "Lacanian Discourse." *Prose Studies* 11 (Dec. 1988).

Alcorn, Marshall W., Jr., and Mark Bracher. "Literature, Psychoanalysis, and the Re-formation of the Self: A New Direction for Reader-Response Theory." *PMLA* 100, no. 3 (May 1985): 342–54.

Bal, Mieke, ed. "Psychopoetics: Theory." *Poetics* 13, nos. 4–5 (Oct. 1984).

———, ed. "Psychopoetics at Work." *Style* 18, no. 3 (Summer 1984).

Bannet, Eve Tavor. *Structuralism and the Logic of Dissent: Barthes, Derrida, Foucault, Lacan*. Urbana: University of Illinois Press, 1989.

Bär, Eugen. "The Language of the Unconscious according to Jacques Lacan." *Semiotica* 3, no. 3 (1971): 241–68.

———. "Understanding Lacan." In *Psychoanalysis and Contemporary Science*, vol. 3. Ed. Leo Goldberger and Victor H. Rosen. New York: International Universities Press, 1974, 473–544.

Bellemin-Nöel, Jean. *Vers l'inconscient du texte*. Paris: Presses Universitaires de France, 1979.

Benveniste, Emile. *Problems in General Linguistics*. Trans. Mary Elizabeth Meek. Miami Linguistics Series, no. 8. Coral Gables: University of Miami Press, 1971.

Benvenuto, Bice, and Roger Kennedy. *The Works of Jacques Lacan: An Introduction*. New York: St. Martin's, 1986.

Bonaparte, Marie. *Life and Works of Edgar Allan Poe*. Trans. John Rodker. London: Imago, 1949.

Bracher, Mark. "Lacan's Theory of the Four Discourses." *Prose Studies* 11 (Dec. 1988): 32-49.

Brenkman, John. *Culture and Domination*. Ithaca: Cornell University Press, 1987.

Brooks, Cleanth. *The Well Wrought Urn*. New York: Reynal and Hitchcock, 1947.

Brooks, Peter. "The Idea of a Psychoanalytic Criticism." *Critical Inquiry* 13 (Winter 1987): 334–48.

———. *Reading for the Plot: Design and Intention in Narrative*. New York: Knopf, 1984.

Camden, Vera, ed. *Compromise Formations: Current Directions in Psychoanalytic Criticism*. Kent: Kent State University Press, 1989.

Cave, Terence. "The Prime and Precious Thing." *Times Literary Supplement*, 4 Jan. 1985, 14.

Clark, Michael. *Jacques Lacan: An Annotated Bibliography*. 2 vols. New York: Garland, 1988.

Crane, R. S. "The Critical Monism of Cleanth Brooks." In *Critics and Criticism: Ancient and Modern*. Ed. R. S. Crane et al. Chicago: University of Chicago Press, 1952, 83–107.

Crews, Frederick C. "Can Literature Be Psychoanalyzed?" Chap. 1 in *Out of My System: Psychoanalysis, Ideology, and Critical Method*. New York: Oxford University Press, 1975.

———. *The Sins of the Fathers: Hawthorne's Psychological Themes*. New York: Oxford University Press, 1966.

Culler, Jonathan. "Textual Self-consciousness and the Textual Unconscious." *Style* 18, no. 3 (Summer 1984): 369–76.

Davis, Robert Con. "Lacan, Poe, and Narrative Repression." In Davis, ed., *Lacan and Narration*, 983–1005.

———, ed. *The Fictional Father: Lacanian Readings of the Text*. Amherst: University of Massachusetts Press, 1983.

———, ed. *Lacan and Narration: The Psychoanalytic Difference in Narrative Theory*. Baltimore: Johns Hopkins University Press, 1983.

Deleuze, Gilles, and Felix Guattari. *Anti-Oedipus: Capitalism and Schizophrenia*. Trans. Robert Hurley et al. New York: Viking, 1977.

de Man, Paul. *Allegories of Reading: Figural Language in Rousseau, Nietzsche, Rilke, and Proust*. New Haven: Yale University Press, 1979.

Derrida, Jacques. *Of Grammatology*. Trans. Gayatri Chakravorty Spivak. Baltimore: Johns Hopkins University Press, 1976.

———. "The Purveyor of Truth." Trans. Willis Domingo et al. *Yale French Studies* 52 (1975): 31–113.

Eco, Umberto. *A Theory of Semiotics*. Bloomington: Indiana University Press, 1976.

Feibleman, James K. *Ontology*. Baltimore: Johns Hopkins University Press, 1951.

———. *The Revival of Realism*. Chapel Hill: University of North Carolina Press, 1946.

Felman, Shoshana. "The Case of Poe: Applications/Implications of Psychoanalysis." Chap. 2 in *Jacques Lacan and the Adventure of Insight*. Cambridge: Harvard University Press, 1987, 27–51.

———. *Jacques Lacan and the Adventure of Insight: Psychoanalysis in Contemporary Culture*. Cambridge: Harvard University Press, 1987.

———, ed. *Literature and Psychoanalysis: The Question of Reading: Otherwise*. Baltimore: Johns Hopkins University Press, 1982.

Fisher, David James, ed. "Psychoanalysis and Interpretation." *Humanities in Society* 4, nos. 2–3 (Spring-Summer 1981).

Flieger, Jerry Aline. "Trial and Error: The Case of the Textual Unconscious." *Diacritics* 11, no. 1 (1981): 56–67.

Forrester, John. *Language and the Origins of Psychoanalysis.* New York: Columbia University Press, 1980.

Foucault, Michel. *The Order of Things.* New York: Pantheon, 1970.

Freud, Sigmund. *Beyond the Pleasure Principle.* Vol. 18 of *The Standard Edition of the Complete Psychological Works of Sigmund Freud.* Ed. and trans. James Strachey. London: Hogarth, 1964.

———. "Constructions in Analysis." In *Standard Edition* 23:255–79.

———. "Creative Writers and Day-dreaming." In *Standard Edition* 9:141–53.

———. "Family Romances." In *Standard Edition* 9:238–39.

———. "On Narcissism: An Introduction." In *Standard Edition* 14:73–102.

———. *The Standard Edition of the Complete Psychological Works of Sigmund Freud.* 24 vols. Ed. and trans. James Strachey. London: Hogarth, 1953–74.

Frisch, Karl von. *Bees: Their Vision, Chemical Senses, and Language.* Ithaca: Cornell University Press, 1950.

Gallop, Jane. *Reading Lacan.* Ithaca: Cornell University Press, 1985.

Green, Andre. "The Logic of Lacan's *Objet A* and Freudian Theory: Convergences and Questions." In *Interpreting Lacan.* Ed. Joseph H. Smith and William Kerrigan. Psychiatry and the Humanities, vol. 6. New Haven: Yale University Press, 1983, 161–92.

Greimas, A.-J., and J. Courtes. *Semiotics and Language.* Trans. Larry Crist et al. Bloomington: Indiana University Press, 1982.

Hall, Gerald. "Appendix: The Logical Typing of the Symbolic, the Imaginary, and the Real." In *System and Structure: Essays in Communication and Exchange,* 2d ed. Ed. Anthony Wilden. New York: Tavistock, 1980, 274–77.

Hartman, Geoffrey. *Beyond Formalism: Literary Essays 1958–1970.* New Haven: Yale University Press, 1970.

———, ed. *Psychoanalysis and the Question of the Text.* 1978. Reprint. Baltimore: Johns Hopkins University Press, 1985.

Hawking, Stephen W. *A Brief History of Time: From the Big Bang to Black Holes.* New York: Bantam, 1988.

Hernadi, Paul. *Beyond Genre: New Directions in Literary Classification.* Ithaca: Cornell University Press, 1972.

Hirsch, E. D., Jr. "Some Aims of Criticism." In *Literary Theory and Structure: Essays in Honor of William K. Wimsatt.* Ed. Frank Brady, John Palmer, and Martin Price. New Haven: Yale University Press, 1973, 41–62.

Holland, Norman. *The I.* New Haven: Yale University Press, 1985.

———. "Unity Identity Text Self." *PMLA* 90 (1975): 813–22.

Jameson, Fredric. "Imaginary and Symbolic in Lacan: Marxism, Psychoanalytic Criticism, and the Problem of the Subject." *Yale French Studies* 55–56 (1977): 338–95.

———. *The Political Unconscious: Narrative as a Socially Symbolic Act.* Ithaca: Cornell University Press, 1981.

Johnson, Barbara. "The Frame of Reference." *Yale French Studies* 55–56 (1977): 457–505.

Kellner, Hans. "Triangular Anxieties: The Present State of European Intellectual History." In *Modern European Intellectual History: Reappraisals and New Perspectives.* Ed. Dominick LaCapra and Stephen Kaplan. Ithaca: Cornell University Press, 1982, 111–36.

Kristeva, Julia. *Desire in Language: A Semiotic Approach to Literature and Art.* Ed. Leon S. Roudiez. Trans. Thomas Gora et al. New York: Columbia University Press, 1980.

——. *Revolution in Poetic Language.* Trans. Margaret Waller. New York: Columbia University Press, 1984.

——. "Within the Microcosm of 'The Talking Cure.' " In *Interpreting Lacan.* Ed. Joseph H. Smith and William Kerrigan. Psychiatry and the Humanities, vol. 6. New Haven: Yale University Press, 1983, 33–48.

Lacan, Jacques. "Desire and the Interpretation of Desire in *Hamlet.*" *Yale French Studies* 55–56 (1977): 11–52.

——. *Ecrits: A Selection.* Trans. Alan Sheridan. New York: Norton, 1977.

——. *The Ego in Freud's Theory and in the Technique of Psychoanalysis, Seminar II, 1954–55.* Ed. Jacques-Alain Miller. Trans. Sylvana Tomaselli, with notes by John Forrester. New York: Norton, 1988.

——. "The Family Complexes." Trans. Carolyn Asp. *Critical Texts* 5, no. 3 (1988): 12–29.

——. *Feminine Sexuality: Jacques Lacan and the "Ecole Freudienne."* Ed. Juliet Mitchell. Trans. and ed. Jacqueline Rose. New York: Norton, 1982.

——. *The Four Fundamental Concepts of Psycho-analysis.* Ed. Jacques-Alain Miller. Trans. Alan Sheridan. New York: Norton, 1978.

——. *Freud's Papers on Technique, Seminar I, 1953–54.* Ed. Jacques-Alain Miller. Trans. John Forrester. New York: Norton, 1988.

——. "The Neurotic's Individual Myth." Trans. Martha Noel Evans. *Psychoanalytic Quarterly* 48 (1979): 405–25.

——. *The Psychoses, Seminar III, 1955–56.* Ed. Jacques-Alain Miller. Trans. John Forrester. New York: Norton, forthcoming.

——. "The Seminar on 'The Purloined Letter.' " Trans. Jeffrey Mehlman. *Yale French Studies* 48 (1972): 39–72.

——. *Speech and Language in Psychoanalysis.* Trans. Anthony Wilden. Baltimore: Johns Hopkins University Press, 1981. Orig. pub. as *The Language of the Self: The Function of Language in Psychoanalysis,* 1968.

——. *Scilicet* 8 (1976).

——. "Of Structure as an Inmixing of an Otherness Prerequisite to Any Subject Whatever." In *The Structuralist Controversy: The Language of Criticism and the Sciences of Man.* Ed. Richard Macksey and Eugenio Donato. Baltimore: Johns Hopkins University Press, 1972, 186–200.

——. *Television: A Challenge to the Psychoanalytic Establishment.* Trans. Denis Hollier et al. New York: Norton, 1990.

Lacan, Jacques, and Wladimir Granoff. "Fetishism: The Symbolic, the Imaginary and the Real." In *Perversions: Psychodynamics and Therapy.* Ed. M. Balint and S. Lorand. New York: Gramercy, 1956, 265–76.

Laplanche, Jean. *Life and Death in Psychoanalysis.* Trans. Jeffrey Mehlman. Baltimore: Johns Hopkins University Press, 1985.

Laplanche, Jean, and J.-B. Pontalis. *The Language of Psycho-analysis.* Trans. Donald Nicholson-Smith. New York: Norton, 1973.

Lavers, Annette. "Some Aspects of Language in the Work of Lacan." *Semiotica* 3, no. 3 (1971): 269–79.

Lemaire, Anika. *Jacques Lacan.* Trans. David Macey. London: Routledge and Kegan Paul, 1977.

Lévi-Strauss, Claude. *Structural Anthropology.* 2 vols. Trans. Claire Jakobson and Brooke Grundfest-Schoepf (vol. 1) and Monique Layton (vol. 2). New York: Basic Books, 1963, 1976.

Loewenstein, R. M. "Some Remarks on the Role of Speech in Psychoanalytic Technique." *International Journal of Psychoanalysis* 37 (1956): 460–67.

Lukacher, Ned. *Primal Scenes: Literature, Philosophy, Psychoanalysis.* Ithaca: Cornell University Press, 1986.

MacCabe, Colin, ed. *The Talking Cure: Essays in Psychoanalysis and Language.* 1981. New York: St. Martin's, 1986.

Macey, David. *Lacan in Contexts.* New York: Verso, 1988.

Macksey, Richard, ed. *Velocities of Change: Critical Essays from MLN.* Baltimore: Johns Hopkins University Press, 1974.

Mahler, Margaret S., et al. *The Psychological Birth of the Human Infant.* New York: Basic Books, 1975.

Mehlman, Jeffrey, ed. "French Freud: Structural Studies in Psychoanalysis." *Yale French Studies* 48 (1972).

Meissner, W. W. *Internalization in Psychoanalysis.* New York: International Universities Press, 1981.

Mellard, James M. *Doing Tropology: Analysis of Narrative Discourse.* Urbana: University of Illinois Press, 1987.

———. "Lacan and Faulkner: A Post-Freudian Analysis of Humor in the Fiction." In *Faulkner and Humor.* Ed. Doreen Fowler and Ann J. Abadie. Jackson: University Presses of Mississippi, 1986, 198–220.

Mitchell, Juliet, ed., and Jacqueline Rose, trans. and ed. *Feminine Sexuality: Jacques Lacan and the "Ecole Freudienne."* New York: Norton, 1982.

Muller, John P., and William J. Richardson. *Lacan and Language: A Reader's Guide to "Ecrits."* New York: International Universities Press, 1982.

Pottle, Frederick A. "Synchrony and Diachrony: A Plea for the Use in Literary Studies of Saussure's Concepts and Terminology." In *Literary Theory and Structure: Essays in Honor of William K. Wimsatt.* Ed. Frank Brady, John Palmer, and Martin Price. New Haven: Yale University Press, 1973, 3–21.

Ragland-Sullivan, Ellie. *Jacques Lacan and the Philosophy of Psychoanalysis.* Urbana: University of Illinois Press, 1986.

———. "Lacan's Seminars on James Joyce: Writing as Symptom and 'Singular Solution.'" In *Compromise Formations: Current Directions in Psychoanalytic Criticism.* Ed. Vera Camden. Kent: Kent State University Press, 1989, 61–85.

——. "The Limits of Discourse Structure: The Hysteric and the Analyst." *Prose Studies* 11 (Dec. 1988): 61–83.

——. "The Magnetism between Reader and Text: Prolegomena to a Lacanian Poetics." *Poetics* 13 (1984): 381–406.

——. "Plato's *Symposium* and the Lacanian Theory of Transference: Or, What Is Love?" *South-Atlantic Quarterly* 88, no. 4 (Fall 1989): 725–55.

Reppen, Joseph, and Maurice Charney, eds. *The Psychoanalytic Study of Literature.* Hillsdale: Analytic Press/Lawrence Erlbaum Associates, 1985.

Rimmon-Kenan, Shlomith, ed. *Discourse in Psychoanalysis and Literature.* New York: Methuen, 1987.

Rose, Jacqueline. "Introduction-II." In *Feminine Sexuality: Jacques Lacan and the "Ecole Freudienne."* Ed. Juliet Mitchell. Trans. and ed. Jacqueline Rose. New York: Norton, 1982, 27–57.

Rosenbaum, Bent, and Harly Sonne. *The Language of Psychosis.* New York: New York University Press, 1986.

Roudinesco, Elisabeth. *La bataille de cent ans: Histoire de la psychanalyse en France.* 2 vols. Paris: Seuil, 1987.

Saussure, Ferdinand de. *Course in General Linguistics.* 1916. Reprint. Ed. Charles Bally and Albert Sechehaye. Trans. Wade Baskin. New York: McGraw-Hill, 1966.

Schneiderman, Stuart. "Afloat with Jacques Lacan." *Diacritics* 1, no. 2 (1971): 27–34.

Silverman, Kaja. *The Subject of Semiotics.* New York: Oxford University Press, 1983.

Skura, Meredith Anne. *The Literary Use of the Psychoanalytic Process.* New Haven: Yale University Press, 1981.

Smith, Joseph H., and William Kerrigan, eds. *Interpreting Lacan.* Psychiatry and the Humanities, vol. 6. New Haven: Yale University Press, 1983.

Spector, Jack. *The Aesthetics of Freud: A Study in Psychoanalysis and Art.* New York: Praeger, 1973.

Thom, Martin. "The Unconscious Structured as a Language." In *The Talking Cure.* Ed. Colin MacCabe. New York: St. Martin's, 1986, 1–44.

White, Hayden V. *Tropics of Discourse: Essays in Cultural Criticism.* Baltimore: Johns Hopkins University Press, 1978.

Wilden, Anthony. "Lacan and the Discourse of the Other." In *Speech and Language in Psychoanalysis* by Jacques Lacan. Trans. Anthony Wilden. Baltimore: Johns Hopkins University Press, 1981, 159–311. Orig. pub. as *The Language of the Self: The Function of Language in Psychoanalysis,* 1968.

Winnicott, D. W. *Playing and Reality.* Harmondsworth, Eng.: Penguin, 1980.

Wright, Elizabeth. "Another Look at Lacan and Literary Criticism." *New Literary History* 19, no. 3 (Spring 1988): 617–27.

CHAPTER ONE

Inscriptions of the Subject:
The Scarlet Letter

> What is being unfolded . . . is articulated like a discourse (the
> unconscious is the discourse of the Other), whose syntax Freud
> first sought to define for those bits that come to us in certain
> privileged moments, in dreams, in slips of the tongue or pen,
> in flashes of wit.
>
> —Jacques Lacan, *Ecrits: A Selection*

Nathaniel Hawthorne's *The Scarlet Letter* will open up our using Lacan
for reading fiction. This work is widely regarded not only as a mas-
terpiece of moral, cultural, and religious insight, but also of prescient
psychoanalytic insight. Just how prescient we shall soon see. The classic
Freudian psychoanalytic reading of the book is by Frederick C. Crews;
there are non-Freudian readings as well, including several recent essays.[1]
But Hawthorne's romance is merely one of any number of works of
fiction that have elicited such readings; it is no more privileged a paradigm of the subject than many other fictions, perhaps even any other
fictions, for literature in general and fiction in particular may well be
our best model of the workings of human subjectivity. Such is in fact
a major premise underlying psychoanalysis, whether initiated by Freud
or reinterpreted by Lacan. Crews has said, for instance, "The historical
prominence of psychoanalysis in literary studies is readily understand-
able. Literature is written from and about motives, and psychoanalysis
is the only thoroughgoing theory of motives that mankind has devised"
(*Out of My System* 4). Lacan makes the point for himself and Freud:
"Indeed, how could we forget that to the end of his days Freud constantly maintained that . . . a training [in literary analysis] was the prime
requisite in the formation of analysts, and that he designated the eternal

universitas litterarum as the ideal place for its institution" (*Ecrits: A Selection* 147). As Ellie Ragland-Sullivan points out, however, "Psychoanalytic meaning is not immanent in a text because it is the medical discourse of a symptom." Rather, "literature operates a magnetic pull on the reader because it is an allegory of the psyche's fundamental structure" ("Magnetism" 381).

Viewed in the light of Lacanian theory, *The Scarlet Letter*, though perhaps not actually more privileged than other texts, does nonetheless provide a particularly useful model for analysis, not least because its dominant symbol is precisely one of Lacan's: the letter. In the one clinical presentation we have by Lacan, he spoke of the man dubbed Gérard Primeau as a patient having a particularly "Lacanian" psychosis (Schneiderman 41); it is equally apparent, I think, that Hawthorne's novel is an almost uniquely Lacanian work of fiction. Perhaps more than James's "Beast in the Jungle," Hawthorne's romance is valuably approached through Lacanian principles not only because it represents important functions (the mirror stage and the Oedipus), but also because it focuses on four major characters whose experiences exemplify versions of subjectivity Lacan determines through psychoanalysis. The first two I shall consider represent "normal"—as opposed to pathological (neurotic or psychotic)—subjects. The discourse of the child, Pearl, is clearly inscribed within the timely processes of the passage through the mirror stage and the Oedipus, and her mother, Hester Prynne, equally clearly, is inscribed as post-Oedipal, but, as a normatively adult subject condemned as "criminal," she exhibits the problematical relation of subjectivity to the gaze within the dynamics of the registers of the Imaginary and the Symbolic. Perhaps most valuably, a Lacanian approach dramatizes the inscriptions of the other two major characters as pathological subjects. Arthur Dimmesdale may be positioned within Lacan's conception of neurosis so that we may examine symptoms and the notion of the cure, and Roger Chillingworth allows us to examine the question of psychosis even as he enfigures the analyst and the Lacanian Other. The four inscribed subjectivities thus dramatize the quaternary subject as constituted of agonistic functions from which may be derived specific types of discourse. Seen finally to suggest a total structuration—both normative and pathological—of any possible subject whatever, the tale's four major figures dramatize the ways in which a Lacanian criticism may look at the interrelations of characters as manifestations of aspects of subjectivity and the irruptions into discourse they entail. In short, Hawthorne's language makes a Lacan thematics seem almost "natural."

The "Normative" Subject: Pearl, the Mirror Stage, and Oedipus

> The function of the mirror-stage as a particular case of the function of the *imago* . . . is to establish a relation between the organism and its reality.
>
> —Jacques Lacan, *Ecrits: A Selection*

Pearl's story, in Lacanian terms, is the most fundamental of those represented in the subject-consciousnesses of *The Scarlet Letter*. In Hawthorne's representation of Pearl, we may follow her passage from infancy (meaning, in Lacan's terms, the *infans* stage of the child-without-speech) through the moment of the mirror stage, to the assumption of gender, and to the resolution of the Oedipus complex in her introjection of the Name-of-the-Father. She is at the *infans* stage when she is first seen on the scaffold of the pillory with Hester at the novel's beginning; there, as an inchoate human subject, her response is directed totally by visual and auditory stimuli. Then, she is shown in the early chapters achieving the first moment of the mirror passage, where she finds in her mother an image of bodily unity, and later finds among animals, playmates, and objects images of Imaginary identification and antagonism. Finally, in the last chapters, she is shown effecting the determinative moment of gender identity and acceptance of Law in the Oedipal passage; this moment, in the assumption of gender, takes her through recognition that the paternal signifier, the Phallus, lies only in the Other and that she herself comes at last under the authority of her father as the representative of Law. Each of these moves clearly exhibits the constitution of subjectivity according to Lacanian principles, for Pearl experiences the world in relation to those dominant images of which Lacan so frequently speaks: the mother and images associated with her, objects symbolizing the other, and intimations of the symbolic presence of the Other to be found in the Name-of-the-Father.

We must say that for Pearl, as normative subject, the whole of the constitution of subjectivity is represented in two moments: first, in her passage through the mirror stage, and, second, in her acceptance of a father to whose authority, vested in the Name-of-the-Father, she might cede her subjectivity. Narratively foreshadowing Pearl's end, Hawthorne (though Lacan would not) gives the latter moment the value of a quest for the infant. An adumbration of this quest occurs in the earliest glimpse readers have of Pearl. Even on the scaffold with Hester, the infant breaks her determined passivity to respond to the sound of Arthur Dimmesdale's voice. That voice, in retrospect, shall represent the intrusion of the paternal metaphor, "the metaphor that substitutes this Name in the place first symbolized by the operation of the absence of the mother" (*Ecrits: A Selection* 200). It is precisely that which, for a prescient moment, takes the place where the mother was, for indeed— as the voice of the community's most revered spokesman—it represents the voice of Pearl's culture, one speaking from the place of knowledge, which is also the place of the Other. As Lacan would have it, Pearl's response is not to words as such, but to the physical materiality of the voice itself. In this response she is little different from the crowd in the square. "The young pastor's voice was tremulously sweet, rich, deep, and broken," Hawthorne tells us, as Dimmesdale speaks over Hester's ignominious display on the scaffold. "The feeling that it so evidently manifested, rather than the direct purport of the words, caused it to vibrate within all hearts, and brought the listeners into one accord of sympathy. Even the poor baby, at Hester's bosom, was affected by the same influence: for it directed its hitherto vacant gaze towards Mr. Dimmesdale, and held up its little arms, with a half pleased, half plaintive murmur."[2] Pearl's gesture here, in every respect, foreshadows the aim and end of the infant's constitutive relation to ego, (m)other, and the Otherness represented in the high place from which the minister speaks.

Although the Oedipal goal (as cultural *telos,* not as conscious aim) of the child's early life, in Lacanian terms, is to enter a normative structural relation with the law, name, or authority of the father, the necessary focus of the neonatal and postnatal infant inevitably is on the mother-as-other and passage through the mirror stage. Because Pearl is isolated not only from her father, but also from the larger community, her early characterization, besides serving Hawthorne's own aims as a storyteller, is especially representative of Lacanian principles. The first image on which the infant ordinarily fastens tactilely is the mother, especially the body of the mother laid down as a Real, unsignifiable image in the unconscious. Generally, the mother's body, particularly in the anaclitic object of the breast, devolves to the *objet a,* that bodily part which in the unconscious becomes the aim of an oral drive. But the mother may also have a scopic dimension linking visual images to other *objets a*. With the development of vision, the infant almost immediately seizes upon the face of the mother as that which represents her. Already the infant is caught in the wake of life, its primal object already begun to be displaced by other objects that desire expects to fill the void left by the *objet a*, by primal loss (see *Ecrits: A Selection* 255).

Thus, caught in what Lacan calls the defiles of the signifier, the law of signification, this image of the mother, by the process of metonymy, normally is displaced by other images. One image signifying the symbiosis of infant and mother is usually the maternal breast or bosom. What happens in Pearl's case, however, is that she quickly shifts the identity of the mother not to the image of the breast, but to the object located on Hester's breast—namely, the scarlet letter A. Though such metonymic displacements (according to Lacan) are not particularly unusual, Hawthorne makes an issue of Pearl's attachment to the emblem: "The very first thing which she had noticed, in her life," writes Hawthorne, "was—what?—not the mother's smile, responding to it, as other babies do, by that faint, embryo smile of the little mouth. By no means! But that first object of which Pearl seemed to become aware was— shall we say it?—the scarlet letter on Hester's bosom!" (96). The scarlet letter becomes Pearl's "first object" in Hawthorne's terms, but the determinative, founding object is not the letter. It is the breast for which, metonymically, the letter A comes to stand. Thus for Pearl the A becomes the enfiguration of the breast, itself the *objet petit a* in the unconscious that stands for (among other things) the mother herself.[3]

Formation of the drives is critical to the constitution of the subject, for there can be no subjectivity without desire, and desire is caused by the separation of the subject from its first object—the mother or the mother's breast. In the discourse of the hysteric, says Lacan, the emphasis is on the primacy of the division of the subject over his or her relation to the object of fantasy. The letter A becomes the object of Pearl's fantasy because it stands in for the breast that itself is the cause of her desire. But as signifier of the *objet a*, the letter cannot yield the satisfaction of the drive that one might expect. Rather, it serves the ambiguous functions Lacan describes as *turn* and *trick*. As that around which the subject's drive turns, it motivates the subject, but as that which is tricked by the drive, it leads to frustration or alienation (FFC 168). On the one hand, the object—the letter A—

provides a focal point around which the interest of the child shall
revolve; on the other hand, the same object merely tricks the child
into believing that to have it will assure satisfaction, though the signifying object, Lacan says, "is in fact simply the presence of a hollow,
a void" that can be "occupied" by any object and whose power to act
upon the subject can be known "only in the form of the lost object,
the *petit a*" (180), the "little *autre*" that stands in a differential, perhaps
mediatory, relation to the "Grand *Autre*," the great Other who represents Law, Authority, Interdiction.

The image, at the outset, indeed stands in for the mother. But as
the child moves further along the path toward differentiation from the
mother (in other words, toward the passage through the mirror stage),
the child develops an ambivalent relation to her and, therefore, to the
images representing her. The ambivalence is illustrated very clearly in
Pearl's behavior. Immediately after the revelation that Pearl's first significant image of Imaginary identification is the scarlet letter, Hawthorne also recounts Pearl's aggressive attack on it. "In the afternoon
of a certain summer's day, after Pearl grew big enough to run about,
she amused herself with gathering handfuls of wild-flowers, and flinging
them, one by one, at her mother's bosom; dancing up and down, like
a little elf, whenever she hit the scarlet letter" (97). Such ambivalence
manifests the mirror process of psychic differentiation, for it acknowledges the child's awareness of the otherness of both self and mother
in the other-directed aggressivity (as Lacan points out in his essay on
that topic).[4] In Hawthorne's text, the ambivalence is also associated
with what we may call the child's Oedipal suspicions, its growing awareness of indebtedness for constitution as a subject not to one, but to
two, not merely to Mother, but also to Father. Pearl's attention here,
Hawthorne shows us, is directed toward the question of paternity in
the Imaginary, not in the Symbolic. When Hester tells Pearl that the
Heavenly Father had sent the child, Hawthorne writes that it is "with
a hesitation that did not escape the acuteness of the child. Whether
moved only by her ordinary freakishness, or because an evil spirit
prompted her, she put up her small forefinger, and touched the scarlet
letter" (98). With her finger on the symbol, Pearl tells her mother that
the Heavenly is not her father, at least not the father she desires. The
symbol under her finger suggests to Pearl that her desired father lies
elsewhere, indeed, lies somewhere behind the letter, the scarlet letter.
Eventually, she will discover that both her desired Imaginary and her

necessary Symbolic father are linked under, but hidden by, the same letter *A*.

The other side of the ambivalent behavior that marks the Lacanian register of the Imaginary is Pearl's exaggerated veneration of the "little object." That veneration is evidence that Pearl has begun to identify herself with the letter, to see herself as much as her mother in the letter. Consequently, in certain moments typical of the ambivalence of the Imaginary identifications with the other or the images representing the other, her aggressiveness is modulated toward what at root is a self-directed, narcissistic affection. In the chapter called "Hester and Pearl," for example, Pearl injures a tiny bird as she flings pebbles at a flock; with its gray coloring and a brightly contrapuntal breast, the bird, by metaphoric similarity, represents Pearl's mother, who dresses in gray but wears the scarlet letter on her bosom. Thus, Pearl's aggressive rock-throwing is characteristic of the child's puzzling hostility toward Hester. But Hawthorne's text, by the further process of metonymy, clearly identifies the tiny birds with Pearl, too. First, we learn that she gave up her throwing "because it grieved her to have done harm to a little being that was as wild as the sea-breeze, or as wild as Pearl herself." Then Hawthorne notes that when the child hears her mother's voice, she flits "along as lightly as one of the little sea-birds" (178). Then in the chain of metaphoric substitutions (bird for mother, and bird for child) the text's attention comes to rest on Pearl's imitation not of the bird, but of the scarlet letter. "As the last touch to her mermaid's garb," which Pearl had made for herself of sea-weed, "Pearl took some eel-grass, and imitated, as best she could, on her own bosom, the decoration with which she was so familiar on her mother's. A letter,—the letter A,—but freshly green, instead of scarlet!" (178). Finally, as if to assure readers of the connections among child, green letter, mother, and scarlet letter, Hawthorne recounts Pearl's pointing once again to the letter on Hester's bosom and inquiring of its signification. Once again, however, the end of this chain of displacements is none other than an invocation not of the maternal, but of the paternal signifier, as Pearl wonders if Hester wears the letter on her breast "for the same reason that the minister keeps his hand over his heart!" (179). Plainly, the letter *A* stands for a mother who is not one, is not *l'Autre*—the figure of the law of the Other or the Name-of-the-Father.

Hester will not answer the child's questions about the letter or the minister's hand over his heart, but it seems clear enough that Pearl's questions will stop only when (through the agency of the letter) she knows her desired Imaginary father and thus can recognize the authority of the Symbolic father and, along with it, the inevitability of the loss of the phallic signifier (associated with the phallic mother and, here, with the scarlet letter) that Lacan defines as alienation into language. The scene in which this phase of the Lacanian mirror stage is depicted occurs most visibly in chapter 19, "The Child at the Brook-Side." This phase of the mirror passage is characterized by the overt emergence, in the consciousness of the subject, of the Oedipal triangle. That the Oedipal question has shadowed Pearl's life throughout is evident in her behavior, her almost mystical intimations regarding the identity of her father, and her inquiries regarding the metaphoric linkage between the letter on Hester's bosom and the hand over the minister's heart. The question, moreover, is central to each of the three scaffold scenes. It is broached in the first, nearly finds its answer in the second, where Arthur should have announced his true paternal relation to the child, and is finally answered in the third, which concludes Pearl's passage through the mirror. But the most dramatic evidence of the Oedipal structuring—a structuring necessary, Lacan contends, if the Symbolic is to enter the child and make it a normally functioning subject—occurs earlier in the dark forest.

There, the brook that separates Pearl from Hester and Arthur serves as the mediating figure of the mirror. The brook, early on, is imaged in the text both as mirror and as child. It is enfigured, for example, as an object that could "mirror its revelations on the smooth surface of a pool," but also as one whose babble is "kind, quiet, soothing, but melancholy, like the voice of a young child that was spending its infancy without playfulness" (186). Later, and most significantly, the brook forms the mirror in which, in remarkable Lacanian terms, Pearl herself is reflected. On the one hand, as Lacan argues concerning the other in the mirror, this projection is idealized (certainly by Hawthorne, almost certainly by Pearl): "it reflected a perfect image of her little figure, with all the brilliant picturesqueness of her beauty, in its adornment of flowers and wreathed foliage, but more refined and spiritualized than the reality" (208). On the other hand, the subject absorbs something of its own being back from the mirror's reflection: "This image, so nearly identical with the living Pearl, seemed to communicate somewhat of its own shadowy and intangible quality to the child herself" (208). Most important of all, however, is the onset of alienation (but, Lacan would say, also of subjectivity and symbolization) that occurs in this reflection in the mirror. "In the brook beneath," Hawthorne writes, "stood another child,—another and the same." The alienation is observed by the mother as much as by the child. Hawthorne tells us that "Hester felt herself, in some indistinct and tantalizing manner, estranged from Pearl; as if the child, in her lonely ramble through the forest, had strayed out of the sphere in which she and her mother dwelt together, and was now vainly seeking to return to it" (208). Pearl—as Hester perceives—now belongs to a world of differences, of otherness even in the same, of identity found only in others or the other. Pearl is entering the world of *as if* and *aphanisis*, a world in which there is no same recuperable by memory or nostalgia. Such, in Lacanian terms, is the fall from grace.

That which will prevent Pearl from returning to the sphere of union with the mother who offers an illusion of totality is the *symbol* of the other—the father. "In the Oedipal complex phase," explains Eugen Bär, "the law imposes itself in the symbol of the father on the infant, separating the latter from the mother" (Bär 513). The contour of the Oedipal structure is plain in the forest scene, though Hawthorne ascribes Pearl's estrangement not to some inevitable passage of the child, but to an act of the mother. After the child has wandered from her mother's side there in the forest, "another inmate had been admitted within the circle of the mother's feelings, and so modified the aspect of them all, that Pearl, the returning wanderer, could not find her wonted place, and hardly knew where she was" (208). Her shock could not have been greater had she found Hester and Arthur copulating. The potent intruder, Hawthorne notes, points out "that this brook is the boundary between two worlds, and that thou canst never meet thy Pearl again" (208). But, for her part, Pearl does not yet know or acknowledge the minister as her father and certainly not as the signifier of paternity or authority awaiting her beyond the mirror. Instead, she directs her attention to the scarlet letter once more, for, again, the letter is the symbol of the child as a little thing that fulfills the desire of the mother, just as it is a symbol of the unity of being the child has identified with the body of her mother. Clearly, the letter has phallic significance for Pearl. When Hester, in a moment of abandon with Dimmesdale, takes the emblem from her breast and tosses it toward the brook, the gesture must represent her recognition of her own castration. Seeing the object symbolizing herself and her mother now separated from her mother, Pearl feels the panic of the child suddenly become aware of castration—its own and its mother's. Her demand, therefore, is for Hester to put it back on, Pearl (like the child in the "Fort! Da!" game) perhaps hoping its return will close the gap and restore the totality lost with the symbolic phallus. But now the letter will not and cannot fill or restore anything in the Real (the Real is always full, says Lacan). Nor will the Oedipal kiss—proffered by Arthur—until it comes (in the third scaffold scene) with the acknowledgment (Pearl's and Arthur's) of actual fatherhood. Then, however, what the father's kiss will accomplish is not restoration of the phallus, but the impress of gender and the lesson of the Law, the Phallus, and castration.

The final step in Pearl's journey through the mirror stage, since it matches Dimmesdale's assumption of the Law of the Father, too, occurs in chapter 23, "The Revelation of the Scarlet Letter." The scene in the forest is, as it were, merely a foreshadowing of the mirror stage: the appropriate Oedipal personages (mother, father, child) are present, but the immediate results are not conclusive for Pearl. Her desire remains invested in the letter as if it were the paternal metaphor. By her imperious demands she forces Hester to don the letter again, and, by her hostility toward the minister, she drives him away from the mirroring, dividing brook. Thus, in the chapter leading up to the minister's revelation, Pearl displays the same intemperate, essentially lawless behavior that has always marked her. Not yet under the rule of law and the phallic authority, Pearl manifests pure, prepotent desire: "Whenever Pearl saw any thing to excite her ever active and wandering curiosity, she flew thitherward, and, as we might say, seized upon that man or thing as her own property, so far as she desired it; but without yielding the minutest degree of control over her emotions in requital" (244). So long as Pearl maintains such a relation to others and the world, she will remain caught in the identificatory web of the Imaginary. For her psychic (and cultural) evolution to occur, she must move into the register of the Symbolic. The Imaginary gives any subject a self (*moi* or ego) and an other, but the Symbolic gives a third, necessary agency: a concept of mediation, one represented in the father. "The child," writes Bär, "has to learn to receive [its] value," its being itself desirable, "from others, from the father, from the sociocultural system.

In this process, [it] is divided into the roles, designed by others, which [it] has to assume, and the impulse of [its] own absolute desires, which [it] has to repress" (Bär 515). What Pearl gains when she is recognized publicly (and recognizes herself) as Dimmesdale's child is the obverse of what she loses. She gains identity under the Law of the Father, but she loses the absolute narcissistic freedom of her "natural" ("pre-mirror") condition. She gains the phallus as a signifier in the register of the Symbolic, but she loses illusory totality in the register of the Imaginary. She loses her identity as a child, finally, but she gains the capability of mature womanhood as defined within her culture. No description of the passage through the Oedipus complex could be better than Hawthorne's account of Pearl's acceptance of her father: "Pearl kissed his lips. A spell was broken. The great scene of grief, in which the wild infant bore a part, had developed all her sympathies; and as her tears fell upon her father's cheek, they were the pledge that she would grow up amid human joy and sorrow, nor for ever do battle with the world, but be a woman in it" (256). In Lacanian terms, it is not Dimmesdale as father in the Real, but the minister as the representation of the Symbolic Name-of-the-Father, the Law of the Father, that is critical in Pearl's assumption of post-Oedipal subjectivity. Thus, however much one may wish to disavow the legitimacy—certainly the "naturalness" or permanency—of this particular culture's definition of womanhood, at the moment of Pearl's ascenscion to it, that definition is all she has to keep her from neurosis, perhaps even psychosis.

Pearl's assumption of gender and her relation to culture have been much debated issues in recent years. I think Lacan offers some useful answers to important questions raised, for example, by feminist readings of *The Scarlet Letter*. T. Walter Herbert, Jr., for example, has discussed the way in which "interactive selfhoods" relate in the "cultural construction of gender." Herbert's approach is not very rigorously psychoanalytic in Freudian or any other terms, but the essay would have made better sense had it been Lacanian, particularly had it been rooted in a conception of the primacy of language within culture. Herbert writes as if a culture acts without mediation. Herbert's comment on Pearl would have made perfectly good Lacanian sense: "Little Pearl is made to enact the qualities that most troubled Hawthorne in his daughter [Una], and she is eventually delivered from them. Hawthorne surrounds little Pearl, that is to say, with a therapeutic program, which includes a diagnosis of her difficulty and a prescription for cure, grounded on the gender categories that he considered natural and that defined a femininity he hoped his daughter would grow into" (287). The "cure" of which Herbert speaks is simply, in Lacanian terms, Pearl's accepting or introjecting the law with the *name* of the father. Herbert bases his interactive reading of Hawthorne, Una/Pearl, and *The Scarlet Letter* on what Stephen Greenblatt calls a "cultural poetics," but that poetics—as a Lacanian will recognize—is essentially a *psycho*poetics of culture and cultural objects. What Lacan brings to the reading of a figure such as Pearl is a way to link up Hawthorne's highly metaphorical language and the cultural determinations that can be seen to operate through it in the constitution of subjectivity, including one's gender.

Imaginary, Symbolic, and the Gaze: Hester

> Lacan insists on the difference, and the opposition, between the Imaginary and the Symbolic, showing that intersubjectivity cannot be reduced to the group of relations that he classes as Imaginary.
>
> —J. Laplanche and J.-B. Pontalis, *The Language of Psycho-Analysis*

The second of the two nonpathological subjects of consciousness in *The Scarlet Letter* is Pearl's mother, Hester Prynne. The dynamics of Hester's first appearance manifest several Lacanian concepts, for the power of the cultural gaze to which she is subjected will activate the dialectic of the Imaginary and the Symbolic that develops in the mirror stage Pearl passes through. Forced to emerge from a dark jail into the bright noontime sun, then to stand exposed on the scaffold of the pillory of Boston, Hester is made to wear the letter on which her crime insists, but that letter which is also the scopic object focusing her punishment under the communal gaze. Hester's crime—in Lacanian terms—is an expression of her psychic involvement in the Imaginary, her punishment an expression of the dominating authority of the cultural Symbolic. Thus, Hester's ambivalent relationship to the scarlet letter she wears becomes an expression of the general psychic ambivalence manifested in her apparent submission to communal law at the same time she finds a way to deny it. On the one hand, the letter is placed on her by the town fathers so that the gaze—being seen—is the main form of public punishment to which she will be subjected; on the other, she herself has transformed the stigma into such a compelling work of visual art that she and the letter she wears can hardly fail to attract the punitive attention of the gaze. The psychic split is evident in Hawthorne's first description of Hester's encounter with the audience for which her emblem is intended: "wisely judging that one token of her shame would but poorly serve to hide another, she took the baby on her arm, and, with a burning blush, and yet a haughty smile, and a glance that would not be ashamed, looked around at her townspeople and neighbours. On the breast of her gown, in fine red cloth, surrounded with an elaborate embroidery and fantastic flourishes of gold thread, appeared the letter A. It was so artistically done, and with so much fertility and gorgeous luxuriance of fancy, that it had all the effect of a last and fitting decoration to the apparel which she wore" (52–53). All Hester's problems as a subject caught between the Imaginary and the Symbolic are represented here, and it is these problems that Hester, accepting a cultural definition of her gender role, will resolve by the narrative's end.

We are all, according to Lacan, caught in the identificatory webs of the Imaginary. Hawthorne's treatment of Hester suggests just how enmeshed the subject becomes in the images of the Imaginary. The Imaginary, according to Ragland-Sullivan, "is the domain of the *imago* and relationship interaction" (*JLPP* 130–31). Whereas the register of the Symbolic operates "by a differential logic which names, codifies, and legalizes," the Imaginary operates by an "identificatory, fusional logic" (*JLPP* 131). The crucial fact of the Imaginary, where Hester is concerned, is that without adequate recourse to positive identity in the Symbolic she will be incapable of consistent self-reflection or self-awareness. Caught in the identifications of this register, she simply cannot understand or appreciate the drives operating on or within her. In effect, she must deny more than ordinarily the power of the indestructible drives of the unconscious. But, from an analytic perspective, it is clearly possible to make those unconscious drives or forces manifest. They will be evident in the images or figures of speech Hawthorne uses to represent her relation to others within her social environment. The most obvious others, of course, are Pearl, Dimmesdale, and Chillingworth. Hester's psychoanalytic profile can be drawn from her relations with these, for those relations will suggest the images that, within the topography of her psyche, project onto the place of the other and provide glimpses of the ego ideal of secondary narcissism lying on the plane of the cultural Other.

In the Imaginary, all identificatory others (persons, things, sensory impressions) become objects of desire in the field of the subject consciousness—that is, in the subject who relates through desire to those others. Hester—as desiring subject—relates to those identificatory others primarily through the function of sight—what Lacan calls the scopic field. Thus, for Hester, the Lacanian *objet petit a* (the objects that focus her desire) will be visual, and, more than that, will be artistically shaped. The principal example of this scopic identification with an object representing desire is Hester's relation to the infant Pearl on the one hand, and the scarlet letter on the other. But under the gaze, the *objet petit a* is ambiguous. From the first moment of their appearance, the letter A and the infant are joined as tokens signifying Hester's phallic desire, but they also signify her shame. Thus either may substitute, metaphorically, for her sexual desire and for her relation to the dominant, symbolic Other—the community and its punitive agent, the gaze. As signifiers, child and letter (as in the algorithm S/s) stand for the missing phallus that the community desires to see and that Hester determines to keep hidden. That phallus is, quite literally in *The Scarlet Letter*, the name of the father.[5] The index of Pearl's ambiguous objectivity to Hester as a subject lies in the contrapuntal aims of the two. It is the name of the father that Hester will not divulge; it is the father's name that Pearl shall demand. Similarly, the letter Hester wears denies the father's name, but at the same time it, metonymically (part for whole, A for Arthur), reveals it. In this respect, since the community and its gaze represent the Symbolic Other, Pearl and the letter as *objets petit a* mediate a relation for Hester to the unconscious. Thus, not only are Pearl and the letter A links to the name of the father, they also forge links between Hester's conscious and unconscious, Imaginary and Symbolic registers.

Pearl's identity, for Hester, is almost immediately absorbed into that symbolic object represented by the letter. Apparently unconsciously, Hester turns the child into a metaphoric replica of the scarlet emblem, thus fulfilling the signifying configuration seen at the outset when the child and the letter were linked only by metonymic contiguity on Hester's bosom. It is the nature of identifications in the Imaginary that they function either or both by similarity and contrast, sympathy and conflict. Both principles operate in the identificatory connection between Hester and Pearl. The contrast occurs in the drab attire of the mother compared to the bright finery of the child. The relation represented here in the difference is the same as that between the field (gray—or, as Hester's heraldic epitaph has it, sable) on which the letter stands and the letter itself (scarlet—or the heraldic gules) as opposed to the bright finery of Pearl and the field of drab Puritan fashion against which she stands. Of the relation between the exotically embroidered letter *A* and the communal standard, Hawthorne says that it "was of a splendor in accordance with the taste of the age, but greatly beyond what was allowed by the sumptuary regulations of the colony" (53). Of the contrast between Hester's attire, generally, and Pearl's, Hawthorne writes: "Her own dress was of the coarsest materials and the most sombre hue; with only that one ornament,—the scarlet letter,—which it was her doom to wear. The child's attire, on the other hand, was distinguished by a fanciful, or, we might rather say, a fantastic ingenuity, which served, indeed, to heighten the airy charm that early began to develop itself in the little girl, but which appeared to have also a deeper meaning" (83).

The deeper meaning of Pearl as an identificatory other lies in Hester's use of her as a two-sided medium channeling her relation to the community. Pearl (like the scarlet letter) is one side of the artistic expression that Hester permits herself; the other is the "good work," "the exquisite productions of her needle" (83), that she performs for the Puritan community. In effect, Pearl becomes Hester's living letter to the Puritan world. Here the principle of similarity or affinity found in the Imaginary can be seen in operation. Hester mimics through Pearl the luxurious beauty of the scarlet letter so that there can be no doubt of the similarity (and, thus, metaphoric identity) of the one object and the other, the child and the letter. Dressed by Hester all in crimson velvet tunics, "of a peculiar cut, abundantly embroidered with fantasies and flourishes of gold thread" (102), Pearl mirrors the emblem on her mother's breast. The child's garb "irresistibly and inevitably reminded the beholder of the token which Hester Prynne was doomed to wear upon her bosom. It was the scarlet letter in another form; the scarlet letter endowed with life" (102). Thus, for Hester, Pearl is both "the object of her affection and the emblem of her guilt and torture . . . [;] only in consequence of that identity had Hester contrived so perfectly to represent the scarlet letter in her appearance" (102).

The identificatory associations of Pearl and the letter, while representing the contrasting values of affection and punishment, are no more ambivalently expressive of Hester's relation to the community than her other works—the "finer productions of her handiwork" (82) that provide mother and child a livelihood. As the child and the letter both focus and symbolize the punitive gaze of Hester's social structure, so the works of her hands focus and symbolize the submissive relation Hester exhibits to the representatives of authority there. Whereas Pearl and the gorgeous emblem on Hester's bosom flout that authority, her other artisanal creations unconsciously recognize its power. The market she discovers for her products involve major domains of the social Symbolic: birth, death, and "public ceremonies, such as ordinations, the installation of magistrates, and all that could give majesty to the forms in which a new government manifested itself to the people" (82). But because Hester has exhibited a mode of desire (sexual) ordinarily denied the female, she is never permitted to act in that domain of sexuality circumscribed by culture's rituals. She is not permitted "to embroider the white veil which was to cover the pure blushes of a bride," but she is given access through her good work to all the other potent symbols of the law, up to and including the law of mortality: "Her needle work was seen on the ruff of the Governor; military men wore it on their scarfs, and the minister on his band; it decked the baby's little cap; it was shut up, to be mildewed and moulder away, in the coffins of the dead" (83). As Hawthorne points out, the exception made of the bridal veil indicates "the ever relentless vigor with which society frowned upon her sin" (83), but at the same time the various permissions give evidence (in the symbolic difference) of the agency and the potency of the Law.

One of the impressions given by Hester's involvement in the plot of *The Scarlet Letter* is that her psychic conflict as a subject is ended once she steps out into the sunlight flooding the scaffold of the pillory. But awareness of the ambiguity of her relation to Pearl and the letter, on one side, and to the authority of public law, on the other, suggests that indeed there is a conflict that must be resolved. She must finally accept the law, its symbols of authority, and through them the rule of the register of the Symbolic. The signifiers of that register constantly appear in aspects of what Lacan calls the gaze, along with the metonymical imagery associated with it such as the eye, the look, and the stare. Together, these represent one of the most important motifs in the narrative. The gaze, as Lacan might say, cuts in many directions, as it links the subject to the object and by that linkage turns each into the other whenever one reverses (by a shift in point of view) the scopic field. For Hester, in her conscious life, the gaze dominates as a double for the community—the public law to and under whose scrutiny (her "doom") she has been sentenced. Thus, for her, the gaze is even more important as an image of the Imaginary other than her lover, Arthur Dimmesdale, who in the ordinary love story might normally be regarded as the dominant figure of her Imaginary register.[6] But the public's gaze and its symbols also connect Hester's unconscious with the more powerful source of Law, Authority, and the Name(s)-of-the-Father in the Symbolic register. Says Lacan, "The gaze is presented to us only in the form of a strange contingency, symbolic of what we find on the horizon, as the thrust of our experience, namely, the lack that constitutes castration anxiety" (*FFC* 72–73).

Dimmesdale—like many readers—assumes that Hester has escaped psychic torment simply because her sin has been made public. But the power of the gaze and the agency of the eye work their effects into Hester's life just as rigorously as the minister's self-scrutiny does into his. The insistence of the law of the Other that must finally be observed comes to Hester in her punishment.[7] The scarlet letter she wears, for example, is held "up to the public gaze" (55), and she feels the "heavy weight of a thousand unrelenting eyes" (57). Hester can escape the gaze, the eyes, of neither friends nor strangers, nor friends who are strangers, as in the case of Roger Chillingworth, who is really *Prynne* and Hester's husband, lost and presumed dead at the tale's start. Roger is "the stranger" in the opening scene who "had bent his eyes on Hester Prynne" (61), and it is he who looks into her eyes with "a gaze that made her heart shrink and shudder" (72). But actual strangers and familiar faces trouble her, too. "Another peculiar torture was felt in the gaze of a new eye" (85), we are told, yet the "accustomed stare," in its "cool . . . familiarity" (86), is no pleasure for Hester either. Even Pearl—the one closest to Hester—is a constant reminder of the virtually absolute power of the gaze returned from the Other. "Weeks . . . would sometimes elapse," we are told, "during which Pearl's gaze might never once be fixed" on Hester's emblem of sin, "but then . . . it would come . . . like the stroke of sudden death" (96–97). The only gaze not so painful is Arthur Dimmesdale's, but that is because Hester and Arthur share the same pain, as perhaps they wear the same letter on their breasts. Their relation as doubles under the gaze is suggested, for example, in the late forest scene. "Here," in the forest tableau, "seen only by his eyes, the scarlet letter need not burn into the bosom of the fallen woman" (195–96), writes Hawthorne. For her part, what Hester has endured for the seven long years has been, simply, "the world's ignominious stare" (251). That stare is nothing less than the Other of Law, Authority, and the place of the Father Lacan associates with the register of the Symbolic.

Never to be assimilated into the Symbolic is to remain neurotically enmeshed in the images of the Imaginary. Though Hester exhibits traits of the obsessional (in the sense that her "good works" must cheat death), Hester will move from the potentially neurotic entrapment of the Imaginary into the culturally defined freedom of the Symbolic, but there is a suspenseful moment in the tale's plot that suggests she might fail. That moment, in which it appears that Hester will throw away not only the scarlet letter, but also seven years of preparation for absorption by the Symbolic, occurs in the forest scene when she tries to persuade Arthur to escape Boston and the gaze of the Puritan law under which they both are condemned. The escape she plans would take them away from those eyes that seem always overtly to penetrate her and covertly to penetrate Arthur. The covert agent of the communal gaze is Roger Chillingworth, the one who becomes what Hawthorne in another tale would call the bosom serpent. Above all, therefore, the escape Hester plans would take both of them away from Roger. "Thy heart," Hester tells Arthur, "must be no longer under his evil eye" (196). While it may be true that Roger is Hawthorne's figure of evil, there is never a doubt in the book that Roger is also Hawthorne's agent of a religious-cum-communal punishment. What else is the devil, the Black Man, he who is also the ambiguous agent of the symbolic Other, the law of the Father. Consequently, Roger's gaze is equally representative of the communal law under which they suffer and the more universal unconscious—Oedipal—law they had breached together when Arthur took Roger's place—the place of the lawful father—in relation to Hester's child. There is, as Hester discovers, no escaping Roger, for there is no escaping the Symbolic enfigured in the Puritans' "Black Man," who, we are assured, "hath a way of ordering matters so that the mark [of sin] shall be disclosed in open daylight to the eyes of the world" (242). It is because Roger stands for the Other that Hester (with Pearl and Arthur) cannot give him the slip and depart on a ship bound for the "lawless" sea.

One cannot know for certain that Hester would have experienced the same sense of acceptance of the Law of the Other had Roger not foiled her escape and Arthur not chosen to make his public revelation of his own share of her sin. But, psychologically, her acceptance—or capitulation—seems inevitable if we judge from the one instance of that acceptance Hawthorne reports. Although it comes at a moment when she believes they all will indeed escape Roger together, "after sustaining the gaze of the multitudes through seven miserable years as a necessity," Hawthorne writes, "she now . . . encountered it freely and voluntarily" (227). But should one deny the importance of her acceptance here, one ought to consider her return to Boston later in life and to the very site of her public ignominy after she had for awhile sojourned in the Old World with the mature Pearl. Her return is precisely an acceptance of her life under the burden of the Law, under the rule of the Symbolic Other. That acceptance, finally, is vividly symbolized in terms inevitably associated with the most potent reminder of our human submission to the Other. Death is the most emphatic expression of the human limitation represented in the Symbolic by the law of castration. In Hester's tale, the symbol of her final acceptance is the token, the tombstone, erected over her grave, bearing words authored by her and given authority by her submission to the Other: "On a field, sable, the letter A, gules" (264). That escutcheon is the ultimate expression of Hester's existence (*l'ètre*) under the letter and the law of the Lacanian *Autre*. Hester is the one subject—even more than her daughter, Pearl—who, Hawthorne makes it plain, has come to terms with her Symbolic lack, the lack of the symbolic phallus that both engenders her as woman and makes it possible for Hawthorne to hold her up as the emblem of our ordinary existences in a world of limits, boundaries, finitude.

Neurosis, Symptoms, Cure: Dimmesdale

> The primal repressed is a signifier, and we can always regard what is built on this as constituting the symptom *qua* a scaffolding of signifiers. Repressed and symptom are homogeneous, and reducible to the functions of signifiers.
> —Jacques Lacan, *Four Fundamental Concepts*

Arthur Dimmesdale is the figure on whom critics (following Frederick Crews's lead) ordinarily focus when searching for psychoanalytic insights in *The Scarlet Letter*. If one regards Pearl and Hester as more or less ordinary subjects, then it is valid to regard Arthur as extraordinary, as a pathological subject. He suffers symptoms that anyone, including Roger Chillingworth, can read, and those symptoms are such as to persuade just about everyone that Arthur's unconscious has become legible, that, indeed, he is one of our very finest literary exhibits of the unconscious at work. Arthur suffers from a neurosis marked by the symptoms of hysteria rather than of obsession, two of the forms of neurosis Freud notes. Since, as Lacan and others claim, the origin of psychoanalysis itself lies in Freud's discoveries regarding hysteria, Arthur becomes a paradigm case for dramatizing the relations among the hysterical condition, its symptoms, and its cure. Moreover, interpretation here displays the functioning of the unconscious, for, as Lacan insists, the unconscious—in the representations of its symptoms—has already performed an interpretation. Lacan says that "analysis consists in getting [the subject] to speak," for "the symptom is first of all the silence in the supposed speaking subject" (FFC 11). Since in the unconscious the Other of the subject has already spoken, "The analyst's interpretation," says Lacan, "merely reflects the fact that the unconscious, if it is what I say it is, namely, a play of the signifier, has already in its formations—dreams, slips of tongue or pen, witticisms or symptoms—proceeded by interpretation. The Other, the capital Other, is already there in every opening, however fleeting it may be, of the unconscious" (FFC 130).

In *The Four Fundamental Concepts of Psycho-Analysis* Lacan addresses Freud's notion of hysteria. Lacan says that hysteria is related to the subject's desire. The hysteric's specific desire is "the desire of the father, to be sustained in his status" (50). Lacan's claim here means everything for *The Scarlet Letter*, for it identifies not only Arthur's desire, but also the desire of Pearl, Hester, Roger, and, indeed, the entire community of Boston. As subject hysteric, Arthur has foreclosed—though not, as in the psychotic, permanently—the authority of the father—and, thereby, the Authority of the Other. His unconscious, as a consequence, must manifest, in pathological ways, the demand of the Other for control. These ways represent his neurotic symptoms, and Hawthorne's representation of those pathological symptoms fills most of the space in the novel devoted to Arthur. One sees various expressions of the neurosis in Arthur's fasts, dreams, visions, vigils, self-flagellation, and repetitive behavior. All these symptomatic expressions relate to what ails the minister: his relation to the paternal signifier. That relation involves himself as father, of course, but also his relation to the signifier of absolute paternity—to God in his terms and to the *jouissance* of the Other (see *Séminaire* XX). His problem is one of denial, finally, for he is devoured by his attempt to deny fatherhood, the Father, and (psychoanalytically) the Authority of the Other. All these, ultimately, are assimilated to the minister's relation to the letter—the shifting signifier, the polysemous letter *A*.

The letter to which Arthur relates most immediately is that on the bosom of Hester Prynne. Inevitably, the minister's most demanding symptom is his bodily imitation of that letter on his own breast. That "burning torture" or "scorching stigma," in Hawthorne's terms, is a metaphor-cum-symptom, a reproduction in the body of the sign affiliating Arthur with the symbol of his loss. What he has lost—and desires to regain—is the phallus and what it means—paternal authority. In the play of his unconscious, Arthur perceives that Hester now has what he wants, his power and his identity. She has the phallus in the symbol she wears, and in it she also possesses his identity—the letter *A* standing for Authority and Arthur, as well as for Adultery, Adulterer, Able, Angel, and all the other things, in a virtually endless chain, the text suggests it might signify. Thus, although Hester would disagree, Arthur's unconscious sees that the woman now possesses what the man lacks, but it can only be regained symbolically or, if materially, then by submission to the ultimate realm of the Other (that is, to the *jouissance* of the Other, which is death). As the one who wears the letter *A*, Hester herself becomes a figure associated with the Other, though in the dimension of the Real she can be no more than "other" (*l'autre*) to the minister. Hester, by virtue of the authoritative symbol she wears (representing her submission *to* the authority of the Other), is enabled to speak to Arthur from the place of the Other, also the place of the Father, that place Arthur has foregone because of his denial of paternal responsibility. In this chain of relations, therefore, the goal of Arthur's unconscious is to put the minister in the place where Hester stands— really, most aptly, in the most symbolic place where her stance has represented the aim of his desire: the scaffold of the pillory.

Arthur's symptomatic identification with figures of the Other (*l'Autre*) is most vivid in his gestation of the letter *A* in his own body, a hysterical pregnancy, shall we say, suggesting his unconscious assumption of the position of the mother in relation to the paternal signifier associated with the letter. But his symptomatic identification with the place of the Other occurs in compulsively repetitive acts. The most important such act is his return not to the scene of the crime, but to the scene of the punishment. Only by accepting, openly, as Hester has, the punishment for his transgression of the law (not merely Puritan law, either, but the primal Law of the Father, since Hester's husband must represent that law too as the figure of lawful paternity) can the minister regain his appropriate (submissive) relation to the Other. The chapter called "The Minister's Vigil" exhibits Arthur's behavior as "symptomatic" of his neurosis. Hawthorne, indeed, suggests that the episode has the elements of one of the most useful psychoanalytic symptoms; that is, it could have been a dream: "Walking in the shadow of a dream, as it were, and perhaps actually under the influence of a species of somnambulism, Mr. Dimmesdale reached the spot, where, now so long since, Hester Prynne had lived through her first hour of public ignominy" (147). As if indeed in a dream, all the significant figures in Arthur's life appear in the scene around the scaffold. Hester and Pearl, happening by, soon join him on the platform. The old minister John Wilson (a "good Father" figure to Arthur) also happens by, but, significantly, he does not see Arthur in the light of his lantern and so cannot draw him into his "illuminated circle" (150). Similar symbols of Authority or Otherness appear to Arthur by name if not in person: Governor Winthrop, who has just died, and old Governor Bellingham, who hears Arthur's shriek of torment. Likewise, the governor's sister, Mistress Hibbins, the purported witch and consort of the Black Man, also hears Arthur's cry. In his fantastic vision, as happens in dreams, the minister both recognizes and denies his sin. He does both in the way he imagines the results of his discovery there on the pillory by his community: "A dusky tumult would flap its wings from door to door, summoning all the people to behold the ghost—as he needs must think of it—of some defunct transgressor" (151). In other words, while the passage expresses Arthur's desire to take his place beside Hester, the vision's expression of the communal astonishment that it *could* be the minister is also a way to deny his crime.

Two additional figures connoting the Other, linked in the same glance, speak to Arthur on the scaffold of the pillory. These two are God (or Nature) and Roger Chillingworth. Hawthorne's remarks about the means by which the former speaks to the minister are among the most psychoanalytically apt in the book. The word or sign from God Arthur perceives is the formation of the letter *A* in the sky, perhaps, Hawthorne explains, a result of a meteor display: "looking upward to the zenith," the minister "beheld there the appearance of an immense letter,—the letter A,—marked out in lines of dull red light" (155). Hawthorne, coyly imputing Arthur's vision to "the disease in his own eye and heart," suggests that "another's guilt might have seen another symbol in it" (155). In any case, however, Arthur's interpretation of the vision here must be regarded as a symptom; as Hawthorne says, "it could only be the symptom of a highly disordered mental state, when a man, rendered morbidly self-contemplative by long, intense, and secret pain, had extended his egoism over the whole expanse of nature, until the firmament itself should appear no more than a fitting page for his soul's history and fate" (155). Moreover, the minister notes, symptomatically, of course, that all "the time that he gazed upward to the zenith, he was, nevertheless, perfectly aware that little Pearl was pointing her finger towards old Roger Chillingworth, who stood at no great distance from the scaffold. The minister appeared to see him, with the same glance that discerned the miraculous letter" (155–56).

Like Hester, Chillingworth plays a dual role in relation to the minister. Chillingworth is the most important representative for Arthur Dimmesdale of both the other and the Other. As other (*l'autre*) in the Imaginary, the physician is Arthur's double, the secret sharer of the minister's guilt. In the Imaginary, Chillingworth speaks for Arthur's consciousness, the duplicity of his conscience. Like Conrad's sharers, Dimmesdale and Chillingworth share living quarters. As "the two were lodged in the same house" after a time, "it truly seemed that this sagacious, experienced, benevolent, old physician, with his concord of paternal and reverential love for the young pastor, was the very man, of all mankind, to be constantly within reach of his voice" (125). As his double, Chillingworth does for or to Arthur only what the minister does himself. Both of them probe the young man's heart, each like "a treasure-seeker in a dark cavern" (125), each digging into "the poor clergyman's heart, like a miner searching for gold," or "like a sexton delving into a grave, possibly in quest of a jewel that had been buried on the dead man's bosom" (129). These figures are Hawthorne's to describe what Roger does to Dimmesdale, but in fact they also describe what the minister aims for—the "treasure," "jewel," or symbol that stands for the phallus as mark of lack or object of desire that Arthur hopes still to find on his own person. The metaphors all devolve to the dominant signifier in the text, the letter *A*, here metonymically suggested in the word *bosom*, which inevitably draws Hester Prynne and her mystic object back into play. Thus, Roger appears as the sagacious old figure of the father who looks into the minister's heart for the symbol of the Father, just as the minister himself searches his own soul for the symbol that will return to him the thing (paternity, Paternal Authority) he has lost.

As a "diabolical agent" with "Divine permission, for a season, to burrow into the clergyman's . . . soul," Chillingworth is the other in the Imaginary capable of becoming the Other of the analytic transference. The transference is necessary in this relation if Dimmesdale is to achieve what amounts to the analytic cure. The cure hinges on the patient's recognizing his or her desire, the "demand" that drives the patient to behave in a specific way regarded as neurotic. Dimmesdale's desire is a desire *of* the father; his demand is to be desired by the father and so is a desire to stand in the place of the mother. His desire, in short, is *not* to be the father, but to have the father and for the father to have him. His own desire is thus revealed to him in Chillingworth's desire for him. In "The Direction of the Treatment and the Principles of Its Power" (*Ecrits: A Selection* 226–80), Lacan says that in an analysis "the analyst deals . . . with all the articulations of the subject's demand. But . . . must respond to them only from the position of the transference" (256). The effect of Dimmesdale's relation to Chillingworth lies in the apparent transference-relation between them. Through the agency of the transference, therefore, the minister becomes capable of effecting a cure. Once Hester reveals to Arthur the identity of Chillingworth—"That old man," she says, "he was my husband" (194)—the minister undergoes a transformation, connoting a structural change in the ego's relation within the quadrangular subject, that virtually reverses the changes, physical and behavioral, he had suffered the last seven years. With the old man's "help," Dimmesdale begins to identify his ego position with the father, not the mother. This change of identificatory relation has several consequences. First, though the old man is thereby revealed as one against whom Arthur and Hester had sinned, Chillingworth is above all exhibited to Arthur as one who sins more grievously (unpardonably) than the minister alone or the young couple together. By that contrast, Arthur gains some relief from his heavy burden, but more than that he gains from the awareness that Chillingworth is a figure of Otherness who knows. Dimmesdale's symptoms have confessed for him, as it were, and, in the transference, the father-confessor now assumes for the minister the greater burden of both sin and knowledge. Though stated here more simply than it ever really is, all that Dimmesdale has to do now to attain the cure is utter the "proper word" that will reveal the substitutions taking place in his neurotic symptoms. That word, of course, is represented only in its metonymical part—a letter, the A for Adultery that stands for the violation of the law, but also the A that stands for Authority and the place of the Father—the Alpha of He-who-is-Alpha-and-Omega.

Arthur Dimmesdale utters the proper word in "The Revelation of the Scarlet Letter." There, the minister confesses his complicity in sin with Hester Prynne, assumes the position of the masculine ego structure and the responsibility (short-lived, to be sure) of his paternal relation to Pearl, and expresses the ultimate desire that determines his being. That desire is an extension of the hysteric's desire of the father and is represented in the subject of Arthur's sermon: "the relation between the Deity and the communities of mankind" (249). His topic stands in metonymical relation to his own personal identity theme, for it is Arthur's individual relation to the Deity that drives him. Arthur's ultimate goal is to be that part of the community who stands for the whole, and that part who also stands for the Deity. The minister's aim (as it is his professional function) is to stand in for the Son, the treasured symbol of the Father. Arthur's aim—and Hawthorne's as a novelist—accounts for the representations in the text of the minister's Christliness: the immanence in Arthur of the Name-of-the-Father and the congregation's sense of his imminent, sacrificial death. Like Christ, Arthur "so loved them all," that he would give up his life, though "he could not depart heavenward without a sigh" (249). The community senses his passage as that of an angel who "had shaken his bright wings over the people for an instant,—at once a shadow and a splendor" (249); their impression, moreover, is that he bears "the brilliant particles of a halo in the air about his head" (250–51). Most important, the desire of the Father leads Arthur from the pulpit back to the scaffold of the pillory, where his last, most significant acts are rites of passage to the Other. Taking his place in the triangle of Oedipal signification, Arthur assumes paternity, accepts castration (in the punitive gaze of the community, which, as we saw with Hester, is also an expression of the Other), and makes his everlasting peace with his family, his earthly father, and his heavenly Father. As Son, Arthur shows that he wears the mark, "his own red stigma" (255), that brands him, too, as the son of Man, transfigured by death into the psychoanalytic Other that encircles our Hawthornian souls and Lacanian psyches.

Psychosis, Analyst, Other: Chillingworth

> I say somewhere that *the unconscious is the discourse of the Other*. Now, this discourse of the Other that is to be realized, that of the unconscious, is not beyond the closure, it is *outside*. It is this discourse [that] through the mouth of the analyst calls for the reopening of the shutter.
>
> —Jacques Lacan, *Four Fundamental Concepts*

Roger Chillingworth is the character in *The Scarlet Letter* who most nearly seems a function only. In that respect he is perhaps closest to Pearl, who, though easily treated as a subject consciousness, seems often to be largely a means to achieve the ends of Hawthorne's emplotment. The function Chillingworth serves, subsumed in his role as physician to Arthur Dimmesdale, is that of the analyst. Hawthorne himself makes that clear in the text. Although the ostensible role of the old man is that of doctor for physical ailments, the actual role is that of the analyst, manifestly the psycho-analyst. Hawthorne makes it plain that the relation of physical signs to health is like that of the symptom to mental activity. "Whenever there is a heart and an intellect," writes Hawthorne, in the perspective of the doctor, "the diseases of the physical frame are tinged with the peculiarities of these. In Arthur Dimmesdale, thought and imagination were so active, and sensibility so intense, that the bodily infirmity would be likely to have its groundwork there" (124). Chillingworth's method is more like that of the psychoanalyst than of the physician; indeed, his aims are to uncover material from within the mind of his patient, rather than to heal physical infirmities. "Lacan," says Eugen Bär, "thinks of the analyst as the *translator* between the unconscious and conscious meaning systems of the patient. He silently gathers the irruptions of the Other and inverts them into conscious meaning units" (Bär 531). Of Chillingworth's method, Hawthorne writes, "Thus Roger Chillingworth scrutinized his patient carefully, both as he saw him in his ordinary life, keeping an accustomed pathway in the range of thoughts familiar to him, and as he appeared when thrown amidst other moral scenery, the novelty of which might call out something new to the surface of the character" (124).

In his role as analyst, Chillingworth is as much the figure of the artist as the physician. "Lacan's theory emphasizes the artistic character of psychoanalytic technique," says Bär. "It is up to the analyst's intuition, guided by his own unconscious, to detect nodes and especially to detect the infinitely complex individual content of nodes. To do that, the analyst has to be an artist himself, schooled, according to Lacan, in a wide range of disciplines, including among others mythology, comparative literature and religion, history of ideas, and linguistics" (534). Noted for his research, Chillingworth has all the scholarly qualifications for his artistic task. In Hester's earliest recollection of him, the old man is the very "figure of the study and the cloister" (58). To the people of Boston, he becomes a "brilliant acquisition" because of his medical and intellectual gifts. "He soon manifested his familiarity with the ponderous and imposing machinery of antique psychic"; additionally, in his Indian captivity, "he had gained much knowledge of the properties of native herbs and roots" (119–20). And he knows enough of theology, literature, and other arts to comport himself as the scholar he had been in the Old World.

Chillingworth has the rational and imaginative faculties, as well as motive and opportunity, moreover, to probe into his favorite patient's psyche. Of the relation of Dimmesdale (as patient) to Chillingworth (as analyst), Hawthorne writes: "A man burdened with a secret should especially avoid the intimacy of his physician. If the latter possess native sagacity, and a nameless something more,—let us call it intuition; if he show no intrusive egotism, nor disagreeably prominent characteristics of his own; if he have the power, which must be born with him, to bring his mind into such affinity with his patient's, that this last shall unawares have spoken what he imagines himself only to have thought; if such revelations be received without tumult, and acknowledged not so often by an uttered sympathy, as by silence, an inarticulate breath, and here and there by a word, to indicate that all is understood; if, to these qualifications of a confidant be joined the advantages afforded by his recognized character as a physician;—then, at some inevitable moment, will the soul of the sufferer be dissolved, and flow forth in a dark, but transparent stream, bringing all its mysteries into the daylight" (124). Chillingworth is thus more than the "psychoanalyst *manqué*," as Frederick Crews claims in *The Sins of the Fathers* (141); he is the analyst who will both fail and succeed. Indeed, Lacan makes it plain in "The Direction of the Treatment" that the analyst need not be *right* to effect a successful cure.

Chillingworth begins his analysis of Arthur Dimmesdale in what might be regarded as the proper relation. He begins in objectivity. The problem of the minister's (or, at first, merely someone's) guilt is simply a scientific puzzle. "He had begun an investigation, as he imagined," says Hawthorne, "with the severe and equal integrity of a judge, desirous only of truth, even as if the question involved no more than the air-drawn lines and figures of a geometrical problem, instead of human passions, and wrongs inflicted on himself" (129). That is as it should be. In this relation, Chillingworth could sustain the proper role of the analyst to Dimmesdale, but when the old man gets caught up in the personal, vengeful, punitive dimension, he can no longer serve as the Other in the Symbolic (though he cannot invalidate the Other, either). The changed relation between Roger and Arthur (from the old man's perspective as subject) involves the phenomenon of transference, for the relation becomes part of Roger's register of the Imaginary, the old man becoming a double or mirror image of the younger man. "But, as he proceeded," "a terrible fascination, a kind of fierce, though still calm, necessity seized the old man within its gripe, and never set him free again, until he had done all its bidding" (129). From a Lacanian perspective, such a symmetrical, transferential relation between analyst and patient "would mean that the analyst would himself be captured in the trap of the imaginary, that is, in his own illusory autonomy shaped through successive identifications with other persons or social patterns. The analysis resulting from this relationship [would be] a mere narcissistic game between analyst and patient" (Bär 532).

In his identificatory relation to Dimmesdale, Chillingworth undergoes as much of a physical transformation as the minister. The signs of the old man's otherness—his being a dark double to Arthur—appear in his face and body. The wiser folk in Boston see the changes, which are only slightly more overt than those occurring in Arthur. "At first, his expression had been calm, meditative, scholar-like," says Hawthorne. "Now, there was something ugly and evil in his face, which they had not previously noticed, and which grew still the more obvious to sight" (127). The window to a man's soul might well be the eyes, and in the old man's eyes are further signs of his deformation: "Sometimes, a light glimmered out of the physician's eyes, burning blue and ominous, like the reflection of a furnace, or let us say, like one of those gleams of ghastly fire that darted from Bunyan's awful door-way in the hill-side, and quivered on the pilgrim's face" (129). But the transformation is just as evident in Chillingworth's body; though he cannot become a walking, visible letter *A* such as Pearl, he can be an invisible one such as Arthur, who wears his sign under his tunic. Hester sees Roger's change clearly; to her it is a change that makes his demeanor mirror that of his tormented victim. Hester was shocked "to discern what a change had been wrought upon him within the past seven years. It was not so much that he had grown older; for though the traces of advancing life were visible, he bore his age well, and seemed to retain a wiry vigor of alertness. But the former aspect of an intellectual and studious man, calm and quiet, which was what she best remembered in him, had altogether vanished, and been succeeded by an eager, searching, almost fierce, yet carefully guarded look. It seemed to be his wish and purpose to mask this expression with a smile; but . . . the spectator could see his blackness all the better for it" (169).

Chillingworth, moreover, sees the change himself. He even refers to himself as one transformed into a fiend for the torment of one man. "The unfortunate physician . . . lifted his hands with a look of horror, as if he had beheld some frightful shape, which he could not recognize, usurping the place of his own image in a glass. It was one of those moments . . . when a man's moral aspect is faithfully revealed to his mind's eye" (172). But he is too caught in the trap of the Imaginary relation to cease analysis of Dimmesdale now. Since he has left Hester's punishment to the scarlet letter, as he says (173), he will continue to take onto himself the punishment of Arthur Dimmesdale. Alas, for Roger, the reciprocity between the two men must mean that what happens to one will happen to the other. Thus, if the minister dies, so must the physician. "Nothing was more remarkable than the change," writes Hawthorne, "which took place, almost immediately after Mr. Dimmesdale's death, in the appearance and demeanour of the old man known as Roger Chillingworth. All his strength and energy . . . seemed at once to desert him; insomuch that he positively withered up, shrivelled away, and almost vanished from mortal sight, like an uprooted weed that lies wilting in the sun" (260).

Chillingworth represents a figure of the transferential other to Dimmesdale because of their identificatory relation, but the old man really ought to represent the Other, not only for the minister, but also for Hester and Pearl as well. The physician, in one sense, is indeed the Other to them and for several reasons. To Hester and Arthur, he stands in the place of the Father because, though the husband of the young woman, he is also old enough to be her father. As a figure of the parental generation, Chillingworth thus invokes the Oedipal Law, the interdiction of incest. But it is that relation from the Symbolic that he violates. In his relation to Hester, Chillingworth, even before he becomes Dimmesdale's nemesis, is already something of a sinner himself. He admits as much to her: "Mine was the first wrong, when I betrayed thy budding youth into a false and unnatural relation with my decay" (74–75). Given the extent of his complicity with Hester, therefore, the old man, rather than Other, is largely the other to his young wife, as, furthermore, the two become doubled in their plot against Dimmesdale. As Roger says to Hester, "Between thee and me, the scale hangs fairly balanced" (75). Thus, whereas the old man ought to have remained in his proper place as the paternal agent or signifier of the Other to Hester, when he violates his proper role to join her in an Imaginary, "love" relationship he becomes other, really "merely" other.

Even so, in the domain of the Symbolic, Chillingworth must continue to signify the Father, play the role of the Other, an image linked to the Authority of Law found in his other name: Prynne—his name as Other. As Prynne, not Chillingworth, Roger persists—regardless of his own choices—as the Symbolic *Nom* or Name-of-the-Father and, as Lacan would say, as the *Non* or "No-of-the-Father" (see *Ecrits: A Selection* 179–225), the interdiction spoken by the Law. At the very moment Roger Chillingworth enters into an Imaginary relation to the young people, Roger *Prynne* is thrust into the Symbolic realm of their unconscious as the Other whose Law they have actually violated. The name at issue in the novel seems to be Dimmesdale's, but in fact it is equally Prynne's. It is that name about which Hester chooses silence on the scaffold of the pillory, and later that is the name she vows not to reveal to Arthur at the same time she vows not to reveal Arthur's to the old man. But it is Prynne-as-Other who enables Roger to carry out his corresponding vow to discover the name of Hester's lover and Pearl's father. He says to Hester, "Thou wilt not reveal his name? Not the less he is mine. . . . He bears no letter of infamy wrought into his garment, as thou dost; but I shall read it on his heart" (75). The ineluctable presence of Prynne—both Other and the Father in Arthur's unconscious—rather than the presence of Chillingworth as demonic double, is that which, ultimately, elicits the minister's symptoms and final "cure."

The most insistent evidence in Hawthorne's text that Chillingworth directs us to the position of the Other is the constant identification of him with the figure of the devil, Satan, or the Black Man. Neither the Other in Lacanian analysis nor God-the-Father in Puritan religion is unambiguously good; in both, obviously, is the threat of the Law, the intimidating power of punishment for transgressions. Consequently, whereas Hawthorne's Puritans would regard the Black Man as somehow separate from their conception of God-the-Father, Hawthorne's text makes it clear that the two (as in, say, *Paradise Lost*) are tied together. Thus, the demonic acts of the old man may have a divine purpose. The devil is the force of Law *out there* and *in here*, out there in the physical and in here in the psychological realms. Hester, for example, asks of Roger, "Art thou like the Black Man that haunts the forest round about us?" (77). The child Pearl likewise recognizes the old man as an image of the devil who has a grip on the mind of the minister; she warns her mother, "Come away, or yonder old Black Man will catch you! He hath got hold of the minister already" (134). Since the minister's problems lie in acknowledgment of the Other, Dimmesdale, for his part, does not recognize Chillingworth so quickly. On the scaffold at midnight, he asks, "Who is that man, Hester?" Hester must keep silent because of her vow to Roger, but Pearl has made no such vow and offers to inform the minister. As the patient-subject, however, Dimmesdale is not quite prepared yet to understand the child. "Pearl mumbled something into his ear," Hawthorne says, but "if it involved any secret information in regard to old Roger Chillingworth, it was in a tongue unknown to the erudite clergyman" (156). Nonetheless, the intimations Arthur feels regarding the identity of his dark Other prompts the minister the next day to preach "a discourse which was held to be the richest and most powerful, and the most replete with heavenly influences, that had ever proceeded from his lips" (157).

Roger Chillingworth, like Arthur Dimmesdale, represents the pathological in *The Scarlet Letter*. But where the minister is curably neurotic, the old physician is finally incurably psychotic. The psychotic, even more than the neurotic, is dominated by language and the force of the Other. "The psychotic," says Ragland-Sullivan, "paradoxically, is without libido," the drive or "lack-in-being" that aligns him or her to others and the Imaginary. "At the psychotic limit of psychic free-dom," says Ragland-Sullivan, "the individual does not have enough Desire to form adequate identity boundaries and unities. The psychotic literally dreams awake and identifies 'self' with the fragments and im-ages forming that inner-world, patchwork quilt, which most people experience as a unified *moi*" (*JLPP* 116). The result of such perceptions, says Ragland-Sullivan, is that the psychotic subject no longer can make the "normal" distinctions between the Imaginary and the Symbolic and so cannot "function in the Symbolic realm of displacement and sub-stitutions" (157). Instead, the psychotic in an episode may function in a kind of dream in which he or she takes Imaginary material for the Real. In the case of Chillingworth, we see Hawthorne progressively unmasking the pathological subjecthood of the old man. Though La-can contends that in real life subjects do not move from one structural position to another (neurosis to psychosis, for example), narratively, the progress Hawthorne delineates looks like a descent from ordinary subjectivity through neurosis to psychosis. Chillingworth seems merely the ordinary subject as he first appears to Hester at the scaffold and in the jail. He displays himself as perhaps an obsessional neurotic in his unbending demand for the name of Pearl's father and his conse-quent vow of persecution and discovery of the sinner. He ends by displaying his deepest, most fundamental subjectivity as one of psy-chosis. In his final justification of his aims as the destiny set by some force outside himself, it is as if he has turned over his actions and judgments to some "voice" that speaks through him. No ego remains, for, in foreclosing the paternal signifier, he has relinquished his desire totally to the domain of the Other.

The most significant evidence that Chillingworth is psychotic (though in Lacanian terms his pathology may be that of the obsessional) occurs in his justification to Hester of his persecution of the minister: "It is not granted me to pardon," he says, relinquishing one activity of the ego. The power of pardon, he says, belongs elsewhere, to his former religion: "My old faith, long forgotten, comes back to me," he says, "and explains all that we do, and all we suffer. By thy first step awry, thou didst plant the germ of evil; but, since that moment, it has all been a dark necessity. Ye that have wronged me are not sinful, save in a kind of typical illusion; neither am I fiend-like, who have snatched a fiend's office from his hands. It is our fate. Let the black flower blossom as it may!" (174). What Chillingworth says here means almost precisely what Ragland-Sullivan, interpreting Lacan, says of the paranoid psychotic, for what the old man claims is simply that the Other of the Law of Necessity speaks and acts through him. As Ragland-Sullivan says, in words that could easily describe Roger, "In paranoid psychosis the Imaginary representational text recorded in the Other(A) is alluded to in its pristine, hallucinatory purity to show the 'logic' of the fragmentary underside of identity, the subjective underface of reality" (*JLPP* 157).

Whether obsessional or truly psychotic, Chillingworth of course never displays the verbal incoherence, the "word salad" characteristic especially of schizophrenics (see Rosenbaum and Sonne). His psychotic being is largely observed in his crime, and makes one surmise that all the master criminals of history and of fictions, such as the James Bond movies, are largely psychotics. Though Chillingworth's crime—his unpardonable sin—is not actual murder, it is closely related to the murders so often committed by paranoid psychotics. Examples of these range from the Papin sisters, who brutally murdered their female employers, to Richard Speck, who murdered eight nurses in Chicago (1966), and Charles Whitman, the Texas Tower killer (also in 1966), to such serial killers as the peripatetic Theodore Bundy and New York City's "Son of Sam," David Berkowitz.[8] All (apparently) felt themselves to be doing nothing more than the bidding of an Other who spoke directly to or through them. The paradigm is perhaps Berkowitz, the Son-of-Sam murderer who killed, he says, at the behest of a dog owned by a six-thousand-year-old man named Sam. But, of course, Sam was not just any man nor the dog just any dog, for Berkowitz regarded Sam as Satan. Moreover, the inversion of the relation between Sam and dog, Satan and god, provides a Lacanian linguistic turn to the matter, for in the Symbolic Sam is surely god, the Other, and in Berkowitz's madness "god" is simply *dog* inverted. Chillingworth's claim that it is his "old faith," his Puritan religion, that drives him to his monomaniacal persecution of Dimmesdale merely attributes it, by metonymy, to the "Other" source—to God.

Chillingworth belongs among Hawthorne's mad scientists such as Rappacinni of "Rappacinni's Daughter" and Aylmer of "The Birthmark," figures who, like those actual criminals, are willing to commit murder, the unpardonable sin, to discover the secret of life. Though one might not call these other characters in Hawthorne psychotics, it is clear that they illustrate psychotic structures. In Lacan, the paradigm for such structures is found in the Papin sisters, Christine and Lea, who savagely murdered the two women (mother and daughter) who were their employers. Lacan's analysis of this famous case suggests that the sisters were involved in an incestuous and homosexual relationship with each other that had foreclosed the authority of Law, the Name-of-the-Father. In effect, in the murders they were acting out a metaphor, the figurative threat, "I'll tear her eyes out." But the violence of the act, as opposed to the words, came about because the two sisters had never accepted the existence of the Other, of man, since there had never been any but women in their strangely isolated household (Clément 73). Thus, their savage response to the abrupt intrusion of an authority *felt* to be Paternal—though it came in the scolding by the mother and daughter—is a denial, but at the same time it is a quest for knowledge, knowledge of the Other. Says Lacan, "They plucked out their victims' eyes as the Bacchantes castrated their victims. The sacrilegious curiosity that has anguished men since the beginning of time moved them in their desire for their victims, in their search in the dead women's gaping wounds for what Christine, in all innocence, later described to the court as 'the mystery of life' " (Clément 72). It is precisely the quest to solve just this mystery of life that drives Chillingworth, too, not only in his studies in science and alchemy, but also in his study of Arthur Dimmesdale. As he tells Hester, "there are few things,—whether in the outward world, or, to a certain depth, in the invisible sphere of thought,—few things hidden from the man, who devotes himself earnestly and unreservedly to the solution of a mystery" (75).

The source of the ultimate, Phallic mystery for Chillingworth becomes the man who will provide the proper name for Hester's child. "I shall seek this man," he tells Hester, "as I have sought truth in books; as I have sought gold in alchemy" (75). Perhaps the most telling clue that Chillingworth's quest is for the Phallus (the origin of life, plenitude, ultimate *jouissance*) is his insistence upon its possession, not mere recognition or discovery. "I shall see him tremble. I shall feel myself shudder, suddenly and unawares. Sooner or later, he must needs be mine!" (75). It is such an orgasmic, phallic *jouissance* that the old man experiences, indeed, when he has authoritative confirmation of the name of the sinner, the name of Pearl's father, and—as it must be—the Name-of-the-Father. That rapture occurs when he comes upon a view of the minister's naked breast. The sight is as intimidating to the old man as the sight of Jehovah would have been to the Old Testament prophets. So Chillingworth turns his eyes away from the sight: "But with what a wild look of wonder, joy, and horror!" writes Hawthorne. "With what a ghastly rapture, as it were, too mighty to be expressed only by the eye and features, and therefore bursting forth through the whole ugliness of his figure, and making itself even riotously manifest by the extravagant gestures with which he threw up his arms towards the ceiling, and stamped his foot upon the floor! Had a man seen old Roger Chillingworth, at that moment of his ecstasy, he would have had no need to ask how Satan comports himself, when a precious human soul is lost to heaven, and won into his kingdom" (138). Nor would one have to ask how the subject might respond upon discovery of the Phallus, the ultimate signifier, the symbolic domain of the Absolute. Finally, then, we may say that Chillingworth enjoys his psychotic's *jouissance* in the presence of Arthur's "thing," Arthur's letter—the letter (Alpha) in which insists the Phallus, the name of the father (Pearl's Arthur), and the Name-of-the-Father, the "Great Other" who, most ironically, founds the old man's *jouissance* at the same time He/It also confirms the minister's role, privately sought and publicly demanded, as the son of God. There is perhaps a Lacanian lesson in all this for Hawthorne. Those who are spoken by the Other or who seek the secret of life represented in the realm of the Other are also those whom Hawthorne would regard as the unpardonable sinners. They are the ones who will take human lives in the pursuit of that knowledge and at the behest of that Other voice. In his own way, therefore, Hawthorne has shown us the face of psychosis.

Notes

1. Though Crews abandons the Freudian critical approach, see *The Sins of the Fathers* for the most controversial psychoanalytic reading of Hawthorne. I might point out here that a limitation of Crews's interpretation of *The Scarlet Letter* is that it focuses almost exclusively on Dimmesdale—the neurotic subject; Crews and the Freudians in general have little to say about "normal" subjects. For other psychological or psychoanalytic interpretations, see also Adams; Dolis, "Hawthorne's Letter" and "Hawthorne's Morphology of Alienation: The Psychosomatic Phenomenon"; Hilgers; Irwin; and Ragussis. For criticism considered structuralist, post-structuralist, or postmodernist, see also Bell, Colacurcio, Lee, Rowe, and Torgovnick.

2. Hawthorne, *The Scarlet Letter*, p. 67. Further references to this text will be included parenthetically within the chapter.

3. For comments on Lacan's concept of the *objet a* or *objet petit a,* see note 4 to the Introduction. I will have much more to say about the use of *l'objet petit a* in my chapter on *To the Lighthouse.*

4. See "Aggressivity in Psychoanalysis," in *Ecrits: A Selection,* pp. 8–29. It is very important to understand that the *imago* found in the mirror images may be both positive and negative for the subject, and thus treated quite ambivalently.

5. Lacan insists on the primacy of the signifier of paternity, as opposed to the "fact" of paternity in the Real. In the essay "On the Possible Treatment of Psychosis," he explains, for example, that primitive peoples will always attribute paternity to some spirit a woman has met somewhere "if the symbolic context requires it." "It is certainly this," he continues, "that demonstrates that the attribution of procreation to the father can only be the effect of a pure signifier, of a recognition, not of a real father, but of what religion has taught us to refer to as the Name-of-the-Father." He adds, then, "Of course, there is no need of a signifier to be a father, any more than to be dead, but without a signifier, no one would ever know anything about either state of being." Lacan continues in a vein that is especially significant in the context of Hawthorne's novel:

> I would take this opportunity of reminding those who cannot be persuaded to seek in Freud's texts an extension of the enlightenment that their pedagogues dispense to them how insistently Freud stresses the affinity of the two signifying relations that I have just referred to, whenever the neurotic subject (especially the obsessional) manifests this affinity through the conjunction of the themes of the father and death.
>
> How, indeed, could Freud fail to recognize such an affinity, when the necessity of his reflexion led him to link the appearance of the signifier of the Father, as author of the Law, with death, even to the murder of the Father—thus showing that if this murder is the fruitful moment of debt through which the subject binds himself for life to the Law, the symbolic Father is, in so far as he signifies this Law, the dead Father. (*Ecrits: A Selection* 199)

6. See Sandeen for a discussion in which Hester and Arthur would, perforce, remain as objects to each other in Lacan's quadrant (in Schéma L) of the "other."

7. Employing the theory of Lacan and of Jeremy Bentham, Michel Foucault has written of the way in which Bentham's "panopticon" tower in prisons functions as a symbol of the controlling gaze. As a symbol, the tower—from which one has a 360-degree view of the inmates—works whether or not anyone is in it actually to keep watch. In this respect, the tower becomes a symbol of the Other, perhaps of the Phallus as well.

8. The crimes of the Papin sisters were among the subjects of Lacan's thesis in medicine (1932). The analysis of the psychological problems of the two

women is crucial to the development of Lacan's thought. Perhaps the most readable account of the crimes and Lacan's analysis is in Clément. For the sake of comparison, see Abrahamsen's psychoanalytic study of David Berkowitz.

Works Cited

Abrahamsen, David. *Confessions of Son of Sam.* New York: Columbia University Press, 1985.

Adams, Michael Vannoy. "Pathography, Hawthorne, and the History of Psychological Ideas." *ESQ* 29, no. 3 (1983): 113–26.

Bär, Eugen. "Understanding Lacan." *Psychoanalysis and Contemporary Science*, vol. 3. Ed. Leo Goldberger and Victor H. Rosen. New York: International Universities Press, 1974, 473–544.

Bell, Millicent. "The Obliquity of Signs in *The Scarlet Letter.*" *Massachusetts Review* 23 (Spring 1982): 113–26.

Clément, Catherine. *The Lives and Legends of Jacques Lacan.* Trans. Arthur Goldhammer. New York: Columbia University Press, 1983.

Colacurcio, Michael J., ed. *New Essays on "The Scarlet Letter."* Cambridge: Cambridge University Press, 1985.

Crews, Frederick C. *The Sins of the Fathers: Hawthorne's Psychological Themes.* New York: Oxford University Press, 1966.

———. *Out of My System: Psychoanalysis, Ideology, and Critical Method.* New York: Oxford University Press, 1975.

Dolis, John. "Hawthorne's Letter." *Notebooks in Cultural Analysis* 1 (1984): 103–23.

———. "Hawthorne's Morphology of Alienation: The Psychosomatic Phenomenon." *American Imago* 41, no. 1 (Spring 1984): 47–62.

Freud, Sigmund. "Delusions and Dreams in Jensen's *Gradiva.*" In *The Standard Edition of the Complete Psychological Works of Sigmund Freud*, vol. 9. Ed. and trans. James Strachey. London: Hogarth, 1959, 7–95.

Greenblatt, Stephen. *Renaissance Self-fashioning, from More to Shakespeare.* Chicago: University of Chicago Press, 1980.

Hawthorne, Nathaniel. *The Scarlet Letter.* In *The Centenary Edition of the Works of Nathaniel Hawthorne*, vol. 1. Columbus: Ohio State University Press, 1962.

Herbert, T. Walter, Jr. "Nathaniel Hawthorne, Una Hawthorne, and *The Scarlet Letter:* Interactive Selfhoods and the Cultural Construction of Gender." *PMLA* 103 (1988): 285–97.

Hilgers, Thomas L. "The Psychological Conflict Resolution in *The Scarlet Letter.*" *American Transcendental Quarterly* 43 (Summer 1979): 211–24.

Irwin, John. *American Hieroglyphics: The Symbol of the Egyptian Hieroglyphics in the American Renaissance.* New Haven: Yale University Press, 1980.

Lacan, Jacques. *Ecrits: A Selection.* Trans. Alan Sheridan. New York: Norton, 1977.

———. *The Four Fundamental Concepts of Psycho-analysis.* Ed. Jacques-Alain Miller. Trans. Alan Sheridan. New York: Norton, 1978.

Lee, A. Robert, ed. *Nathaniel Hawthorne: New Critical Essays.* Totowa: Barnes and Noble, 1982.

Lévi-Strauss, Claude. *The Elementary Structures of Kinship.* Trans. James Harle Bell et al. Boston: Beacon, 1969.

———. *Mythologiques.* 4 vols. Trans. John and Doreen Weightman. New York: Harper, 1970, 1973, 1978, 1981.

———. *The Savage Mind.* Chicago: University of Chicago Press, 1966.

———. *Structural Anthropology.* 2 vols. Trans. Claire Jakobson and Brooke Grundfest-Schoepf (vol. 1) and Monique Layton (vol. 2). New York: Basic Books, 1963, 1976.

Muller, John, and William J. Richardson. *Lacan and Language: A Reader's Guide to "Ecrits."* New York: International Universities Press, 1982.

Ragland-Sullivan, Ellie. *Jacques Lacan and the Philosophy of Psychoanalysis.* Urbana: University of Illinois Press, 1986.

———. "The Magnetism between Reader and Text: Prolegomena to a Lacanian Poetics." *Poetics* 13 (1984): 381–406.

Ragussis, Michael. "Family Discourse and Fiction in *The Scarlet Letter.*" *ELH* 49, no. 4 (Winter 1982): 863–88.

Rosenbaum, Bent, and Harly Sonne. *The Language of Psychosis.* New York: New York University Press, 1986.

Rowe, John Carlos. "The Internal Conflict of Romantic Narrative: Hegel's Phenomenology and Hawthorne's *The Scarlet Letter.*" *MLN* 95 (1980): 1203–31.

Sandeen, Ernest. "*The Scarlet Letter* as a Love Story." *PMLA* 77 (1962): 425–35.

Schneiderman, Stuart, ed. and trans. *Returning to Freud: Clinical Psychoanalysis and the School of Jacques Lacan.* New Haven: Yale University Press, 1980.

Sheridan, Alan. "Translator's Notes." In *The Four Fundamental Concepts of Psycho-analysis* by Jacques Lacan. Ed. Jacques-Alain Miller. Trans. Alan Sheridan. New York: Norton, 1978.

Torgovnick, Marianna. *Closure in the Novel.* Princeton: Princeton University Press, 1981.

CHAPTER TWO

A "Countable Unity": The Lacanian Subject in "The Beast in the Jungle"

The unconscious is that chapter of my history that is marked by a blank or occupied by a falsehood: it is the censored chapter. But the truth can be rediscovered; usually it has already been written down elsewhere.

—Jacques Lacan, *Ecrits: A Selection*

In "The Magnetism between Reader and Text," Ellie Ragland-Sullivan speaks of the way literary works represent a reader's ego to itself through the language of the text. The literary text, she suggests, exerts a "magnetic pull" on readers "because it is an allegory of the psyche's fundamental structure" (381). But the psyche—the ego—of any subject is always in a process of constant creation and recreation; it is not stable, fixed, determinant; it is always "in play" through a constant interaction of features motivated by substitutions, displacements, and other functions such as condensation and contiguous referentiality. The ego, in Lacanian terms, always comes, moreover, *from* the other; it is assumed—in all its motility—from external sources, *and* it is made up: it is a fiction. As a "fiction," the ego is exchanged constantly with the egos of others, the fictive symbols of other selves, in a social environment. This exchange, along with the constant process of transformation (as image displaces image, symbol substitutes for other symbol), also functions in one's relation to a literary text. A literary work offers a formally controlled context within which a reader may try out other identifications, may position itself at any of the four points of the quadrangular structure of the subject. The literary work thus offers the subject a means of replaying both its mirror-stage and its Oedipal functions. Though any given work may permit equal possibilities for identification with both functions, some texts will feature one much more than the other. James's "Beast in the Jungle" is a tale that features the constant play of mirror-stage identifications in its dominant fictional subject. In fact, James's tale becomes a metaphorical—or allegorical— rendering of the way in which human subjectivity comes into being. Indeed, it is likely that the tale remains so fascinating to generations of readers precisely because it so actively and repetitiously recreates that moment of the mirror stage when the subject discovers itself in its identificatory other. John Marcher constantly relives that moment, and through him readers are enabled to relive those moments in their own lives as well.

Perhaps the most difficult—and the most basic—notion in Lacan is that regarding the constitution of subjectivity. Since Lacan does not posit an a priori self or ego, his conception of the origin of the subject does not accord with the ordinary ways we think about causes and effects. If the ego is not present from birth, how does it come to exist? And once it exists, how does it change, if it does ever change? As if the constitution of the subject were not difficult enough to understand, then, Lacan adds to the difficulty questions of growth, development, or maturation in human subjectivity. To be sure, Lacan does not posit "logical, genital, or genetic developmental sequences of maturation in his epistemology," writes Ragland-Sullivan (*JLPP* 283), but as I indicated in the Introduction, he nonetheless identifies transitional moments toward what one associates with the human maturity so closely linked to cultural values and socialization. In my Introduction, I looked at these moments in several ways. In my reading of *The Scarlet Letter* I looked at the specific example of Pearl's passage through the mirror stage and the dissolution of the Oedipus complex. Here I want to take another look at those moments and connect them to another means of explanation. This other explanatory model has to do with number. I want to use James's tale and Lacan's notion of the subject's "countable unity" to elucidate concretely Lacan's rather difficult conception of subjectivity.

Lacan expressly links the moments of the constitution of the subject and its development to a deeply fundamental sense in humans of counting. Any ordinary human has a sense of the countable. But for Lacan counting can explain his conception of human subjectivity. For example, counting has to do with the only sort of "unity" an always divided subject may have. Counting, says Lacan, is "unity in another light." This unity is appropriate for the subject because it is not "a *unifying* unity but the *countable* unity one, two, three" ("Of Structure" 190; my emphasis). Counting permits Lacan to explain the anomalies of human identity—its sense of unity despite its divisions. Lacan sees this paradox in the distinction between language and number. As he suggests in "Of Structure," number represents the difference of identity and permits the appearance of history (temporality) even when there is none, but language represents the identity of difference and suggests the appearance of synchrony (unity) even when it is impossible (193). The human perception of number, therefore, is very closely related to that conception of the constitution of subjectivity that begins in the mirror stage and occurs fully (in the normative subject) in the Oedipal passage. Human subjectivity (identity) begins to emerge because of a process of covering over (psychoanalytically, the repression) of a dyadic first object (mother, infant). Lacan explains that process in terms of set theory. In set theory, that dyadic object is the set formed of 0 + 1; in the birth of the child as human subject, the set is normatively comprised of child and mother or other primary nurturer. Regarding each integer as a set, where, for example, 1 is the set formed by 0 and 1, Lacan says that it "is necessary that two constitute the first integer which is not yet born as a number before the two appears. You have made this possible because the *two* is here to grant existence to the first *one*: put *two* in the place of *one* and consequently in the place of the *two* you see *three* appear" (191). In each instance, a number (comprising a "set") comes into existence because of the "fading" of another number, also comprising a set (192). Subjectivity, Lacan suggests, occurs in a similar way: "The question of the two is for us the question of the subject, and here we reach a fact of psychoanalytical experience in as much as the two does not complete the one to make two, *but must repeat the one to permit the one to exist*. This first repetition is the only one necessary to explain the genesis of the number, and only one repetition is necessary to constitute the status of the subject" (191; my emphasis). In this way, using set theory to explain counting, Lacan ends by explaining the functioning of the mirror stage in the constitution of the subject.

The metaphor of counting thus becomes a useful concept for organizing the paradoxes of Lacan's conception of the subject, its apparent temporal (diachronic) phases in relation to the synchronic (unitary) moments of psychogenesis. Both Ragland-Sullivan and Stuart Schneiderman suggest this possibility. Schneiderman has given us a kind of thematics of the way the first several sets relate to one another in Lacanian theory: "The empty set, whose name is zero, corresponds to the empty grave," he says; it also "represents the mother's lack of a phallus." One "is the signifier," suggests Schneiderman, but it is also "the phallic function, so important to Freud and Lacan." "The number two," he says, "appears commonly in psychoanalytic theory as the ego and its object, as me and you, as mother and child." Similarly, for its part, three "refers to the triangulation of the Oedipus complex in Freud, and Lacan used it in theorizing the imaginary, real, and symbolic orders" (7). Where Schneiderman relates unconscious counting to the thematics of signifying structures, Ragland-Sullivan relates such counting both to those synchronic themes and to the diachronic (temporal) order in which the unconscious ordinarily encounters the signifiers. "I interpret Lacan's 0 as the number of primary identification or of elemental representationalism," Ragland-Sullivan says. One, in turn, "is the number marking the infant's attainment of a sense of body unity by mentally identifying with a *Gestalt* exterior to it." Next, "as the post–mirror-stage number of separation, 2 denotes the split (*Ichspaltung*) internalized by an infant when language and the Name-of-the-Father reveal the necessity of psychic differentiation from the mother. "The number three is pivotal in measuring the progress toward sociocultural maturation, for it connotes "the Oedipal gender myth that situates the mother and father in cultural identity concepts of masculine and feminine" (*JLPP* 134). Together, Schneiderman and Ragland-Sullivan suggest that the process of human subjective maturation, as we ordinarily experience it, is figuratively nothing more than learning to count, learning to count *others* in a significant way in the structure of one's lived engagements. In the process, as a subject, one achieves a countable—though not a fixed, centered, or totalizable—unity. Although Lacan considers countable phases beyond number three, I shall focus on the moves up to three in "The Beast in the Jungle," for these embrace the functions of the mirror stage (which dominates James's text) and the too long awaited dissolution of Marcher's Oedipus complex. These functions, Lacan says, enable the constitution of the human subject, and they continue of course to play a role in the subject's life ever after, but, as Marcher's life story suggests, they do not play equal roles in all lives.

Zero: The Empty Set

Zero refers . . . to the pre–mirror-stage infant whose experience of the world occurs in bits and pieces.
—Ellie Ragland-Sullivan, *Jacques Lacan and the Philosophy of Psychoanalysis*

I want to begin by suggesting that James's tale provides a metaphor of the constitution of the Lacanian subject. I do not mean to suggest in the following discussion that John Marcher has not achieved normative subjecthood by the opening event of James's tale. Rather, I mean to suggest that the tale recapitulates—many times over—the structure of the constitution of the subject. The tale thus suggests the way in which one's life *repeats* the two dominant moments of one's constitution (or "identity," in the ordinary parlance)—the moment of the mirror stage and the moment of the Oedipus complex. James's tale thus accounts for the preoccupation in narrative of stories of separation from the figure of the other, of stories revealing figures of the other (the double of the mirror), and of stories of conflicts and resolutions with the father (the Other of law, authority). Specifically, James's "Beast in the Jungle" recapitulates in a variety of ways Marcher's mirror-stage identification with the (m)other; only late does it suggest the separation necessary for a normative move to the Oedipus encounter with the father-become-the-Name-of-the-Father. The tale's incredible redundancy is the result of the power of the first, the mirror, identifications necessary to the constitution of an ego-subjectivity. But if the tale exhibits a satisfactory conclusion for most readers, it does so because Marcher finally achieves a long-delayed dissolution of the Oedipus complex. In ordinary terms, Marcher at last grows up and positions himself as a man in his structuration as a subject.

The constitution of the subject, as Lacan explains it, explains one of the puzzling, though usually unrecognized, features of James's characterization of John Marcher: he has no apparent past. There seems to be no history, no family history, not even any parentage before he meets May Bartram at Weatherend at the beginning of "The Beast in the Jungle." The only past he has seems to be that earlier meeting with May in Italy. But that meeting is the real puzzle. Since Marcher has no real recollection of it as a moment in his life, it literally has no existence until May creates it for him. The development of book 1 of "The Beast in the Jungle," consequently, establishes the existence of this void or zero phase in Marcher's psychic life and, then, fills the empty set through the device of an "other." The other who forms the mirror for Marcher, thereby permitting him to count an Imaginary "one," is, of course, May Bartram. The void as the empty set is suggested from the very first words of the story: "What determined the speech that startled him in the course of their encounter scarcely matters," James writes of Marcher's response, adding, significantly, "being *probably* but some words spoken by himself quite without intention" (61; my emphasis). To begin with, one sees that Marcher is not quite certain what the origin is of his and May's decision to pursue their relationship. Now, in the conclusion of that first sentence, Marcher speaks of the "*renewal* of acquaintance" (61), but in fact, when (in the story's second paragraph) he recounts their first meeting at Weatherend, he does not actually recall anything about her. Her face, James writes, was "a *reminder*, yet not quite a *remembrance*" (62). That face, moreover, "had begun merely by troubling him rather pleasantly. It affected him as the sequel of something *of which he had lost the beginning*" (62; my emphasis).

Marcher continues to ruminate in this vein because he clearly has not established a set, a being, without May. In effect, without her creating the first integer to bound the set, he himself is not yet constituted. Not only does he feel that the meeting is a "continuation," though he "didn't know what it continued" (62), he also believes even "without a direct sign from her" (62) that May "hadn't lost the thread," though she would not "give it back to him, he saw, without some putting forth of his hand for it" (62). All this he detects without speech or signs, despite "the fact that at the moment some accident of grouping brought them face to face he was still merely fumbling with the idea that any contact between them in the past would have had no importance. If it had had no importance he scarcely knew why his actual impression of her should so seem to have so much; the answer to which, however, was that in such a life as they all appeared to be leading for the moment one could but take things as they came" (63). Thus, when Marcher detects May's drifting toward him, he feels it may have been the result of her somehow being aware "that he had, within the couple of hours, devoted more imagination to her than to all the others put together, and had thereby penetrated to a kind of truth [about May herself] that the others were too stupid for" (63). In James's assessment, May and Marcher find themselves mirrored in the face of the other, but Marcher only flatters his memory when he suggests that "she remembered him very much as she was remembered—only a good deal better" (63–64). In fact, as James will suggest very shortly, Marcher simply does not have a recollection. Like the subject in the process of constitution, he has only a construction—itself built of bits and pieces supplied by some other subject.

Marcher exists, metaphorically, in these moments as if an infant in a sort of preverbal universe, a mystical realm of magical signs, hints, and intimations of physical and psychic unity. As if at base zero, Marcher is the infant, "unaware that its primordial unities come from identificatory fusion with body parts and imagistic fragments"—as Ragland-Sullivan says (*JLPP* 134). "By the time they at last thus came to speech they were alone in one of the rooms ..., and the charm of it was that even before they had spoken they had practically arranged with each other to stay behind to talk" (64). Marcher feels the charm of many things at this moment at Weatherend, but perhaps the most significant is May's having singled him out for her special attention, but giving him the power to reject it if he should so desire. "It was most of all perhaps in the way she came to him as if ... should he choose to keep the whole thing down, [he might] just take her mild attention for a part of her general business" (64) as the whole group's tour guide. He chooses to pursue her attention, of course, and—in language that suggests the jungle beast eventually to be figured forth in the story—James writes that Marcher "almost jumped at it to get there," that is, to get to the memory "before her" (64). Marcher thinks that as "soon as he heard her voice, ... the gap was filled up and the missing link supplied" (64), and he blurts out, "I met you years and years ago in Rome. I remember all about it" (64). But if May is the judge, then he is wrong; for "to prove how well he did [remember] he began to pour forth the particular recollections that popped up as he called for them. Her face and her voice, all at his service now, worked the miracle ... yet he was really still more pleased on her showing him, with amusement, that in his haste to make everything right he had got most things rather wrong" (64–65).

Figuratively, Marcher as subjectivity is at locus zero and awaits the countable unity conferred by another who bounds the set of zero and

1; in this move, he achieves "oneness." As Ragland-Sullivan says, "One, by contrast [to zero], is the number marking the infant's attainment of a sense of body unity by [its] mentally identifying with a *Gestalt* exterior to it. Therefore, it is the number of symbiosis, denoting both mirror-stage psychic fusion and corporal identification with the human form. This dual fusion gives rise to the countable unity of the 'self' that is taken on in the other's mirror and substituted for a preceding disunity" (*JLPP* 134). The plethora of May's details correcting Marcher reduces to the fact that before her appearance there is *in* Marcher only zero. He simply has no memory of her or their first meeting in Naples. May points out this moral to him: "he *really* didn't remember the least thing about her; and he only felt it as a drawback that when all was made strictly historic there didn't appear much of anything left" (65). Such an impasse at zero would have led to nothing further had not both been eager to fill the void by establishing a set—0 + 1. James tells us, "They looked at each other as with the feeling of an occasion missed; the present would have been so much better if the other, in the far distance, in the foreign land, hadn't been so stupidly meagre" (66). What is left, of course, is imagination, really, the Lacanian Imaginary. As if in support of a Lacanian perspective, James says that Marcher "would have liked to invent something, get her to make-believe with him that some passage of a romantic or critical kind *had* originally occurred. He was really almost reaching out in imagination" (67). It is a moment of high drama, with the enigma of the lost fortune or the mystery of "two paths diverging" in life presiding over it. If one of them does not do something, "They would separate, and now for no second or no third chance" (67). But it is May, not Marcher, who saves the moment. Once more, she seems to have prestidigitated a missing link: "What she brought out," James says, "quite cleared the air and supplied the link—the link it was so odd he should frivolously have managed to lose" (67–68).

The remainder of book 1 effectively dramatizes the Lacanian notion of the constitution of the subject. It offers a scene in which May and Marcher slowly constitute around a void the secret core of Marcher's life. That is the most Lacanian theme of all: the "self" is built around a void. But so is James's story. Most readers—all, indeed, as far as I can tell—assume that there is a factual basis not only to their original meeting in Naples, but also to the confession that Marcher had made there to May.[1] But actual textual evidence in the scene does not bear out such a conclusion any more than the exposition preceding it. The scene begins with May's saying that he had told her something in that first meeting: "I've never forgotten," she says, and it has since often made her think of him. "What I allude to was what you said to me, on the way back [from a boat excursion to Sorrento], as we sat under the awning of the boat enjoying the cool. Have you forgotten?" (68). Indeed, Marcher has "forgotten," and even wonders if perhaps he has made a pass at May—made "some imbecile 'offer' " (68). But the assumption that May herself remembers something makes him conscious of "a loss," so he claims to remember the Sorrento day she mentions (68). When May rather doubts that, Marcher goes on to suggest that he must have made an ass of himself. Not at all, May corrects. "If I had only thought you foolish," she says, "the thing I speak of wouldn't so have remained with me. It was about yourself" (69). The narrative exposition is explicit regarding Marcher's memory: "She waited as if it might come to him; but as, only meeting her eyes in wonder, he gave no sign, she burnt her ships. 'Has it ever happened?' " (69).

The Lacanian dance around the void—the empty set—continues between the two people, each an other to the other. If this were a scene true to an ego-centered notion of subjectivity, in the next movement Marcher would himself divulge precisely what constitutes the secret, the origin of his being. That he does not and cannot is precisely the Lacanian element in James's presentation. Readers are forced to look at it in great detail, for James draws it out to enormous length. In all this scene, the really significant *Lacanian* point is that Marcher never says what *his* version of the secret is. Moreover, he suggests by his evasions of it that in fact he does not have one. He must, instead, rely upon whatever May claims is the "truth." There is no truth, of course, other than the subject's truth. The subject's truth is that there is only the void, the empty set, the *mise en abîme*. That being the case, why not allow the other to constitute his past for him and, in so doing, constitute for him a unity he can count on, as well? One might say, as I have suggested, that Marcher has undergone a repetition of the mirror stage of the infant. Within that structure, May Bartram has become Marcher's other, the one who defines his being. She tells him: "You said you had had from your earliest time, as the deepest thing within you, the sense of being kept for something rare and strange, possibly prodigious and terrible, that was sooner or later to happen to you, that you had in your bones the foreboding and the conviction of, and that would perhaps overwhelm you" (71). This moment might have been propitious for Marcher to confirm absolutely, unequivocally that her version is the real or true one. But he does not, and when May asks if he still has such a belief, he says only, "Oh!" and James "explains," "There was too much to say" (72). Too much, indeed. He now has gathered enough from his mirror-other, however, to *be* a subject; he now claims that "it" has not yet come, and he extrapolates from what she has given him in the way that any blank subject might. "It" is not something he will do or be famous or admired for. No, let's say it will be something to "wait for—to have to meet, to face, to see suddenly break out in my life; possibly destroying all further consciousness, possibly annihilating me; possibly, on the other hand, only altering everything, striking at the root of all my world and leaving me to the consequences, however they shape themselves" (72). It is not going to be, he says, anything as trivial as falling in love. It is not even going to be anything that he "wants," nor is it going to be something "violent." It is, he says, simply "*the* thing" (73). And, since he exists only in her eyes, May Bartram is going to be present—even, perhaps, "at the catastrophe" (73). Now joined in the mirror, "it was as if the long look they exchanged held them together" (74).

What Marcher has encountered in this metaphorical moment of his constitution as a subject is the phenomenon Lacan, borrowing the term from Ernest Jones, calls *aphanisis*. *Aphanisis* is the name Lacan gives to the moment in which the subject comes into being as a result of a signifier—and not just any signifier, either, but a signifier of/from the other—and simultaneously disappears under it. There is no a priori ego, in other words; there is only a subject represented as a signifier for another signifier. The subject is constituted, Lacan insists, in what can only be regarded as fundamentally a social relation. For Lacan, "a signifier is that which represents a subject for another signifier" (*FFC* 207), and that other signifier is taken from the social order. May Bartram is that other, of course, but the consequence of Marcher's realization is his disappearance beneath that signifier she has provided. He is now, in May's view, at an indeterminate place. "What we find," says Lacan, "is the constitution of the subject in the field of the Other. . . . If he is apprehended at his birth in the field of the Other, the characteristic of the subject of the unconscious is that of being, beneath the signifier that develops its networks, its chains and its history, at an indeterminate place" (*FFC* 208). Marcher counts to one—

reaches oneness, that is—by covering over a void, a zero, a locus that he is incapable of filling by himself or even of recognizing without the other—the *second* person—who calls him into being. The scene with May in Naples is momentous, then, not because it really exists—Lacan would say, Who cares?—but because it calls into existence John Marcher as a subject, Marcher as a subject for another, a subject for another signifier identified in May Bartram.

Thus the scene at Weatherend, it turns out, is momentous because it introduces Marcher to desire and alienation. Desire is the desire of the other that originates in alienation. Lacan says the emerging subject's alienation occurs in the operation of separation that comes in the mirror stage's opening up of the primal, mother-child dyad. "By separation, the subject finds the weak point of the primal dyad of the signifying articulation." The weak point is that "it is alienating in essence." The dyad opens a space of desire, says Lacan. "It is in the interval between these two signifiers [subject and other] that resides the desire offered to the mapping of the subject." That mapping occurs in the subject's "experience of the discourse of the Other, of the first Other he has to deal with, let us say, by way of illustration, the mother" (FFC 218). Identity, alienation, and desire are all generated in the subject's relation to this figure Lacan calls sometimes the (m)other. "It is in so far as his desire is beyond or falls short of what she says, of what she hints at, of what she brings out as meaning, it is in so far as his desire is unknown, it is in this point of lack, that the desire of the subject is constituted" (FFC 218-19). As we shall see, what May Bartram has given Marcher, structurally speaking, in giving him access to the signifier of a self, is desire, her desire, the desire of the Other. It is in pursuit of the object(s) of desire she represents for him that Marcher will spend virtually the remainder of his days.

One: Imaginary Unity

The first meeting between an infant and the Real is symbolized by Lacan as the *objet a,* which refers both to the primordial gap between body experience and perception and to the images which quickly fill in this gap. . . . From the start, *objet a* carries the dual meaning of "lack" and that which compensates for lack.

—Ellie Ragland-Sullivan, *Jacques Lacan and the Philosophy of Psychoanalysis*

What, in Lacanian terms, comes next for James's paradigmatic subject? What has he achieved thus far? In the first book of "The Beast in the Jungle" John Marcher, metaphorically, has found his identificatory *imago* in the mirror of May Bartram. Thus from her he has assumed bodily unity and begun to assume an ego, an ideal-ego, the moment of the *first* narcissism encountered in the mirror-stage function. Realized *in* an other, he realizes, in Lacan's terms, a speaking I as a subject for an other I, another signifier. The analysis of book 1 demonstrates conclusively that, whatever James's intentions, for Marcher, as metaphorical, inchoate subject, there is *no* original ego identity before the appearance of the otherness represented in May. Lacan makes that point repeatedly in his work: identity is conferred by another upon the individual; it is not worn as an a priori existent. It comes to the individual from outside and fills a lack, a gap, a void in being. Thus what comes next for the emerging subject is the *objet a,* those identificatory objects with which the ego in its experiences is inextricably fused. The *objets a* are those images and objects first perceived to fill this void. For Lacan, these images are linked to desire as the subject's motivating causes, and so are ordinarily involved with the subject's primary drives. The drives—oral, anal, scopic, and invocatory—are represented in the breast, excrement, the gaze, and the voice (FFC 103–4; JLPP 73–75). For John Marcher, in his relation to May Bartram, the primal images are the gaze and the voice, especially the gaze, which may include images of the eyes and of the face as well. In James, the emphasis lies there because, as Lacan says, the visual or scopic drive "most completely eludes . . . castration" (FFC 78). For it is castration—always subjective, rather than physical—that Marcher aims to evade. Indeed, one may say that virtually the entire tale after Marcher's "birth" as a subject from the meeting with May at Weatherend is involved in Marcher's determination to avoid castration, that is, the *structure* of alienation that embodies Lacan's concept of castration. His aim is forever to live in the fullness of the eyes of the (m)other—here represented by May.

Working in tandem, these two Lacanian themes have the power to prolong James's story virtually indefinitely. The denial of castration and the repetitions of the scopic drive are established by the end of the first book. There, when James focuses the climax of the final scene on Marcher's demand that May watch with him for the appearance of his expected catastrophe, Lacan would surmise that it can be that they await nothing other than castration, loss of Marcher's obsession, his "poor old thing." The affect associated with his demand is suggested in the scene's repetition of the word *afraid*. When Marcher first lays down the condition that May must watch with him, she asks if he is afraid (74). His response is an evasion—"Don't leave me *now*," he begs. When she repeats the question, he evades again, asking in return if she thinks him "a harmless lunatic" (74). When she answers his question, he asks her a very important one:

> "You mean you feel how my obsession—poor old thing!—may correspond to some possible reality."
> "To some possible reality."
> "Then you *will* watch with me?" (74)

But, for a third time, May refuses to answer his question until he has answered hers about his being afraid. Significantly, he reveals once more his void of memory regarding the putative original meeting.

> "Did I tell you I was—at Naples?"
> "No, you said nothing about it."
> "Then I don't know. And I should *like* to know," said John Marcher. "You'll tell me yourself whether you think so. If you'll see." (74)

The crucial Lacanian element in May's promise to watch with Marcher is the satisfaction, for Marcher, of the scopic drive. This drive involves both the eye—the organ of vision or watching—and the gaze—the sense of being judged as separate from the eye. Lacan suggests that the gap or split between the eye and the gaze manifests the scopic drive in the subject, who is trying to fill a lack or absence in being. "The gaze," says Lacan, "is presented to us only in the form of a strange contingency, symbolic of what we find on the horizon, as the thrust of our experience, namely the lack that constitutes castration anxiety" (*FFC* 72–73). Thus, May's understanding with Marcher that she will watch with him places Marcher in the scopic field, but he is there not as the one watching so much as the one being watched. In accord with the function of the gaze, then, her watching assists Marcher's covering over the gap or lack in his existence exhibiting castration, at the same time, metonymically, that it fills that gap. In Marcher's earlier word, May's watching him supplies the missing link, or, since it is the phallus that is missing, supplies the link—the poor old thing—

that is missed. May thus is involved in Marcher's denial of castration, not merely in permitting him to avoid anxiety, but also in permitting him to feel he has in fact avoided castration altogether. Thus May plays the role of the mother who permits the child to believe that he is all to or for her. That role, as Lacan suggests in his discussion of Judge Schreber in "On a Question Preliminary to Any Possible Treatment of Psychosis" (*Ecrits: A Selection* 179–225), is often the precursor of mental pathology.

Once the Lacanian context has been established, one may see all these implications in book 1 of James's tale. Thus, retroactively, I would like to reread the tale's opening scene. Here, as in psychoanalysis, certain themes become visible only after the fact—*Nachträglichkeit* is Freud's word for the phenomenon. The scene of Marcher's encounter with May at Weatherend is an example of that "strange contingency" calling attention to what one normally misses or has missed of which Lacan speaks. The scene (here narrated, not dramatized) begins with unidentified persons: a subject (the "he") and an object (the "she").[2] As typically in James, the scene is much more scopic than auditory. James's language quickly begins to assume the values of possession and mastery, both economic and sexual. The tropes are strange outside an analytic context, for they evoke the primal scene and represent *objets a* to Marcher for possession and purposes of representation: "There were persons to be observed, singly or in couples, bending toward objects in out-of-the-way corners with their hands on their knees and their heads nodding quite as with the emphasis of an excited sense of smell. When they were two they either mingled their sounds of ecstasy or melted into silences of even deeper import, so that there were aspects of the occasion that gave it for Marcher much the air of the 'look round,' previous to a sale highly advertised, that excites or quenches, as may be, the dream of acquisition" (61–62).

While desire permeates this scene, Marcher dissociates himself from it as an unsavory, rather sexualized scene of "ecstasy." His aim, exhibiting denial, seems to have more to do with the oral drive than the genital. The image James uses would seem to dissociate Marcher even from that, but the image (Lacan would say) cannot be merely contingent or accidental in this context. Picking up on "the emphasis of an excited sense of smell" attributed to the guests, James suggests that Marcher's "impulse was not, as happened, like the gloating of some of his companions, to be compared to the movements of a dog sniffing a cupboard" (61). The fact that the two drives are joined in Marcher's needs, however, is suggested in his impulse's having issue, offspring, as it were: "It had an issue promptly enough in a direction that was not to have been calculated" (62). That issue is a face—May Bartram's, which (as we saw) "was a reminder, yet not quite a remembrance" (62) of Marcher's forgotten past. *It* (the face) and *she* (May) provide Marcher "a thread" (62) and a "link" (64), a connection to the "poor old thing" missed, but it also provides substitutes for the thing as well:

> Her face and her voice, all at his service now, worked the miracle. (64)

> As soon as he heard her voice, . . . the gap was filled up and the missing link supplied. (64)

> [I]t was as if the long look they exchanged held them together. (74)

The look or gaze, augmented, to be sure, by the invocatory "voice," is precisely the *objet a* providing the connection between Marcher and May Bartram. Making him a subject by virtue of his being acknowledged within her scopic field, May fills the absence of being in Marcher, fills momentarily the empty set signified by zero, and confers upon him "oneness," the potential of his being a signifier in a set—0 + 1—formed by the two of them in a signifying relationship. For all practical purposes, Marcher's initial encounter with May represents his entry to—not passage through—the mirror stage. There, his need is transformed into desire. The shift is indicative of what almost every perceptive reader sees in Marcher: his infantile, narcissistic, self-directed egotism. Need is passive, intransitive, we are told, but desire is active, transitive, acquisitive: "the prespecular infant is invaded by . . . archaic images commensurate with corporal experience and sensation. In the mirror stage need matures into desire via recognition from the other" (*JLPP* 73–74). As secondary energy, Desire is imaged by Lacan as the "*dérive de la jouissance.*" The imagery Lacan uses here is especially applicable to Marcher's state.

> *Dérive* means the hollowed-out drift or wake—thus, an aftermath or effect—left by a boat in water or an aircraft in the sky. I interpret this metaphor to mean that Desire (as a motivating energy throughout life) comes from the effects or traces left in human beings by

key images. Lacan also described the human subject as afloat (*a la dérive*). *A la dérive* refers to a boat cut loose from its moorings. Detached from any direct access to its own unconscious knowledge, the human subject is also adrift. (*JLPP* 75)

Marcher is, then, the subject adrift. James uses such imagery to describe the situation in which Marcher finds himself with May following the first encounter at Weatherend. Marcher is denied the ancestral past given May. She has a great-aunt "under whose wing, since losing her mother, she had to such an extent found shelter" (75). Moreover, the lost mother and her surrogate have left May a home in London. That provision of a home for May provides Marcher a substitutive satisfaction: "Nothing for a long time had made him easier than the thought that the aching [from the aunt's death] must have been much soothed by Miss Bartram's now finding herself able to set up a small home in London" (75). Marcher's warm feelings are a result of the desire he himself feels (it is a desire of the mother, of course), and the fact that May's good fortune will be displaced toward him. Now he will be able to see May—and be seen by her—more regularly: "They were literally afloat together; for our gentleman this was marked, quite as marked as that the fortunate cause of it was just the buried treasure of her knowledge. He had with his own hands dug up this little hoard, brought to light . . . the object of value the hiding-place of which he had, after putting it into the ground himself, so strangely, so long forgotten" (76). Nonetheless, their situation after May's ancient benefactress dies does not result in all the satisfaction Marcher desires. Marcher is now indeed caught in the *dérive* of his desire. Rather than recovering the "taste of their youth and their ignorance" (76) as they had at first, "they were, to Marcher's sense, no longer hovering about the headwaters of their stream, but had felt their boat pushed sharply off and down the current" (76). This journey eventually will take Marcher to another moment—the Oedipal—of subjectivity, but the journey will end up taking years and years. If we may say anything about Marcher, it is that his maturation is not timely.

Two: The M(other) in the Jungle

The number two appears commonly in psychoanalytic theory as the ego and its object, as me and you, as mother and child.

—Stuart Schneiderman, *Jacques Lacan:
The Death of an Intellectual Hero*

The Lacanian question arising now pertains to that lost object found again in the face, voice, eyes, and gaze of May Bartram. We know that, in Lacan, this object has to be the phallus, that which the substitutes (face, gaze) somehow replace. But the question in any text—literary or psychoanalytic—is precisely how the phallus—and, perhaps, the associated castration—is to be represented. In this tale, as the Freudians have already told us, it is represented in that titular "Beast in the Jungle."[3] Marcher cannot—or does not—name the catastrophe/castration earlier; May does that. But Marcher does name the dominant figure of the phallic catastrophe. The image of the beast is the one thing Marcher himself provides: not she, but he himself had made it or made it up. He does not have to defer to May Bartram, although—inevitably—the thing arises because of her. It arises because Marcher has to explain to himself why he cannot marry her. Marcher's fiction that gives James the title of his fiction is the beast in the jungle.

James provides a series of linguistic displacements for castration that finally produces the beast. The displacements are gradual (this, after all, is James), but they are very clear in their phallic implications. James begins by suggesting just how insistent Marcher will be in fulfilling his own needs apart from any May might have. But he would not be "in the least coercive" or unmindful that "her affairs, her requirements, her peculiarities . . . would come into their intercourse" (78–79). The displacements of Marcher's language are revealing, for the cat, as it were, is out of the bag: "All this naturally was a sign of how much he took the intercourse itself for granted. There was nothing more to be done about *that*. It simply existed; had sprung into being with her first penetrating question to him in the autumn light there at Weatherend. The real form it should have taken on the basis that stood out large was the form of their marrying. But the devil in this was that the very basis itself put marrying out of the question" (79). So, one asks, why is marrying a problem? James answers for Marcher: that about which Marcher, narcissistically, is obsessed—though that is not how James says it—is "a privilege he could [not] invite a woman to share" (79). In his narcissism and from the vantage of the Imaginary unity May has conferred upon him, Marcher thinks he has the privileged *it*, the phallus, the "little old thing." But of course he neither is it nor has it; he may have only its replacement, and that replacement (part or part-object) is signified by or in May herself. What he ought to realize is that he can have "it" by having May. But to take her on as a lover would be to give her up as a figure of the mother. And *that* he works hard to avoid, for it would bring into the picture the necessity of a phallic father to replace the desire of the phallic mother.

Protecting himself from the spectre of the Oedipus and castration, he thus, in a complex transformation, turns May into the phallic mother who needs *his* protection: "Something or other lay in wait for him amid the twists and the turns of the months and the years, like a crouching beast in the jungle. It signified little whether the crouching beast were destined to slay him or to be slain. The definite point was the inevitable spring of the creature; and the definite lesson from that was that a man of feeling didn't cause himself to be accompanied by a lady on a tiger-hunt. Such was the image under which he had ended by figuring his life" (79). Turning the "it" into a thing dangerous *to* May herself, he can now be a hero in protecting *her* from it. Chivalrously, he would not have her see it spring up within her presence. So the threatened *it*—the desired thing, "the little hoard," the "buried treasure" that connects to Lacan's *objet a*—becomes even more threatening when it becomes an object that, metonymically, is itself transformed into the threat. *Objet a* and *jouissance* are conjoined in Marcher's dealing with interdiction, the forbidden pleasure coming from the violation of it. *It* becomes the "beast," and the beast certainly represents the forbidden phallic *jouissance* he thinks he possesses in the place of the Name-of-the-Father he unconsciously hopes to supplant.

Obviously, the beast, figuratively, is much in evidence in the tale, but the really important Lacanian fact is that it waits until the second book to appear and, indeed, can never claim originality as the image of Marcher's expected disaster. Since he is not constituted as a subject before the encounter with May, Marcher must find it, too, in the mirror with her. If this were Hawthorne, the figure of the beast would first appear on, say, a brooch decorating the bosom of Miss Bartram. Consequently, it would be no feat to move, metonymically, from the decorative figure on the brooch to the location of the brooch, and then to say that what Marcher really, ambivalently, both seeks and fears is the beast-cum-*breast*-in-the-jungle. Then, the move—again, metonymically—from May's breast to her face would be simple enough. In fact, something like this does occur. Though this is James, the displacements of the beast almost invariably end at May Bartram's face. Her face—the face of the subject-creating other—is also, as Lacan notes, ordinarily that of the mother as well. In the Imaginary, the mother's face represents the first other, the first lover, and the first, unconscious splitting of the subject through its offering a narcissistic, identificatory trajectory. But in the Symbolic, that face bears marks that are represented in the Other, along with the Father, the Imaginary figure of the Law. The mother's face, by becoming effaced through repression in the unconscious, will eventually have become the figure that teaches Marcher to count beyond the narcissistic one, it being "the *two* here to grant existence to the first *one*" (FFC 191).

Every reader of "The Beast in the Jungle" has become aware of just how little "happens" in the tale and, more, just how repetitive it is. But, as Lacan insists, repetition is the means by which the ego establishes itself, and so James's tale represents the way subjectivity works. Indeed, James establishes Marcher's ego by the repetitions of the text. The repetition throughout is essentially the same as that in book 1: that is, a premise is established through exposition heavily dependent upon metaphors (rather than metonymies), and then the focus of the exposited premise (the *mise en abîme* of Marcher's memory in book 1, for instance) is broken into bits, thoroughly "treated" (in James's lexicon), and moved very little (if at all) beyond the original naming operation.[4] In book 1, for example, the action is no more than to unveil a void, give it a name ("catastrophe"), and then agree to watch for its coming. In book 2, the plot is much the same: the void unveiled in one is renamed "the beast" in two, and together May and Marcher await its appearance, she now beginning to assume that his "secret" is the "secret of her own life, too" (81). This secret, I have argued, is quite literally—and paradoxically—a *represented* nothing—a void or absence; and May Bartram probably knows as much, and so realizes that *nothing* in fact is precisely what is going to happen—for her or to Marcher. Consequently, she makes the point that must be made about James's tale. When Marcher asks her, "How shall I ever repay you?" (92), her answer is precise: "By going on as you are" (92). That is what he—the ego—does until her death, and that is what the story does too, until after she is in her grave.

The variation that occurs in the tale is itself a product of the repetition. What is repeated in the text is desire; what is varied are the images in which the desire is located, though one must realize that the images are all linked together in metonymic signifying chains. For instance, in the beginning of the account the face of May Bartram is the image (so Marcher claims) that links him to the scene of his buried past, buried treasure, even his secret self. Along the way, the face—in the figure of its eyes—becomes not merely the reminder of the source of Marcher's secret; it also becomes the metonymical link to the source in the Real itself. Just one of many examples of the metonymic transfer occurs as Marcher questions May about his (perhaps *their*) fear: "Marcher softly groaned as with a gasp, half-spent, at *the face,* more uncovered just then than it had been for a long-while, of the imagination always with them. It had always had its incalculable *moments of glaring out,* quite as with *the very eyes of the very Beast,* and, used as he was to them, they could still draw from him the tribute of a sigh that rose from the depths of his being" (87; my emphasis). May's face, the face that watches with Marcher, thus becomes the face of the beast that watches him, too. Moreover, when Marcher tries to rationalize his not thinking about the spring of the beast, it shows up nonetheless in another figure: "he in fact didn't care, always to be talking about it. Such a feature in one's outlook was really like a hump on one's back. The differences it made every minute of the day existed quite independently of discussion. One discussed of course *like* a hunchback, for there was always, if nothing else, the hunchback's face. That remained and she was watching him" (79–80).

Marcher's denial of castration, along with his desire of the mother, causes a series of transformations of the basic phallic signifier. For example, the face *that watches* becomes *itself watched.* Marcher watches May's face for signs of a future he has absorbed from her. In book 3, for example, Marcher begins to dread losing May to some catastrophe before she is able to reveal to him the imminent nature of his own. While, rationally, Marcher realizes that May "had no source of knowledge he hadn't equally," he nonetheless confers upon her the power to be one of those "conductors and revealers" able to sound the "depths" and measure the "abyss" (93). His thought is this: "What if she should have to die before knowing, before seeing" (94). Very shortly, of course, May becomes the source of "an answer to his long riddle" (95). She becomes the sphinx (as, elsewhere, she is a sibyl): "Almost as white as wax, with the marks and signs in her face as numerous and as fine as if they had been etched by a needle, with soft white draperies relieved by a faded green scarf on the delicate tone of which the years had further refined, she was the picture of a serene and exquisite but impenetrable sphinx" (98).

But the transformations always fail to cover over the fear of loss, castration, his being all to or for the mother. Inexorably, the face that becomes the sphinx, as it must in any good Oedipal turn, returns to the being of the mother. But since May Bartram is now approaching her death, it is the mother's departure (one is reminded of Freud's *Fort! Da!*) that now troubles Marcher. Even so, it is not May he mourns in advance. He mourns the answer she possesses to his question: "She was 'out of it,' to Marcher's vision; her work was over; she communicated with him as across some gulf or from some island of rest that she had already reached, and it made him feel strangely abandoned. Was it—or rather wasn't it—that if for so long she had been watching with him the answer to their question must have swum into her ken and taken on its name, so that her occupation was verily gone?" (99). His anxiety before her answer is an anxiety of castration, of loss of the one in whom he would remain whole. Having decided that, indeed, she knows, that she possesses knowledge, he begs her for it before she departs from him forever. Again, he looks to her face, starting with her eyes, "beautiful with a strange cold light" (100), eyes "one of the signs" (101) that she now possesses what he wants—knowledge of a fate even more "monstrous" (103) than the beast he himself had enfigured. He had thought that the two of them together had "looked most things in the face" (101), and he even thinks he could have "faced" the worst alone (102), but he fears what she must now know: "I see in your face and feel here, in this air and amid these appearances, that you're out of it. You've done. You've had your experience. You leave me to my fate" (102). His is the anxiety of the child "abandoned" by the mother before the child has realized that he cannot have her, cannot be her everything, cannot be the phallus for her.

Marcher does not abandon his intense primary narcissism, nor does May Bartram abandon Marcher to his fate at this moment. Marcher's narcissism is seen always in the tropes of James's language. In another figural turn, for example, the imagery associated with May represents her once again as the warm, nurturing figure of Marcher's maternal past. Just how dependent on May-as-Imaginary-other Marcher remains can be seen in a statement May makes to him. While Marcher worries that what is to happen will include "all the loss and all the shame that are thinkable" (103), May reminds him that *all* "we're speaking of, remember, is *only my idea*" (103; my emphasis). His dependent response is to assert that her "belief" is enough for him, and, childishly, he repeats his fear of her abandoning him without her giving him "more light on it" (103). Thus he presses her for answers to a few more questions that, narcissistically, still focus on *him*, on *his* demands, questions such as will he "consciously suffer" (104) and can it be "the worst" not to *know* when it comes? As always, he looks into her face for his answers. But what he thinks he sees (which is never articulated) is not "it" either. Though it is she who is dying, he wonders if she is just being kind to him to save him at the end. His narcissism is plain: "It seemed to him *he should be most in a hole* if his history should prove all a platitude" (105; my emphasis). He wonders if indeed he has "lived with a vain imagination, in the most besotted illusion?" But May affirms, "Whatever the reality is, it *is* a reality" (105). So is something else to come? James writes, "She waited once again, always with her cold sweet eyes on him. . . . It had become suddenly, from her movement and attitude, beautiful and vivid to him *that she had something more to give him;* her wasted face delicately shone with it—it glittered almost as with the white lustre of silver in her expression. She was right, incontestably, for what he saw in her face was the truth. . . . This . . . made him but gape the more gratefully for her revelation, . . . her face shining at him" (105–6; my emphasis). Enigmatically, as always, the "truth" that Marcher sees in May's shining face is contained in her eyes, but they have been veiled from him, giving him a "something else"—what Lacan calls "*jouis-sens*"—that seems to reside behind "the mere closing of her eyes" (106). Thus, at the end of this book, May's "truth" is, reflexively, turned back toward the emptiness Marcher has never really filled; moreover, it becomes *his* gaze, his "stare" (106), the text now highlights, not hers, as she imparts her word. Marcher's "What then has happened" is completed in her "What *was* to [happen]" (107). As Lacan says, "What is realized in my history is not the past definite of what was, since it is no more, or even the present perfect of what has been in what I am, but the future anterior of what I shall have been for what I am in the process of becoming" (*Ecrits: A Selection* 86). What has happened is what was to happen to him. Marcher, we may say, is now the man he will have been.

Three: Oedipus at Last

Three . . . refers to the triangulation of the Oedipus complex in Freud, and Lacan used it in theorizing the imaginary, real, and symbolic orders.

—Stuart Schneiderman, *Jacques Lacan:
The Death of an Intellectual Hero*

The text's pattern of repetitions, its variations on Marcher's narcissistic ego theme, will continue through two more books. Marcher repeats the same empty gestures with May Bartram through book 5 before he finally suffers the loss of her. This loss, in Lacanian terms, represents castration in the subject's recognition not of its own lack, but the *mother's* lack. Lacan says that the "signification of castration" is clinically important because it represents the "discovery [of] the castration of the mother" (*Ecrits: A Selection* 282). Castration also insists upon the differentiation of the subject from the mother, who as phallic mother has to this point in the subject's life represented the object of every need, demand, desire. In these connections Julia Kristeva has said, "As the addressee of every demand, the mother occupies the place of alterity. Her replete body, the receptacle and guarantor of demands, takes the place of all narcissistic, hence imaginary, effects and gratifications; she is, in other words, the phallus. The discovery of castration, however, detaches the subject from his dependence on the mother, and the perception of this lack [*manqué*] makes the phallic function a symbolic function—*the* symbolic function" (47). In Lacan, the mirror phase and acceptance of castration are successive moments in the constitution of the subject. The latter moment—which Lacan sometimes calls "the phallic stage" (*Ecrits: A Selection* 282)—puts "the finishing touches on the process of separation that posits the subject as signifiable, which is to say, separate, always confronted by an other" (Kristeva 47). Thus, it seems plain that while Marcher has entered the mirror phase of identification with an imaginary other, with May as *imago* and mother, he has yet to pass through castration and, therefore, overlay the Imaginary with the register of the Symbolic.

Book 5 of James's text, in its vitiating, "merely" Imaginary repetition of Marcher's primary narcissism, illustrates profoundly the way in which Marcher is virtually trapped in the first, identificatory moment of the mirror phase, seemingly unable ever to give over his identity to the Symbolic, triangulating knowledge of castration.[5] As in the tale's previous books, book 5 shows again and again how Marcher sees his life absorbed by May Bartram. Caught in his mirror-stage, narcissistic repetitions, he does not regard her as independent other so much as merely an extension of himself. His thought, for example, upon awareness of the imminence of her death is typical. When May is too ill to open her house to him, Marcher feels "defeated and sore, almost angry" (108). "She was dying and he would lose her," he thinks; worse yet, from his still narcissistic perspective, "she was dying *and his life would end*" (108; my emphasis). He begins to see some glimmering of what loss, loss of the desire of the (m)other, might mean, but he does not yet accede to such knowledge: "What could the thing that was to happen to him be, after all, but just this thing that had begun to happen? Her dying, her death, his consequent solitude—*that* was what he had figured as the Beast in the Jungle, that was what had been in the lap of the gods" (108). The Oedipal moment is out there, but Marcher shall deny as long as possible.

His perspective remains narcissistic, infantile, mirror- or *imago*-bound. Consequently, after her death, he does not recognize that the *lack* that had caused him to have no claim to mourning—to be, that is, one marked or signified as *capable* of mourning, or "the man markedly bereaved" (115)—has nothing to do with her absence or an absence *in* her. It is his lack, the missing signifier, the accession to the domain of the Symbolic phallus, that would have marked both their lives had he achieved it. Clearly, however, he is getting closer to the normative subject's necessary truth: "It was as if in the view of society he had not *been* markedly bereaved, as if there still failed some sign of it, and as if none the less his character could never be affirmed nor the deficiency ever made up" (115). So long as Marcher is stuck in merely Imaginary relations as laid out in the mirror stage, May Bartram can be for him only a symbol of a mother assumed still to possess that phallus which can deny his own "deficiency." She dies, true enough, and is lost to Marcher, but that does not prevent his assuming that somehow he can fill his lack and regain the totality of being she had represented. In this maternal guise, she is indeed—as Kristeva says of the mother—the phallus for Marcher. Consequently, in a predictable metonymic transfer, May, who originally helped Marcher see the beast, but who then was to be saved from the beast, eventually *becomes* the beast. The latter occurs when Marcher transfers his feelings of loss associated with her death to his feelings about the beast in the jungle. It, too, is gone, alas: "the Jungle had been threshed to vacancy and ... the Beast had stolen away." Now "Marcher waded through his beaten grass, where no life stirred, where no breath sounded, where no evil eye seemed to gleam from a possible lair, very much as if vaguely looking for the Beast, and still more as if acutely missing it" (116). In the "as if," Marcher is rehearsing the recognition—of "missing it," the phallus—that eventually shall come to him.

Slowly, Marcher is getting to the point of demonstrating for us the accession of the Imaginary to the Symbolic, of the shift from primary to secondary narcissism. But the displacements will continue for a time after May's death. Marcher metonymically transfers both May and the image of the beast, for example, to the "passion" that forms the contents of his thoughts. He desires to recapture both May and the beast by recapturing "the lost stuff of consciousness" (117) that contains them. And with this quest comes a different image, for Marcher finally begins to see his loss in relation not to a maternal, but to a signifier of paternal authority. Belatedly, Marcher sees himself as a father and thus transforms May. May becomes—along with that beast—the lost child. "The lost stuff of consciousness became thus for him as a strayed or stolen child to an unappeasable father; he hunted it up and down very much as if he were knocking at doors and enquiring of the police" (117–18). But what he finally has to acknowledge, as he is on the verge of an Imaginary paternity, is the Symbolic authority of death, negation, the tomb. At May's tomb, he begins to feel some of the emotions he ought to have felt years before: "He stood for an hour, powerless to turn away and yet powerless to penetrate the darkness of death; fixing with his eyes her inscribed name and date, beating his forehead against the fact of the secret they kept, drawing his breath, while he waited, as if some sense would in pity of him rise from the stones. He kneeled on the stones, however, in vain; they kept what they concealed; and if *the face of the tomb* did become *a face for him* it was because her two names became *a pair of eyes that didn't know him*" (118; my emphasis). At May's tomb, finally, he is thrown back to square zero, to the empty set, the grave emptied of recognition of him. With such knowledge will come—none too soon, one might say—the knowledge of castration and the rule of the Law of the Other.

Book 6 dramatizes, finally, Marcher's counting to three. Three comes in his accession to the register of the Symbolic as a result, finally, of his recognition of the phallic signifier and its meaning as castration. Much of this meaning, indeed, is exhibited in Marcher's ability to count, though the counting, at first, is not what he thinks. After a year's absence from May's grave, following that other visitation, he returns to it as to a "garden of death" (121) that, now, makes him feel more alive than any of those exotic foreign places he had lived in during the intervening months. "It was as if, being nothing anywhere else for any one, nothing even for himself, he were just everything here . . . by clear right of the register that he could scan like an open page" (121). This register is the tomb, as it is also the register of the Symbolic, and he begins his counting there, though he still does so narcissistically: "The open page was the tomb of his friend, and . . . there the backward reaches in which he could lose himself. He did this from time to time with such effect that he seemed to wander through the old years with . . . his other, [not May, but] his younger self; and to wander . . . round and round a third presence—not wandering she, but stationary, still, whose eyes . . . never ceased to follow him" (121). In this renewed Imaginary relation with May, Marcher may think he is counting to three, but, the fact is, the only integer that matters is the one formed of himself (zero) and his other, his "I" "feeding" on her gaze even now for his "support" and "identity" (121). He has not really faced castration yet, but at last he is ready for it; moreover, it will come in another image of a face, this one not maternal, but paternal and phallic.

Marcher assumes the Law of castration in an encounter with the Other. The face that cuts Marcher loose from his primary narcissism is that of a stranger. Marcher's encounter with it, though perhaps inevitable, is accidental. The face belongs to a man who is visiting a fresh grave in May's cemetery. Marcher becomes conscious in that man's face of a "scarred passion," but also of something that "roused, startled, shocked" him into an inexplicable "envy" (124) that is truly Oedipal. To feel envy, Marcher must recognize that he is not all, that there is something to want, something, indeed, that he wants. What he has omitted always in relation to May is *lack*, and it finally, paradoxically, is lack that he attains. In language that is peculiarly apt, the stranger's face symbolically initiates the castrating moment, for it touches Marcher's "ache" and makes it bleed "with an expression like the cut of a blade. He felt it . . . so deep down that he winced at the steady thrust" (122). What Marcher envies in the man is his acknowledged loss, his ability to *feel* lack, privation. Marcher finally understands, moreover, that what he has missed in life is knowledge of the lack and the passion that such knowledge permits—a passion associated, in his case, with loving a woman for herself and, it follows, the ability to mourn her for herself when that time comes, too: "what he presently stood there gazing at was the sounded void of his life. He gazed, he drew breath, in pain; he turned in his dismay, and, turning, he had before him in sharper incision than ever the open page of his story. The name on the table [of May's tomb] smote him as the passage of his neighbor had done, and what it said to him, full in the face, was that *she* was what he had missed" (125). To sound that void is not only to face the death of the other, but also to face the fact that one's being is founded upon a void.

Marcher's belated knowledge is that May Bartram was not only an other in whom he might see himself (as the child sees itself in the mirror of the mother's face or gaze); she also might have signified an Other whose presence could have formed in him—instead of a law of narcissism, which was the "law that had ruled him" (110)—a recognition of castration and the Law of the Father. We may see that inchoate recognition in his last scene with May while she is alive. There, Marcher persuades himself that she is indeed his "sibyl" who speaks with "the true voice of the law" (110), but he never understands what that law is until the stranger's face—no doubt, as some Freudians have said, the resurrected image of the father—makes the "incision" that cuts him to the void. This knowledge of both the other and the Other casts Marcher back upon the tomb, no longer empty now and now destined to suffer under the sign of the phallic Law in which we see the final transformation of the beast: "He saw the Jungle of his life and saw the lurking Beast; then, while he looked, perceived it, as by a stir of the air, rise, huge and hideous, for the leap that was to settle him. His eyes darkened—it was close; and, instinctively turning, in his hallucination, to avoid it, he flung himself, face down, on the tomb" (127). But Marcher's action, in its apparent effort to evade the Law, merely affirms Lacan's theme that the human subject is caught between castration and death. But it is not a question of one *or* the other. For the normative subject, it is always both. Thus, finally, in the beast, Marcher recognizes his castration and the Law of the Father, and therefore he learns, as it were, to count to three: *moi*, mother, and father; image, difference, identity myth. But it is a counting—or an accounting—too little and too late for Marcher to enjoy the fruits of his triumph, though, narcissistically, readers can do so in his stead.

If this analysis of "The Beast in the Jungle" accomplishes anything it should be the demonstration that the subject is a creation of a social relationship, the creature not only of language, but also of the Other in whom language resides for the subject. John Brenkman has discussed this aspect of Lacanian theory. "Lacan's project," says Brenkman, "has been the attempt to give language and intersubjectivity primacy within the theory as well as the practice of psychoanalysis." Brenkman goes on to consider that what Lacan calls "the *Umwelt*, the environment or outer world, of even the newborn is preeminently social. From birth," says Brenkman, "the human being is affected by actions, gestures, wishes, and intentions that are already imbued with the symbolic and that occur within the constraints of specific, historically determined institutions. In Lacan's terms, the subject is, from the outset, radically dependent on the field of the Other—for objects of one's satisfactions, for the benchmarks of one's identity, and for the language that will make one's interaction with others possible" (152). It is easy enough to fit James's tale into this model. As we have seen, May Bartram becomes the other, the mother, and the community of one within which John Marcher has his being as a subject. His extreme dependence upon her has the larger significance, one might suggest, of indicating just how dependent the individual subject is upon the community that provides him or her a place as a signifier within a system of signifiers. But his dependence also suggests that there must be a signifier beyond, above, or outside the community as well. The dyad of the mother and child may represent the origin of the social community, but it must be breached by the signifier of the father if there is to be the Symbolic triangulation that will permit change, growth, transformation within that social structure. Neither a community nor a person should remain locked within a narcissistic self-worship. It is not that Paternity—the signifier of the Father—is "better" than Maternity—the signifier of the Mother; it is only that the subject, whether individual or community, must be able to see around the other, to envision possibilities of thirdness, of an other kind of otherness, to permit the transformations of culture that have marked human history.

Using Lacan, we may go further. Lacan suggests that we may divide the cycle of human subjectivity into two macrophases that account for genetic and cultural demands made on it. The two have a recursive relation to each other. The first phase accounts for the maturity of the normative subject-as-subject. It is represented in the individual's learning to count from zero to three. Though Lacan almost always separates biology from psychogenesis, in fact the latter has a relation to the former determined always by the subject's relation to death. Death, says Lacan, expresses "the limit of the historical function of the subject" (*Ecrits: A Selection* 103). Biologically, the aim of that maturation is to bring the subject to the point preparatory of procreation; culturally, that phase is represented in exogamy or marriage and is symbolized in Lacan's number four. Thus four begins a recursive descent from the point that three represents.

Oedipus and Gender

3

Separation   2 4   Marriage
Body Unity 1   5 Parentage
Birth 0   6 Death

Beyond three's inscription of the Oedipal structure, we see that four's exogamous, matrimonial union thus repeats *socially* number two's *spaltung* of the individual's *Ich,* though this time, because of the departure of the erstwhile child, the thing split is not the I but the originating family unity that shall, in due course, lead to the child's becoming a subject, encountering the Oedipal conflict, assuming gender, and beginning the cycle all over again.[6] Beyond four is five's phase of paternity/maternity; this phase repeats on the social level of the family the individual's assumption of the illusion of a unitary identity—in the bond with the mother—that must inevitably be split as a result of the normative child's Oedipal passage. Beyond five is six representing the end of the line, the point opposite the void prior to birth and beyond which is the void of death. But six also represents an opening onto a beginning, the onset of a genetic and cultural lineage that involves the biological *and* cultural male and female. Six thus represents the establishment of a line of descent that subsumes in the subject the biological and genetic command of the culturally Symbolic imperative to pass along a family name, an identity that will assure the immortality of the "line" even if not of the "point" represented by the individual subject.

To conclude: Lacan's theory of the life cycle of the subject will explain much about "The Beast in the Jungle." There Marcher's progress toward ordinary subjectivity can be measured by means of Lacan's countable stages taken as structural metaphors. Figuratively, Marcher begins at/in zero, the void, and his end occurs at/in three. He achieves—albeit very slowly—the countable unity of the normative subject, but he does not go beyond it to begin the recursive descent that might send up progeny in his name. Marcher can never have the satisfaction of the remaining moments: four and marriage, five and paternity, six and the perpetuity in lineage that conferral of his name upon children could give him. A Lacanian way of looking at "The Beast in the Jungle" will thus say something about the "content" and the "form" of the tale. In terms of content, the failure—metaphorical, of course, since Marcher is not a psychotic—the failure to go beyond three is an index of Marcher's nearly life-long *primary* narcissism (he arrives at the second narcissism much too late to engage in the work of genetics or culture). Since just to get to three is a tremendous struggle for Marcher as a paradigmatic subject consciousness, it should be clear by the end of my analysis why he never does the "proper" things, the genetically or culturally "timely" things in relation to May Bartram. Formally, moreover, it should be clear as well that his relation to her activates the process of James's scrupulous stylistic displacements. It is those displacements that account for the length and repetitiveness of a story in which almost nothing seems to happen. In fact, much is happening, but the "events" occur internally and "happen" within James's tropes more than, externally, between two characters. My Lacanian reading of the story, finally, will resolve the question of why its interpretations may be so contradictory, for the Lacanian theory identifies the two dominant contradictory features. The positive achievement of Marcher, as Lacan might say, is the slow process by which, metaphorically, he at last constitutes himself as a mature subject in the effacement of zero by one, one by two, and, very belatedly, two by three. The negative element is Marcher's failure to go beyond three in a timely fashion; it is a problem of belatedness. We may say, finally, that James's subject is created by the numbers, but it is the missing numbers, not those covered, that make the story tragic or at best merely ironic. For the form of the story is a life history that really covers only half a life. Thus if Marcher's is an entire life, it is one lived only halfway.

Notes

1. One of the interesting ironies of the tale is that in the preface to the volume in which it appears, James alleges not to recall the precise origin of the story itself; it simply appears full-blown in his notebooks, as if it were always already in his consciousness (see ix).

2. For discussions of some of James's stylistic techniques and quirks in "The Beast in the Jungle" and other works of the later phase, see Dawson, Peinovich and Patterson, Shapland, Smit, and Tompkins.

3. See essays by Nance and Rogers, for example; other psychological approaches to the tale are included in Chapman and Van Kaam and Healy. Other

approaches that yield useful insights into image patterns that themselves can be interpreted psychoanalytically can be found in Beck and Jones.

4. For a discussion of the ways in which tropes function in narrative discourse, see White.

5. It must be understood that the "passage through" the Imaginary to the Symbolic does not mean the subject goes beyond the Imaginary. In the constitution of the subject, the Symbolic enters the subject. Thereafter both registers will persist in the subject's display of itself in behavior and verbal repetitions. The Symbolic enters the subject to give an illusion of one's being fully formed, and will reveal itself in the interactions of Imaginary and Real. "Normality," whatever that is, is a result of the interaction only when the goal is to follow social law.

6. Lacan uses the example of the Möbius strip as a means of explaining the paradox of the birth of subjectivity: "This diagram can be considered the basis of a sort of essential inscription at the origin, in the knot which constitutes the subject" ("Of Structure" 192). He uses this concept as a model in part because the sphere simply will not work for his notion of the subject. The subject is never precisely where one would locate it; it is always somewhere else, displaced, at a distance from its posited origin. "I am where I do not think," Lacan says; "I think where I am not." The analogy of the Möbius strip is useful to Lacan because, in cutting it on the line inscribed along its midpoint, one simply continues to create other repetitions of the Möbius, albeit thinner and thinner—a process of continual division that clearly models Lacan's notion of "identity." It is this identity that language affords, the identity of constant difference and repetition. The Möbius strip also provides a model, I would suggest, of the way individual subjects continually split off within the unit of the family; the continual substitution—both of subject and "family"—is represented, but so also is the continuity of lineage the concept of the family gives us. I would suggest that the slope of numbers formed in the schema by 0, 1, 2, and 3 relates largely to the individual subject; the slope formed by 3, 4, 5, and 6 relates largely to the subject in the context of the family as a social model. Clearly, the model supplied by the Möbius strip has especially Lacanian possibilities.

Works Cited

Beck, Ronald. "James's 'The Beast in the Jungle': Theme and Metaphor." *Markham Review* 2, no. 2 (Feb. 1970): 17–20.

Berthold, Michael Coulson. "The Idea of 'Too Late' in James's 'The Beast in the Jungle.' " *Henry James Review* 4, no. 2 (Winter 1983): 128–39.

Brenkman, John. *Culture and Domination.* Ithaca: Cornell University Press, 1987.

Chapman, Sara S. "Stalking the Beast: Egomania and Redemptive Suffering in James's 'Major Phase.' " *Colby Library Quarterly* 11 (1975): 50–66.

Dawson, Anthony B. "The Reader and the Measurement of Time in 'The Beast in the Jungle.' " *English Studies in Canada* 3, no. 4 (Winter 1977): 458–65.

Hirsch, E. D., Jr. *Cultural Literacy: What Every American Needs to Know.* Boston: Houghton Mifflin, 1987.

James, Henry. "The Beast in the Jungle." In *The Novels and Tales of Henry James,* vol. 17. New York: Scribners, 1907–9, 61–127.

Jones, O. P. "The Cold World of London in 'The Beast in the Jungle.' " *Studies in American Fiction* 6 (1978): 227–35.

Klein, Melanie. "The Role of the School in the Libidinal Development of the Child." Chap. 2 in *Contributions to Psycho-analysis 1921–1945.* New York: McGraw-Hill, 1964, 68–86.

Kristeva, Julia. *Revolution in Poetic Language.* Trans. Margaret Waller. New York: Columbia University Press, 1984.

Lacan, Jacques. *Ecrits: A Selection.* Trans. Alan Sheridan. New York: Norton, 1977.

——. *The Four Fundamental Concepts of Psycho-Analysis.* Ed. Jacques-Alain Miller. Trans. Alan Sheridan. New York: Norton, 1978.

——. "Of Structure as an Inmixing of an Otherness Prerequisite to Any Subject Whatever." In *The Structuralist Controversy: The Languages of Criticism and the Sciences of Man.* Ed. Richard Macksey and Eugenio Donato. Baltimore: Johns Hopkins University Press, 1972, 186–200.

Miller, G. A. "The Magical Number Seven, Plus or Minus Two." *Psychological Review* 63 (1956): 81–97.

Nance, William. " 'The Beast in the Jungle': Two Versions of Oedipus." *Studies in Short Fiction* 13 (1976): 433–40.

Peinovich, Michael P., and Richard F. Patterson. "The Cognitive Beast in the Syntactic Jungle: A Study of James's Language." *Language and Style* 11 (1978): 82–93.

Ragland-Sullivan, Ellie. "Counting from 0 to 6: Lacan and the Imaginary Order." In *Working Paper No. 7.* Ed. Kathleen Woodward. Milwaukee: Center for Twentieth Century Studies, 1984, 1–21.

——. *Jacques Lacan and the Philosophy of Psychoanalysis.* Urbana: University of Illinois Press, 1986.

——. "The Magnetism between Reader and Text: Prolegomena to a Lacanian Poetics." *Poetics* 13 (1984): 381–406.

Rogers, Robert. "The Beast in Henry James." *American Imago* 13 (Winter 1956): 427–53.

Schneiderman, Stuart. *Jacques Lacan: The Death of an Intellectual Hero.* Cambridge: Harvard University Press, 1983.

Shapland, Elizabeth. "Duration and Frequency: Prominent Aspects of Time in Henry James' 'The Beast in the Jungle.' " *Papers on Language and Literature* 17, no. 1 (Winter 1981): 33–47.

Smit, David. "The Leap of the Beast: The Dramatic Style of Henry James's 'The Beast in the Jungle.' " *Henry James Review* 4, no. 3 (Spring 1983): 219–30.

Tompkins, Jane. " 'The Beast in the Jungle': An Analysis of James's Late Style." *Modern Fiction Studies* 16 (1970): 185–91.

Van Kaam, Adrian, and Kathleen Healy. *The Demon and the Dove: Personality Growth through Literature*. Pittsburgh: Duquesne University Press, 1967.

White, Hayden V. *Metahistory: The Historical Imagination in Nineteenth-Century Europe*. Baltimore: Johns Hopkins University Press, 1973.

———. *Tropics of Discourse: Essays in Cultural Criticism*. Baltimore: Johns Hopkins University Press, 1978.

CHAPTER THREE

Using Lacan: Reading *To the Lighthouse*

[O]n the level of interpretive codes Lacan's position is not one
of substituting linguistic for classical psychoanalytic concepts,
but rather of mediating between them.
— Fredric Jameson, "Imaginary and Symbolic"

To the Lighthouse is perhaps the most often written about of all the
novels of Virginia Woolf. One reason for the interest in it is that it
has seemed to many critics and scholars among the most autobiographical of her fictions, particularly as it pertains to Woolf's formative
years and relations with her family. It has also seemed among the most
brilliant of modernist novels in its combination of shifting perspectives
and highly poetic uses of language.[1] Thus the novel has been subjected
to virtually every critical approach imaginable, ranging from biograph-
ical and New Critical readings of patterns of imagery to various forms
of psychological critique.[2] The latter have been especially attractive to
critics because of Woolf's troubled early life in the family of a prominent nineteenth-century man of letters (Leslie Stephen) and a "famous
beauty" (Julia Jackson Duckworth), a widow who brought three children to the marriage to Woolf's father. Those half-siblings contributed
to Virginia's early traumas, for apparently she was subjected to an
incestuous relation with one of Julia Duckworth's sons (perhaps even
both Gerald and George Duckworth). Compounding Virginia's troubles, Julia died when the writer was thirteen, leaving the half-sister
(Stella Duckworth) to become a mother surrogate to Virginia during
her adolescence. But Stella herself died just two years later, a few
months after marrying, so Virginia was left at fifteen without either
mother or surrogate mother. Finally, to further compound her prob-

lems, Virginia's father was a somewhat troubled man, however gifted and influential, and his needy personality rent another hole in the fabric of the child's psychosocial formation.[3] Safe to say, Freudian critics have found a rich vein to mine in Woolf and *To the Lighthouse*.[4] Thus perhaps the most necessary means of approach to the novel today is that through Lacan. Indeed, *To the Lighthouse* is so sweeping in its psychoanalytic range that it supports what Freud (though not Lacan) would call a metapsychological reading, here the reading being within Lacanian terms.

The metapsychological reading is possible, even inevitable, because Lacan's three cognitive registers (the Imaginary, the Real, and the Symbolic) seem so fully manifested in the novel's three large divisions—"The Window," "Time Passes," and "The Lighthouse." A quick inspection of the novel may suggest immediately why the parallels to the registers may occur.[5] To begin with, as every critical reader has noted, the novel's opening section focuses most insistently on the figure of the mother, the third on the figure of the father, and the middle one on time and death, history and ineffably contingent reality. Within the structure of Lacanian analysis these foci might lead one to conclude that since the mother in "The Window" is the dominant signifier, there the Imaginary will be the dominant register; that since the father in "The Lighthouse" is the dominant signifier, there the Symbolic will be the dominant register; and since time and death are the dominant signifiers in "Time Passes," the Real (not quite, as Fredric Jameson says, either a register or an order ["Imaginary and Symbolic" 349]) will be dominant, but as the signified, in the second—appropriately a "mediating"—section. Such an approach will be useful for purposes of analysis, but one must remember that *all* registers *always* interact, and so any separations such as proposed here are totally arbitrary. With that said, the divisions may usefully be considered in the order of their appearance in the novel so as to show, in the words of Ellie Ragland-Sullivan, the broad distinctions of "the Imaginary order [as] the domain of the *imago* and relationship interaction," of the Symbolic as "the sphere of culture and language," and of the Real as "that which is concrete and already 'full'—the world of objects and experiences" (*JLPP* 130–31). More than that, discussion of the registers will ultimately involve all Lacan's major restructuring or reinterpretation of Freudian concepts. Thus, each of the next three sections will address a different register as it is manifested in one of the three chapters of *To the Lighthouse*.

The Imaginary and "The Window"

> Lacan defines the essence of the imaginary as a dual relationship,
> a reduplication in the mirror, an immediate opposition between
> consciousness and its other in which each term becomes its opposite
> and is lost in the play of reflections.
>
> —Anika Lemaire, *Jacques Lacan*

In "The Window," the longest of the three parts of *To the Light-house*, Virginia Woolf produces a virtual paradigm of the various features of the Lacanian Imaginary. Characters (that is, the subjects of unconscious desire) in this passage are almost totally caught up in the dualities brought on by the completion of the mirror phase. That means, as Lacan points out in the essay on that phase, that subjects are involved in identificatory or aggressive contacts with others, whether these others (*les autres*) represent aspects of the intra- or the intersubjective configuration. "From the point of view of intrasubjectivity," says Anthony Wilden, "the concept of the Imaginary order accounts for the narcissistic relation of subject and *moi*"—that is, the Ideal Self (*Speech and Language in Psychoanalysis* 174-75). On the other hand, "From the point of view of intersubjectivity, the Imaginary is the dual relationship of [subjects outlined in] the Schema L—the capture of the *moi* [or self] by another, in an erotic or aggressive relationship" (175). Thus the Imaginary is both social and highly individual as it draws real images into the intrapsychic realm of symbols and symbolization. The moment, says Lacan, "in which the mirror-stage comes to an end inaugurates, by the identification with the *imago* of the counterpart and the drama of primordial jealousy ... the dialectic that will henceforth link the *I* to socially elaborated situations" (*Ecrits: A Selection* 5). Moreover, says Lacan, "It is this moment that decisively tips the whole of human knowledge into mediatization through the desire of the other, constitutes its objects in an abstract equivalence by the co-operation of others, and turns the I into that apparatus for which every instinctual thrust constitutes a danger, even though it should correspond to a natural maturation—the very normalization of this maturation being henceforth dependent, in man, on a cultural mediation as exemplified, in the case of the sexual object, by the Oedipus complex" (5-6).

Oedipus and *Jouissance*

The very first section of "The Window" establishes the divisions of the subject in a quite primal way—the conflict of son with father across the body of the mother. The section, moreover, establishes this conflict in Lacanian terms—the "No" of the father (cum Father of the Symbolic) that defines difference versus the "Yes" of the mother (the primal other) that defines the same, similarity, or nondifferentiation of one (I, me) from the other (only incipiently a *you*). Woolf's initial (and youngest) subject is James, the Ramsays' six-year-old son.[6] At that age he still belongs, as Woolf writes, "to that great clan which cannot keep this feeling [of extraordinary joy] separate from that [feeling], but must let future prospects, with their joys and sorrows, cloud what is actually at hand" (9). Woolf attributes the boy's propensity here to a personality type, to "such people" in whom "even in earliest childhood any turn in the wheel of sensation has the power to crystallise and transfix the moment upon which its gloom or radiance rests" (9). But the psychological fact is that the extreme pleasure the child attaches to the mother's positive words—her "Yes, of course, if it's fine tomorrow" (9)—are much more likely to occur in the child of any "sort" who has not yet really internalized the Symbolic word or Law of the Father, the child who in short has not yet accepted the lessons of the Oedipal condition. At the moment of his mother's "Yes," young James remains more firmly attached to the other who is also (m)Other than to the law of difference and negation to come. His powerful libidinal investment in Mrs. Ramsay thus, as Woolf suggests, not only transfixes the moment, it also "endows" other objects (in the type of metonymical transfer one would expect) with the same joy, even "endowed the picture of a refrigerator, as his mother spoke, with heavenly bliss" (9).

Perhaps the most significant aspect of this moment in setting the tenor of the novel is its expression of *jouissance*. But more than that, this moment suggests how a literary text is created as a textual unconscious and mirrors the human unconsciousness, which for Lacan is an unconscious texture if not precisely a text. The active function inhabiting a text is *jouissance*. *Jouissance*, as Lacan defines it, is more than mere pleasure or enjoyment. "There is no adequate translation in English of this word," writes Alan Sheridan in his translator's note to *Ecrits: A Selection;* " 'Enjoyment' conveys the sense, contained in *jouissance*, of enjoyment of rights, of property, etc. Unfortunately, in modern English, the word has lost the sexual connotations it still retains in French. (*Jouir* is slang for 'to come.') 'Pleasure,' on the other hand, is pre-empted by 'plaisir'—and Lacan uses the two terms quite differently. 'Pleasure' obeys the law of homeostasis that Freud evokes in

'Beyond the Pleasure Principle,' whereby, through discharge, the psyche seeks the lowest possible level of tension. *'Jouissance'* transgresses this law and, in that respect, is *beyond* the pleasure principle" (x), though as Ragland-Sullivan notes it still obeys the law of homeostasis and so places joy in death.[7] In James's extraordinary bliss there is clearly this sense of the sexual contained in his *jouissance,* as well as a sense of his transgression of law. The law is here especially Oedipal, for James, illustrating Lacan's dictum that "Desire is a metonymy," expressly transfers his desire for union with his mother to the objects around him. "It," Woolf writes of this moment for James, "was fringed with joy. The wheelbarrow, the lawnmower, the sound of poplar trees, leaves whitening before rain, rooks cawing, brooms knocking, dresses rustling—all these were so coloured and distinguished in his mind that he had already his private code, his secret language" (9–10). His "language" is no more than the "secret language" of desire and the unconscious. While it would not be proper to call this the birth of desire and the unconscious in James, it clearly mimes that birth in the advent of the Oedipal realization.

The birth of desire, the development of language (that is, of symbolization), and the Oedipal conflict are all conjoined in Lacan's conception of a *jouissance* discovered in the pre–mirror-stage objects that cause desire. This concept represents an advance on the Freudian notion of humans as essentially pleasure-seeking animals. "By placing the roots of the pleasure principle in the Imaginary union between infant and (m)Other," says Ragland-Sullivan, "Lacan redefined the pleasure principle as *jouissance* or a sense of Oneness, and reshaped the reality principle to refer to the separation evoked by language and Law (Castration), which ends the mirror stage" (*JLPP* 139). The moment Woolf portrays here in James underscores the "sense of Oneness" of the child with the mother, but already there exists the displacement of the child's feeling from her to the objects surrounding her. The moment suggests, in other words, that young James has indeed passed through his mirror phase (as everyone but the autistic does) and is already aware of his differentiation from his mother and of his necessary submission to the father's law. The at least symbolic castration effected by the Oedipal passage has thus occurred, a psychic fact suggested in further details Woolf gives of that moment's showing the difference between James's inward and outward orientations, as well as his mother's investment in him (contra the father) of something of the Law: "all these were so coloured and distinguished in his mind . . . , though he appeared the image of stark and uncompromising severity, with his high forehead and his fierce blue eyes, impeccably candid and pure, frowning slightly at the sight of human frailty, so that his mother, watching him guide his scissors neatly round the refrigerator, imagined him all red and ermine on the Bench or directing a stern and momentous enterprise in some crisis of public affairs" (10).

Whereas Mrs. Ramsay only imagines her son on the bench (as a symbol of the Law), the Law as it appears in the Imaginary father is in fact present in this moment. It is expressed in Mr. Ramsay, the boy's father, who utters the fateful word of negating contrariety—"*But.*" " 'But,' said his father, stopping in front of the drawing-room window, 'it won't be fine' " (10). This *but* represents the Symbolic No-of-the-father, the principle of contradiction and differentiation that counters the desire for union or oneness symbolized by the mother and expressed in *jouissance*. With the father's word comes the end of James's moment of bliss, but with it also come the hostilities of the Oedipal conflict. Woolf is explicit. The weapon (phallic) the boy wants (lacks) is represented in the father (phallic):

> Had there been an axe handy, or a poker, any weapon that would have gashed a hole in his father's breast and killed him, there and then, James would have seized it. Such were the extremes of emotion that Mr. Ramsay excited in his children's breasts by his mere presence; standing, as now, lean as a knife, narrow as the blade of one, grinning sarcastically, not only with the pleasure of disillusioning his son and casting ridicule upon his wife, who was ten thousand times better in every way than he was (James thought), but also with some secret conceit at his own accuracy of judgement. (10)

Each point of the Oedipal triangle is represented here in son, mother, father. And the imagery—of phallic weapons, of a phallic father, and of a universally valorized mother—is just right for the termination of the momentary transgression of the Law in James's *jouissance*. But Woolf herself does not permit her text to remain caught in James's or the mother's position, for she makes it plain that young James has indeed learned the Oedipal lesson, even if he has not yet fully internalized it (a development to be left for the novel's third section, "The Lighthouse"). If anything, the force of the Law of Oedipus is exaggerated, and, no doubt, represents an Imaginary assessment of a Symbolic value:

> What he said was true. It was always true. He was incapable of
> untruth; never tampered with a fact; never altered a disagreeable
> word to suit the pleasure or convenience of any mortal being,
> least of all of his own children, who, sprung from his loins, should
> be aware from childhood that life is difficult; facts uncompro-
> mising; and the passage to that fabled land where our brightest
> hopes are extinguished, our frail barks founder in darkness (here
> Mr. Ramsay would straighten his back and narrow his little blue
> eyes upon the horizon), one that needs, above all, courage, truth,
> and the power to endure. (10–11)

But even if the Oedipal Law is represented too Imaginarily here, James's thoughts (fused, apparently, not only with some of his father's words but also some of his mother's) underline the force of the Symbolic order, whose law is quest, not final triumphant union, whose mathematics is not $1 + 1 = 1$, nor even $1 + 1 = 2$, but, in its displacements of desire, $1 + 1 = 1 + 1 + 1 + \ldots n$, with n stopping, says Lacan, at the structure that delineates a subject *as* desiring. But, effectively, there is never an end to desire. Desire, as we will learn, has only disappointments.

The miniature Oedipal drama Woolf represents in the opening paragraphs of "The Window" establishes the section's modality of character relations and internal drives. The focus of this longest of the novel's sections is, simply, pleasure, *jouissance,* the fulfillment of the desire (in Lacan's terms) that translates physical (biological) needs into demands. The direction of intra- and intersubjective relations here is always against the current of the Oedipal Law, the rule that "pleasure is therefore destined to be bittersweet and deceptive ever after," as Ragland-Sullivan points out. For pleasure "proceeds paradoxically along the Desiring path of investing passion in simultaneous efforts to recreate the bonds of an impossible unity through substitutes and displacements and, thereby, to deny the reality principle of Castration" (*JLPP* 139). But, as young James's experience in this inaugural moment portends, this paradoxical motivation (both to recreate an original plenitude and to substitute for it or to displace it in other directions) does not separate Desire and Law, but, rather, conjoins them in the very structuration of the subject. " 'Beyond the Pleasure Principle' Lacan found Desire, which is not opposed to reality/Law but is, instead, inseparable from it," says Ellie Ragland-Sullivan. "By recasting the reality principle as constraint (*Zwang*)—the phallic signifier—or as suffering (*unterlegt, untertragen*) that commands the detours and displacements of the quest for *jouissance,* he showed that Desire and Law—pleasure and reality—are opposed only insofar as their conflicting injunctions make up the structure of the human subject itself" (*JLPP* 139).

Desire and *L'Objet Petit A*

The remainder of part 1 of "The Window" extrapolates the Oedipal drama seen in the child's relation to mother and father. It also suggests how desire and objects (or aims) of desire operate to create a textual unconscious, as James's portion had, but also how the vicissitudes of desire generate suspense or *narrative* drive in the unconscious of the text. Mr. and Mrs. Ramsay (as virtually all critics notice) stand for the mother and the father in the text and in their relations to all other characters. "The Window" in effect belongs to Mrs. Ramsay, the figure of the mother. Thus the focus of events (which, in the novel, are essentially moments of consciousness rather than action) is this woman on whom the others project their desires. The mother is always the primal source of the subject's desire, although her role as source is repressed into the unconscious after the passage through the mirror stage and the Oedipal realization. In the beginning, the pre–mirror-stage subject is in a relation of being to the mother: that is, the child simply *is* that which the mother desires; after the mirror stage, the child is in a relation of having or wanting to have: that is, it desires to possess that which the mother desires, though the child does not (and can never) have it (the phallus) nor can the mother either, since the lesson of the Oedipal rule imposed by the father is that she too lacks (is lacking) it. What happens thereafter is that the subject finds substitutes or displacements for the missing thing, now repressed into (and thereby forming) the unconscious. Those substitutes or displacements thus fill the space of Desire, and will ever after represent an alienation of the subject from that which it desires, now symbolized in objects, Lacan's other "little things" representing the *autre*—the *objet petit a*. This dialectical movement from recognition of lack to a desire to fill it is well illustrated in the Ramsays' relations with Charles Tansley.

Like young James, Charles Tansley is still visibly struggling with his Oedipal relationships. Since Tansley obviously is beyond the mirror stage in his psychic development, his desire is represented in substitutions for his mother and father. Mr. and Mrs. Ramsay are those substitutes. The very evident substitution in his attempts to *be* Mr. Ramsay means of course that he wants to be the *thing* desired by the mother. In his turn, Tansley also is the focus of substitutory displacement, for the Ramsay's children displace hostility toward their father onto Tansley. The language of their disapproval, however, suggests just how little Tansley possesses the thing he desires—the phallus: "He was such a miserable specimen, the children said, all humps and hollows" (15)—that is, to them he represents more a feminine (in those humps and hollows) than the masculine image he longs to project. To have that masculine image he operates by way of imitation. He expropriates the dictum (the words of the Law) of the real father: " 'There'll be no landing at the Lighthouse tomorrow,' said Charles Tansley" (15). And he imitates Mr. Ramsay in other ways, particularly in his peripatetic and intellectual habits. "They knew what he liked best—to be for ever walking up and down, up and down, with Mr. Ramsay, and saying who had won this, who had won that, who was 'brilliant but I think fundamentally unsound' " (15). Object of jealous projections, Tansley is roundly disliked, but perhaps he is disliked most for making so obvious what he wants and wants to be—the thing desired by Mrs. Ramsay, for that is precisely what all the novel's subjects (children and adults alike) desire. Thus he is roundly detested because he reminds others of their castrations, at the same time he competes with them for the object of their desires.

Against all odds, Tansley does have his moment of *jouissance* with Mrs. Ramsay. It comes as a result of her recognition of him and is localized in the displacement/substitute of the *objet a*, Lacan's *objet petit a*. First comes the desire to be desired, recognized, by the Other here represented in Mrs. Ramsay. That recognition occurs because Mrs. Ramsay—ever one to attempt to cover over "strife, divisions, difference of opinion" (17)—takes pity on Tansley and asks him to join her in an errand to town. Mrs. Ramsay thus engages Tansley in a "plot" of advance and retreat, small gains followed by immediate losses. We see in it the rhythm of desire. Talking with her, for example, makes Tansley "better pleased with himself than he had done yet." Then appears the *objet a* of displacement, for immediately he focuses his desire not on her person so much as, metonymically, on one of the objects—"her little bag" (20)—associated with her. He asks to carry it for her, but even when she demurs, saying she always carries it herself, there comes a swell of emotion, the onset of a soon-to-be realized affect that links him to his forbidden *jouissance*. "She did too. Yes, he felt that in her. He felt many things, something in particular that excited him and disturbed him for reasons which he could not give" (20). One of those unknown reasons, clearly, is represented in his fantasy of recognition by the (m)Other: "He would like her to see him, gowned and hooded, walking in a procession" (20). Recognized by her, he feels for a moment the omnipotence of the infant at the bosom of the mother: "A fellowship, a professorship, he felt capable of anything" (20).

But Tansley's joy is short-lived in this mini plot of small successes and minor retreats, for that moment is quashed when he notices she is not even watching him. She is watching someone else, and not just anyone else, but a man who has just one arm pasting a bill advertising a circus. Both the one-armed man and the circus poster evoke again Tansley's sense of lack, inadequacy. Yet once more Mrs. Ramsay draws him out. Asking him if he had never been taken to circuses, Mrs. Ramsay surmises that she had "asked the very thing he wanted; had been longing all these days to say, how they did not go to circuses," that, instead, he was from a large, but poor family, and had "paid his own way since he was thirteen" (21). Thus she provides him a moment of recognition, a moment to explain himself, a moment to recover his self-confidence. He is on the verge once more of continuing his narcissistic ramblings when, inevitably, Mrs. Ramsay interrupts him with an exclamation. She is captured by the beauty of the prospect of "the hoary Lighthouse, distant, austere," "in the midst" of a "great plateful of blue water" before them. Once more, in the remark that the lighthouse, in effect, is the possession of Mr. Ramsay, Mrs. Ramsay reminds Tansley of his lack of that which he desires (23).

But his complete capture by *jouissance* in the company of Mrs. Ramsay is merely interrupted, not forestalled entirely. He may still come in touch with it: "Under the influence of that extraordinary emotion which had been growing all the walk, had begun in the garden when he had wanted to take her bag" (24), Tansley begins to "see himself, and everything he had ever known gone crooked a little" (24). But, strange to him, he feels that somehow this woman can restore him to a lost vision of himself; as Lacan might say, she is the woman who is man's symptom. He even decides in what her power lies. Her power somehow resides in "her little bag," and, "determined to carry it," he simply takes it from her. Taking the *objet a* from her, he thus, symbolically, takes her as well; at the same time, the other's gaze, directed at her as the valued possession, takes him in, but also reifies his triumph: "a man digging in a drain stopped digging and looked at her, let his arm fall down and looked at her; for the first time in his life Charles Tansley felt an extraordinary pride; felt the wind and the cyclamen and the violets for he was walking with a beautiful woman. He had hold of her bag" (25). Because of the obviousness of the connection, it is perhaps needless to point out the relation between Mrs. Ramsay and her bag, on the one hand, and the (m)Other and the object associated with her (the breast), on the other. What might need pointing out is the way in which the successful achievement of Tansley's desire, however momentary, is a model of the way narrative texts operate in or upon readers. Tansley's story is an allegory of desire.

Modes of *Jouissance*

The passages involving James and Tansley seem closer to the primally Oedipal situation than most of the other passages through *jouissance* in "The Window." For that reason, their passages represent most graphically the objects/objectives of the unconscious on a text and the text (especially the narrative text) as an unconscious. But other subjects in "The Window" also provide examples of desire and its culmination in different modes of *jouissance* that one may expect in texts and the unconscious. The others (involving virtually every other named character, from Lily and Bankes to Carmichael, Paul and Minta, and Mr. and Mrs. Ramsay) are much more evidently distanced from the Oedipal and the expression of primary libido. What one finds are expressions of *jouissance* representing the repressions of the other (in the image of the mother), but without the sense of intrusion from the father (the phallic signifier, represented by James's real father for him and Tansley both)—except in the case where Mr. Ramsay is the subject consciousness in a relation to wife and son (see section 7, 57–62). Fairly typical of the other expressions of *jouissance* is the relation between Lily and Bankes. Virtually proving Lacan's premise that "desire is the Desire of the Other," these two contemplate a relationship because of the (m)Other—that is, Mrs. Ramsay, whose own law is "they all must marry" (77). Though Lily wants "her own exemption from the universal law" (77), she nonetheless feels that Mrs. Ramsay possesses "treasures," "tablets bearing sacred inscriptions" that could teach her "everything" (79). "Everything" for Lily at bottom is the desire to become one again with the other, to become, "like waters poured into one jar, inextricably the same, one with the object one adored" (79). Lily herself feels that people are "sealed" off one from another, but she can at least wonder if love might "make her and Mrs. Ramsay one" (79). Lily knows enough to realize about herself that it is "not knowledge but unity that she desired" (79). Not only that, shortly afterward, she achieves just such a feeling of oneness, but it is not with Mrs. Ramsay. Rather, it is with Bankes. It occurs through a displacement, in the fusion of Lily's gaze with his upon her link to her *objet a*—her painting. In her moment of ecstatic union with Bankes she feels much as young James had felt in his glorious moment with his mother:

> But it [her canvas] had been seen; it had been taken from her. This man had shared with her something profoundly intimate. And, thanking Mr. Ramsay for it and Mrs. Ramsay for it and the hour and the place, crediting the world with a power which she had not suspected—that one could walk away down that long gallery not alone any more but arm in arm with somebody—the strangest feeling in the world, and the most exhilarating—she nicked the catch of her paint-box to, more firmly than was necessary, and the nick seemed to surround in a circle forever the paint-box, the lawn, Mr. Bankes, and that wild villain, Cam, dashing past. (83)

If Mrs. Ramsay provides the focal image of the universal mother, the figure of primal fusion, for others, it is also the case that she has her other too. In the Real, her other with whom she desires to merge is simply Mr. Ramsay. But as with other subjects, Mrs. Ramsay experiences her moments of *jouissance* in Symbolic displaced images of that Other. For her the dominant such image or *objet a* is the lighthouse and its emanation, the beam of light it casts across the seascape. Sometimes feeling the weight of the symbolic burden she carries for others, she comes to feel a need to be herself, "a wedge-shaped core of darkness" (95). To lose her sense of herself as a subject, a "personality" (96), she begins to merge herself with the third stroke of the lighthouse light. Doing so, "she became the thing she looked at" and becomes a conduit through whom the Other speaks, saying, "We are in the hands of the Lord" (97). The light's third stroke and her eyes have merged, permitting it to search "as she alone could search into her mind and her heart" (97). And from her mind there rose "from the lake of one's being, a mist, a bride to meet her lover" (98). Still, she questions the words of that Other, and wonders what sort of Lord could have made such a world as she lives in, one caught, as Lacan might say, in the defiles of the signifiers of desire, where "no happiness lasted" (98). Even so she recognizes that one might come out of solitude by "laying hold of some little odd or end, some sound, some sight" (99). For her that odd or end, her *objet a*, becomes again the light. Her moment of desire, but linking to the forbidden of *jouissance*, comes upon her:

> She saw the light again. . . . [S]he looked at the steady light, the pitiless, the remorseless, which was so much her, yet so little her, which had her at its beck and call (she woke in the night and saw it bent across their bed, stroking the floor), but for all that she thought, watching it with fascination, hypnotised, as if it were stroking with its silver fingers some sealed vessel in her brain whose bursting would flood her with delight, she had known happiness, exquisite happiness, intense happiness, and it silvered the rough waves a little more brightly, as daylight faded, and the blue went out of the sea and it rolled in waves of pure lemon which curved and swelled and broke upon the beach and the ecstasy burst in her eyes and waves of pure delight raced over the floor of her mind and she felt, It is enough! It is enough! (99–100)

That "The Window" belongs to the order of the Imaginary and particularly to the figure of the (m)Other is powerfully demonstrated in its climactic (though not final) scene, section 17 (pp. 125–68). That scene is Mrs. Ramsay's *pièce de résistance*, the one in which she sits at one head of the dining table (opposite, appropriately enough, her husband) regarding the others "like some queen who, finding her people gathered in the hall, looks down upon them, and descends among them, and acknowledges their tributes silently, and accepts their devotion and their prostration before her" (124). The climactic dinner scene reifies the position of the various subjects to the other, but, at the same time, it does so without being able to suggest that the Imaginary relations can finally resolve difference (that is, the order of the Symbolic). At the scene of the dinner Mrs. Ramsay either enters into an Imaginary relation with each of the others and thereby effects a momentary *jouissance* in them or she causes a surrogate (usually Lily, but sometimes an object) to cause such Imaginary rapture. As Woolf tells us, the entire Imaginary transaction—that is, "the effort of merging and flowing and creating" (126)—rested on Mrs. Ramsay, whose place in the Lacanian schema is as the "other" (*l'autre*) who instigates desire, that "*dérive de la jouissance*" (the wake of pleasure) hollowed out by Mrs. Ramsay and followed by Lily Briscoe, watching "her drifting into that strange no-man's land where to follow people is impossible and yet their going inflicts such a chill on those who watch them that they always try at least to follow them with their eyes as one follows a fading ship" (127).[8] The dining table here becomes a playground for desire. In "real" life, too, one sees the play of the Imaginary between lack and its satisfaction, as well as the dualities of the Imaginary often expressed around the dining table—identificatory fusions and aggressive conflicts. In art—theater and fiction—the dining table is readily and frequently used as the setting for the working out of narrative desires. The reason for its usefulness is clear. Just about all the basic forms of desire are manifested around that table. The forms range from the anal and oral through the scopic and the aural. These forms relate, in Lacan's view, to the "four causes of Desire: the void, the voice, the gaze, and the Phallus (as well as the four 'drives' and images or related fantasies which support Desire)" (*JLPP* 75). The primal images associated with these drives are linked together, Lacan argues, to "make up the perceptual matrices to which other images attach themselves and form 'hallucinatory' meaning networks" (*JLPP* 73). These meaning networks are activated, moreover, through the drive and assume a dominant role in forming "personality," as we think of it. For each individual, a particular part object (related to breast, excrement, the gaze, or the voice) will be localized in those *objets petit a* to which one's desires will be attached. But regardless of what that *objet* is or to what bodily function (oral, anal, visual, aural) it relates, the feeling desired through possession of any *objet* will be rooted in the primal, maternal *jouissance*, that feeling that "refers to the ecstatic sense of unity which preceded an infant's knowledge of separation from the mother, a metaphorical Garden of Eden before the dividing third term—the serpent—brings knowledge of sin" (*JLPP* 75). In other words, "the void, the voice, the gaze, and the Phallus," in Lacan, "are simply different manifestations of *objet a,* functioning alternatively as mnemic traces which first filled in a void; as structuring principles of human identity; and also as the lost object(s) of Desire that are later replaced by substitute objects, activities, and goals" (*JLPP* 80).

The miniature dramas around the Ramsay's dining table are played out between "lack" and "plenitude"—between the men Mrs. Ramsay pities because "they lacked something" (129) and the women whom she never pities because "they had something" (129). While it is not fair to say that Woolf's women never lack anything (after all, Minta loses her brooch), it is fair to say that they must provide for the men around them in ways the men cannot provide for themselves. At bottom the function is maternal—that is, whether the woman is Mrs. Ramsay or Lily, she must provide the objects toward which the men may focus their joy, rapture, *jouissance*. Mrs. Ramsay provides the anaclitic focal point for William Bankes and Augustus Carmichael, who both are enabled to move from alienation to union through images of food. Carmichael finds his *objet a* in a plate of fruit, in which—through a voracious gaze—he is united with Mrs. Ramsay: "to her pleasure (for it brought them into sympathy momentarily) she saw that Augustus too feasted his eyes on the same plate of fruit, plunged in, broke off a bloom there, a tassel here, and returned, after feasting, to his hive. That was his way of looking, different from hers. But looking together united them" (146). Bankes finds his object of pleasurable union with the other in the meal's main course, the beef dish, the *Boeuf en Daube*. Of Bankes, Woolf writes: "He had eaten attentively. It was rich; it was tender. It was perfectly cooked. How did she manage these things in the depths of the country? he asked her. She was a wonderful woman. All his love, all his reverence, had returned" (151).

As for Mr. Ramsay, he is enjoying and suffering a rather anal moment of anxiety and a desire to give: angry with his wife's attention to the oral needs of Carmichael (who, greedy soul, had asked for a second plate of soup), "He was screwing his face up, he was scowling and frowning, and flushing with anger. . . . He loathed people eating when he had finished. She saw his anger fly like a pack of hounds into his eyes, his brow, and she knew that in a moment something violent would explode" (143–44). To make full sense of Ramsay's reactions to his wife's attention to others such as Bankes, it is necessary to refer back to the contretemps between husband and wife in section 7. There, the intrusive third party is the child, James. We have seen the Oedipal conflict from the side of the child, but not from that of the father.

The issues actually remain the same, for in this relation the father is not the Other: he is merely an other entered into an Imaginary relation with the wife-mother. The third term, the Phallus, which for Lacan creates the triangle, is here the child, or, more properly, the child-as-Phallus. In section 7, the relation is absolutely clear. James, represented standing "stiff" between Mrs. Ramsay's knees, is that which Ramsay desires or desires to be: the desire of the mother, which is the Phallus. Though the passage (60–61) actually represents moments of *jouissance* for each member of the triangle (child, father, mother), the seemingly most regressive moment is Ramsay's: "Filled with her words, like a child who drops off satisfied, he said, at last, looking at her with humble gratitude, restored, renewed, that he would take a turn; he would watch the children playing cricket" (60). It is Ramsay's desire to return to such a moment of satisfaction that prompts him at the dinner table to mind his manners, to obey the Law, not to *be* the Law, which exists elsewhere for him. Consequently, because he seeks his wife's (his other's) maternal approval, Mr. Ramsay controls himself like a good little boy in the scene at the dinner table. Thus, "thank goodness! she saw him clutch himself and clap a brake on the wheel, and the whole of his body seemed to emit sparks but not words" (143–44). Having exhibited such control, Mr. Ramsay will have his moment. It comes later through the voice. He is a man who desires praise, encouragement that his work is valued, will last. By a metonymical transfer of interest from his own work to those of "the greats," he is enabled to satisfy his needs by talking of Scott and Shakespeare. Eventually, as the pleasure of orality takes over, he begins to tell stories and soon, as Mrs. Ramsay observes, is "in great spirits" (165). Best of all, his voice—the voice as *objet a*—is joined by voices of others telling stories, and all become one hallowed voice—"as if they were voices at a service in a cathedral. . . . [T]hen one voice . . . speaking alone, reminded her of men and boys crying out the Latin words of a service in some Roman Catholic cathedral. She waited. Her husband spoke. He was repeating something, and she knew it was poetry from the rhythm and the ring of exultation, and melancholy in his voice" (165–66).

Thus the scene of the dinner ends with the *jouissance* of the *invocante,* of all focused in the voice, become more than the voice of the father, become now the voice of the Other in which resides all desire, all satisfaction (however fleeting) of desire. " 'And all the lives we ever lived and all the lives to be are full of trees and changing leaves.' She did not know what they meant, but, like music, the words seemed to be spoken by her own voice, outside her self, saying quite easily and naturally what had been in her mind the whole evening while she said different things" (166). Then her husband's voice gives way to that of Augustus Carmichael, who dons a table napkin to take the role of the chanting, enraptured cleric, giving the final religious glow to the ending scene, all accomplished in "homage" to her. "With her foot on the threshold she waited a moment longer in a scene which was vanishing even as she looked, and then, as she moved and took Minta's arm and left the room, it changed, it shaped itself differently; it had become, she knew, giving one last look at it over her shoulder, already the past" (167-68). Like all human joy, this moment of communally shared *plaisir* linking to humanity's forbidden *jouissance* fades in time, becomes a thing of the past. But, for that moment, in the presence of the *objet a* that fills the void, it pacifies the almost limitless human longing that marks our plight after our fall into the divisive world of the symbol, the realm of the infinite deferral of desire.

The Real and "Time Passes"

> The "real" for Lacan seems to be the order of brute fact.
>
> —Muller and Richardson, *Lacan and Language*

One of the most difficult concepts of a most difficult theoretician is Lacan's notion of "the Real." Similarly, one of the difficult passages of a difficult modernist novel is the middle section of Woolf's *To the Lighthouse*. In Lacan's terms, the first section, "The Window," seems extraordinarily marked by the register of the Imaginary and expressions of fusional desire and forbidden *jouissance*, but the second, "Time Passes," seems equally marked by Woolf's effort to create what can only be called the Lacanian Real. In Lacan's thought, the Real is not regarded as a register or an order quite on the same plane as either the Imaginary or the Symbolic, though inevitably it is inmixed with them. Although it is implicated in Freud's notion of the reality principle, it is neither meant to be Lacan's translation of that term, nor meant to refer to the naive realism of simple dictionary definitions: "that which exists," "of or relating to fixed, permanent things," and so on. Lacan's term would embrace most simplistic definitions, however, for his Real does include the fixed and permanent, though for him those qualities of the Real are beyond human apprehension in any direct way. The Real for Lacan is of course much involved with his conception of "Reality," but since Reality, for Lacan, equals "fantasy" and draws one into the domains of the Imaginary and the Symbolic, both of which are specifically human realms, the Real is not the same as Reality. As Ellie Ragland-Sullivan says, "The Real itself is unmoveable and complete. But man's interpretations of the Real are moveable. The latter combine language with 'self'-experience. The resulting interpretations compose 'reality,' but not the Real. The 'real' Real is both beyond and behind Imaginary perception and Symbolic description. It is an algebraic x, inherently foreclosed from direct apprehension or analysis. The Real, therefore, is that before which the Imaginary falters, and over which the Symbolic stumbles" in their efforts to incorporate the unincorporable (*JLPP* 188; see *Séminaire* I, 298). Thus the Real involves the confrontation of the "brute fact" of the phenomenological with the transformations of the Symbolic, whether regarded in Lacanian or Idealist terms.

The short middle section of *To the Lighthouse* may help us to understand what Lacan means by "the Real," but at the same time the concept will help us understand the novel, as well as how difficult it is to interpolate the Real in a verbal medium. Though there is no subject consciousness dominating "Time Passes" as there is in each of the other two sections, it is nonetheless accurate to say that what occurs in this section is both existential and phenomenological. It seems, in fact, that Woolf's project here is much like that of Wallace Stevens and other Modernist poets concerned with the relation of subjectivity to a distant world of phenomenological objects. Indeed, the phenomenologists' assessments of the relation between subject and object may help us here. We may see that Woolf shares Lacan's sense of the Real, since overtones of Heidegger surface in "Time Passes" as they do in Lacan. Eugen Bär points out that in *Being and Time* (1927), for example, Heidegger addresses the relation of reality and the subject. The subject for Heidegger is the scientist. The philosopher "states that a scientific attitude toward reality presupposes the real as that which is prior to any form of investigation" (Bär 518).

Our human understanding of the world thus involves a projection of things that, for Heidegger, "make up the reality of the world for a given subject ('Dasein')"; that projection, moreover, "presupposes the real by taking it as that which is prior to being [either] experience or thought by the subject" (Bär 518). The real, in short, is always already there for the subject, but the subject is always and irremediably outside the real. For Heidegger, therefore, the most apt illustration of our relation to the real is our relation to the fact of death. "Death as the total reduction of a person's possibilities is called by Heidegger 'the totally real,' since it can only be described 'from within,' i.e., being alive. For Lacan," too, Bär points out, "the real is in a similar way that which can only be described [from] *within* the symbolic . . . [just as] the imaginary . . . [is] that which is *beyond* it" (Bär 518). And for Woolf, likewise, the effort in "Time Passes" seems explicitly to involve as much as possible not only the displacement of the subject from the text, but also the subject's replacement by those objects that fill our phenomenological existences.[9] By the end of "Time Passes," however, Woolf has initiated the process by which the subject may return—does indeed return in the form of Lily Briscoe. In fact, what this section accomplishes, through a process analogous to mourning, is essentially the reconstitution of the subject and the reassertion of the power of the Symbolic over death and the Real.

Time and Brute Fact

The Real seems to have been a necessary passage in the structure of *To the Lighthouse*. The dominance, in "The Window," of Imaginary fusions with what Lacan calls *objets a* would seem to suggest that human *being* (Heidegger's *Dasein*) could somehow be complete without acknowledging the Real. Following the false or misleading plenitude of the novel's first section, what seems mandated is a passage through raw existence, a confrontation with "the order of brute fact" and the domain of Symbolic and Imaginary time—or, in Jameson's term, of "history" ("Imaginary and Symbolic" 384, 387)—and the "totally real" Heidegger calls death. While space and time are intertwined in the novel, we may begin with time. On the face of it, indeed, the aspect of time dominates "Time Passes." The first sentence of the section is "Well, we must wait for the future to show" (189). But such a remark by an actual conscious subject (here Mr. Bankes) is not characteristic of the section, for most of the temporal markers are located in the larger phenomenological framework of days and nights, weeks and months, and, especially, the rhythm of the seasons and the years. Woolf writes, for instance, "But what after all is one night? A short space, especially when the darkness dims so soon, and so soon a bird sings, a cock crows, or a faint green quickens, like a turning leaf, in the hollow of the wave. Night, however, succeeds to night" (192). Beyond these markers are others tracing a longer rhythm. "Nothing it seemed could break that image, corrupt that innocence, or disturb the swaying mantle of silence which, week after week, in the empty room, wove into itself the falling cries of birds, ships hooting, the drone and hum of the fields, a dog's bark, a man's shout, and folded them round the house in silence" (195).

Beyond the diurnal rhythm and the passage of weeks, of course, are the cycles of the seasons. These regularly mark off the passing years (ten in all) as the house stands vacant of human subjects. Early in the section Woolf records a winter that "holds a pack" of dark nights "in store and deals them equally" (192). Shortly thereafter, she mentions "autumn trees" that "gleam in the yellow moonlight, in the light of harvest moons, the light which mellows the energy of labour, and smoothes the stubble, and brings the wave lapping blue to the shore" (192). Later, she records the spring in which Prue Ramsay marries, "the spring without a leaf to toss, bare and bright like a virgin fierce in her chastity" (198), followed by Prue's fatal summer, when "the evenings lengthened" and "there came to the wakeful, the hopeful, walking the beach, stirring the pool, imaginations of the strangest kind" (198). Finally, there is winter again, one in which "nothing said no" (208) to the forces of destruction such as rats, wind, and thistles. Thus while objects in space may represent the narrative's content, time is the most insistent medium in which this narrative moves, and one entire brief section (7) is devoted to its recording: "Night after night, summer and winter, the torments of storms, the arrow-like stillness of fine weather, held their court without interference. . . . [N]ight and day, month and year ran shapelessly together" (202–3).

Besides insisting through repetitions that time is a reality outside human control or being, Woolf equally insists on a spatial realm of "brute fact" or materiality that acts as it will, apart from human intentions or meanings, regardless of any meaning to which one might subject it. In the world of physics, space is almost inextricably linked to light. One may say that space exists because it provides a container for, even if it does not create, light. As a measure of space, light thus becomes the virtual subject of space and time. Significantly, Woolf creates a metaphorical human world, a world containing—but out-side—human consciousness, by use of a conventional metaphor of light.

When there is no light, there is no subject or consciousness to fill Woolf's space. Thus darkness (and, as we shall see, death) subtends consciousness; it underlies so as to include the domain of subjectivity. "So with the lamps all put out," she says at the beginning of part 2 of "Time Passes," with "the moon sunk, and [with] a thin rain drumming on the roof, a downpouring of immense darkness began" (189). In this "profusion of darkness," human objects have lost their definition: "Not only was furniture confounded," she writes; "there was scarcely anything left of *body or mind* by which one could say, 'This is he' or 'This is she' " (190; my emphasis). Eventually, light as it is perceived in nature does return to Woolf's Real domain here, but when it returns it does so without any metaphorical sense of its *being* consciousness. Instead, the lights represent objects searching *for* consciousness. "And so, nosing, rubbing, they went to the window on the staircase, to the servants' bedrooms, to the boxes in the attics; descending, blanched the apples on the dining-room table, fumbled the petals of roses, tried the picture on the easel, brushed the mat and blew a little sand along the floor" (191). Because section 2 ends with a rare moment of conscious subjectivity, one is made more aware of its almost pervasive absence, for that moment occurs in one of those "holes in the Real" rent by death that, as we shall see, Lacan associates with mourning and the reconstitution of the subject. It occurs in one of those bracketed moments of human consciousness Woolf occasionally gives readers. When Woolf tells us here that Augustus Carmichael reads Virgil, therefore, she presages, by the allusion, the deeper descent in "Time Passes" into the netherworld of human subjectivity represented by Lacan's notion of the unspeakable, "impossible" Real.

In a world without a subject, the forces of the Real, of brute fact and physical materiality, take over. For Woolf, this Real is something hidden behind a curtain, though no doubt Lacan would say it is only a curtain of language. Unfortunately, like any poet, the only way Woolf may represent the unrepresentable is in language. So whether behind language or some other veil, the Real is never available to us in any material way. Thus, while Woolf's aim within this passage seems evident enough, it is also true that even here the Real must truly remain hidden behind words, symbols, language. It neither speaks nor thinks itself before the advent of language and subjectivity in the human being. In the world without the subject, in that almost mythical prehistory of the subject Kristeva calls the *chora* and that is also the moment in the infant's life before the mirror stage occurs, there is only a body, but it is a body in fragments, representing a world that is itself made only of fragments. The mirror stage, says Lacan, "is a drama whose internal thrust is precipitated from insufficiency to anticipation," the insufficiency represented in dreams and fantasies as a "fragmented body," the anticipation by images of a *Gestalt* found in the other (*Ecrits: A Selection* 4). Woolf gives us the jumping off place—in the *vel* or veil of alienation—for the inchoate Lacanian subject: "It seemed now as if, touched by human penitence and toil, divine goodness had parted the curtain and displayed behind it, single, distinct, the hare erect; the wave falling; the boat rocking, which, did we deserve them, should be ours always. But alas, divine goodness, twitching the cord, draws the curtain; it does not please him; he covers his treasures in a drench of hail, and so breaks them, so confuses them that it seems impossible that their calm should ever return or that we should ever compose from their fragments a perfect whole or read in the littered pieces the clear words of truth" (192–93). The anxiety regarding wholeness is one Lacan's subject must share with Woolf's text. If that text insists on gaps or breaks, such gaps occur everywhere in human experience. The gaps exist, Lacan insists, between the subject and its unconscious just as they exist between the Real and language. Thus Woolf's remarks here suggest a favorite theme of Lacan, for if the Real is beyond ego or consciousness, so are our symbols: "Like the symbol," says Ragland-Sullivan, "the Real both exists outside the psychic economy and witnesses to an inner conjuncture between the personal and diachronic domain [of time] and the verbal synchronic one [of space]" (*JLPP* 189; *Séminaire* III 76). Moreover, says Ragland-Sullivan, "Psychically speaking, when Lacanians talk about 'reality,' they refer to *moi* [or Imaginary] discourse. The Real, on the other hand, points beyond *moi* fixations to the fragments or residues that reveal the Other(A) as the netherside of the subject" (189). In "Time Passes" Woolf, indeed, insists on that nether, dark, hidden side of the subject, the veiled origin of subjectivity, of consciousness.

The Disappearance of the Subject

The realm of brute fact extends in "Time Passes" to the domain of the human, but it is a metonymical human that Woolf represents. As it is a space once associated with the human, so now it becomes a

Dasein or human being *minus* consciousness or subjectivity. As space gives time substance, so human habitations offer consciousness a possible locale. One form of the human that *might* include consciousness is thus represented metonymically by the Ramsays' abandoned vacation house at Skye. Woolf's use of the house is like that of T. S. Eliot in "Gerontion." In Eliot the subject is seen as a house; in Woolf the house is seen in relation to its former subjects. Woolf's main theme is *vacancy;* it is developed through a figure of "airs," that which fills empty space; like lights, they seem to seek subjectivity, some human occupant. "So with the house empty and the doors locked and the mattresses rolled round," says Woolf, "those stray airs, advance guards of great armies, blustered in, brushed bare boards, nibbled and fanned, met nothing in bedroom or drawing-room that wholly resisted them but only hangings that flapped, wood that creaked, the bare legs of tables, saucepans and china already furred, tarnished, cracked" (194).

As the house represents the body to be inhabited by mind, so human garments represent other metonymical forms of the body once inhabited by conscious subjects. Thus garments provide metonymical images of the diminished human, the human shape or form minus the awareness of the subject. These images, like the house, come under the sway of time and decay. "What people had shed and left—a pair of shoes, a shooting cap, some faded skirts and coats in wardrobes," writes Woolf, "those alone kept the human shape and in the emptiness indicated how once they were filled and animated; how once hands were busy with hooks and buttons" (194). More than mere human presence, however, these images lead Woolf to another image that perfectly represents Lacan's own image of the moment of constitution of the subject. In her way, Woolf captures the mirror stage when she suggests that those garments express "how once the looking-glass had held a face; had held a world hollowed out in which a figure turned, a hand flashed, the door opened, in came children rushing and tumbling; and went out again" (194). These are lovely images indeed, but what they represent is loss, absence, vacancy—what might have been or what might well come to be again, a nostalgia less for the past than for the future.

Even after the advent (in Mrs. McNab) of an inchoate consciousness early on, the world vacated by the Ramsays remains dominated by a brute reality without consciousness. Much of that material Real manifests itself in what it does to the house. The house stands as Woolf's major representation of the body's potential for subjectivity. She catalogs in minute detail the displacements of a potentially mental space by the detritus of a brutish Real signifying death, death itself represented in the house-as-dead-body:

> The house was left; the house was deserted. It was left like a shell on a sandhill to fill with dry salt grains now that life had left it. The long night seemed to have set in; the trifling airs, nibbling, the clammy breaths, fumbling, seemed to have triumphed. The saucepan had rusted and the mat decayed. Toads had nosed their way in. Idly, aimlessly, the swaying shawl swung to and fro. A thistle thrust itself between the tiles in the larder. The swallows nested in the drawing-room; the floor was strewn with straw; the plaster fell in shovelfuls; rafters were laid bare; rats carried off this and that to gnaw behind the wainscots. Tortoise-shell butterflies burst from the chrysalis and pattered their life out on the window-pane. Poppies sowed themselves among the dahlias; the lawn waved with long grass; giant artichokes towered among roses; a fringed carnation flowered among the cabbages; while the gentle tapping of a weed at the window had become, on winters' nights, a drumming from sturdy trees and thorned briars which made the whole room green in summer. (206–7)

Woolf suggests here that the incursions of natural fact, "the sensibility of nature" (207), cannot be blocked by mere unconscious desire, by a dream such as Mrs. McNab's "dream of a lady, of a child, of a plate of milk soup" (207). There is no Symbolic here, no voice of the Father to set boundaries, to establish the law. There seems, Woolf says, nothing to say "no to them" (208), not even the phallic lighthouse that once, when subjects were present, "had laid itself with such authority . . . in the darkness" (199–200).

Regarding human subjectivity, Lacan argues, the most insistent fact of the brute world outside of or beyond consciousness is death. Death is the great "No" of life. As in Freud, in Lacan death has its place at the base of being and identity. For the subject to become a subject, Lacan insists, it must encounter death—the "No" of the Father—in some form; whatever the specific form, it represents castration. In Woolf's novel it is clear that one drive is toward the negation of death. Perhaps the most troubling feature of "Time Passes," indeed, is the death of consciousness represented in the disappearance of the subject and, worse, the subject's being relegated to a mere hole in the Real. Those half dozen bracketed passages in this section vividly express death and the loss of the subject, though at the same time they represent the gap within the Real through which subjectivity may reemerge. Since the very symbol of subjectivity in the novel's previous chapter, "The Window," is Mrs. Ramsay, her loss portends the greatest loss in the entire novel. But in the course of "Time Passes" that loss is represented as a trivial moment, nothing more than a slight rent in the fabric of the Real—a mere punctuation mark in the discourse of time. The brackets signifying that hole, it is important to note, are Woolf's:

> [Mr. Ramsay, stumbling along a passage one dark morning, stretched his arms out, but Mrs. Ramsay having died rather suddenly the night before, his arms, though stretched out, remained empty.] (194)

In his essay on *Hamlet,* Lacan speaks of the devastation caused by such a loss of "the object whose loss is the cause of his desire, an object that has attained an existence that is all the more absolute because it no longer corresponds to anything in reality. The one unbearable dimension of possible human experience is not the experience of one's own death, which no one has, but the experience of the death of another" ("Desire in *Hamlet*" 37). Half the bracketed passages in "Time Passes" rip those immitigable holes in our experience of the novel. The other two deaths are Prue's and Andrew's.

> [Prue Ramsay died that summer in some illness connected with childbirth, which was indeed a tragedy, people said, everything, they said, had promised so well.] (199)

> [A shell exploded. Twenty or thirty young men were blown up in France, among them Andrew Ramsay, whose death, mercifully, was instantaneous.] (201)

In these passages bracketing death, Woolf shows that brute reality takes no notice of the human. In the large perspective of time and space, the human being is of no especial consequence. The pain of that recognition, however, will begin to regenerate a perspective, a subjectivity, that will again valorize life, mind, consciousness.

Death for the human being is not simply negation, for in Lacanian thought the fact of death permits, even insists on, the reemergence of the subject from the Real. In the perception of death, the nascent subject emerges through the formation of the register of the Symbolic. In "Desire and the Interpretation of Desire in *Hamlet*," Lacan says the Symbolic fills those holes in the Real through the process of mourning. Death, says Lacan, creates the hole in the Real that calls forth mourning in the subject, and mourning, with the aid of the primal signifier, begins to reestablish the subject against the screen of the Real. "Just as what is rejected from the symbolic register reappears," says Lacan, "in the real [in psychosis], in the same way the hole in the real that results from loss sets the signifier in motion. This hole provides the place for the projection of the missing signifier," he says; moreover, this signifier, known by Lacan and other post-Freudians as the Phallus, "is essential to the structure of the Other" (38). What this process of mourning entails, Lacan says, is the reestablishment of the *logos;* the *logos* is that order founded on community and culture and identified by Lacan as the Symbolic. "The work of mourning is first of all performed to satisfy the disorder that is produced by the inadequacy of signifying elements to cope with the hole that has been created in existence, for it is the system of signifiers in their totality which is impeached by the least instance of mourning" (38). But in the end, Lacan insists, the work of mourning is essentially to create—or, more properly, to recreate—the subject itself in what amounts to a repetition of the mirror stage.

From Death to Mourning

The narrative trajectory of "Time Passes" thus represents the move from death to mourning to the reconstitution of the subject. Woolf's focus on death and mourning, of course, has not been missed by critics. From a Freudian perspective, Corsa focuses specifically on mourning in the novel. She writes, for example, "It is how the novel comes to grips with death that interests me—how some of the characters work through their mourning over the death of Mrs. Ramsay, and how the whole novel, in its pattern and movement, evokes, recreates, and delineates the mourning process." Moreover, she says that what Woolf did "was to create by character, by situation, by narrator's voice a symbolic reenactment of the work of mourning that corresponds in somewhat simplified terms to the pattern of mourning outlined by Freud and by others since then" (115, 116). Lacan's perspective is at least equally enlightening. What the passage through mourning amounts to, Lacan suggests in his essay on *Hamlet*, is a repetition of the mirror phase, the moment in the life of the subject when identity asserts itself through mirror reflections and creates the possibility of the Oedipal conflict and its attendant moment of castration. In the structure of *To the Lighthouse*, "Time Passes" represents castration through the loss of subjectivity and the imposition of the fact of death, especially the loss through death of the primal object, the mother. But "Time Passes" also represents the reemergence of subjectivity as well. It occurs through the mediation of none other than Mrs. McNab.[10] Woolf tells us, in indirect discourse attributed to the old woman: "So she was dead; and Mr Andrew killed; and Miss Prue dead too, they said, with her first baby; but every one had lost some one these years" (205). Clearly, the mourning process has begun. Lacan says that "ritual introduces some mediation of the gap [*béance*] opened up by mourning. More precisely, ritual operates in such a way as to make this gap coincide with that greater *béance*, the point x, the symbolic lack. The navel of the dream, to which Freud refers at one point, is perhaps nothing but the psychological counterpart of this lack" ("Desire in *Hamlet*" 40). In her recognition of the "greater *béance*," Mrs. McNab begins to mediate between brute insensibility and human subjectivity. By her process of mourning the lack of Mrs. Ramsay, the Symbolic lack and the lack of the Symbolic, the old woman presides over the birth of human subjectivity in the Symbolic, in the ritual of things done (the house cleaning in preparation for the Ramsay's return), and the language of things said. Functioning as the Symbolic, these take care of the mourning and establish the power of the Symbolic over or in the face of the Real.

The human world is hollowed out of the Real by the Symbolic in the same way as the subject is formed in the mirror stage by a splitting of specular images. In "Time Passes," that human, Symbolic world has been represented as departed or diminished or fragmented. Thus what has remained is a metonymical world of objects associated with the human that are now seeking a human subject. It is a world where shadows "for a moment darkened the pool in which light reflected itself" (195), where there is nothing else but light to engage in the act of *reflection*—in any sense of the term. Though not pervasive in criticism of the novel, the view proposed here has its proponents. Maria Di Battista, for example, speaks of "Time Passes" in terms of "that eclipse of consciousness when sleep overcomes the mind, sealing it off from the light by which the world is perceived or reflected." What's more, she says, " 'Time Passes' is an extension of that visionary night when consciousness is overwhelmed and submits to the darkness that surrounds it." Likewise, she adds that "the narrative mind approaches autism in the face of this insensibility of nature" (94, 96). Autistic, insensate, virtually without thought, such is the world, then, as Woolf represents it just before that inchoate consciousness in the form of Mrs. McNab returns to the premises: "Once only a board sprang on the landing; once in the middle of the night with a roar, with a rupture, as after centuries of quiescence, a rock rends itself from the mountain and hurtles crashing into the valley, one fold of [Mrs. Ramsey's] shawl [covering the boar's skull] loosened and swung to and fro. Then again peace descended; and the shadow wavered; light bent to its own image in adoration on the bedroom wall, and Mrs. McNab, tearing the veil of silence with hands that had stood in the wash-tub, grinding it with boots that had crunched the shingle, came as directed to open all windows, and dust the bedrooms" (195–96).

But the threshold of consciousness represented by Mrs. McNab for a long time hardly diminishes the grip of the brute Real on Woolf's landscape. Early on, this old woman seems barely more sensate as a subject than those abandoned clothes of the Ramsays. She would seem to be a negative counterpart to Mrs. Ramsay. Though T. E. Apter seems not to be concerned with the slow rebirth of consciousness in "Time Passes" as it might be represented in a figure such as the lowly Mrs. McNab, he does make a relevant point about the relation of the two women. For Apter, the point of the novel's middle section is to display the *absence* of Mrs. Ramsay: "Since Mrs. Ramsay so thoroughly penetrates her world, her death unbalances and distorts everything." Thus, he says, " 'Time Passes' traces the effects of her illness and death from the point of view of a disembodied spectator in and around the house in Skye who reports fragments of the house's activities, thus giving each movement and each reported remark a symbolic point" (87). From a Lacanian viewpoint, therefore, we may say that if Mrs. Ramsay is the soul of consciousness now missing from the house, then the old servant woman is like the minus one (-1) that exists only because of its dialectical relation to the plus one $(+1)$. Together, plus and minus one comprise the square root of minus one, and that imaginary minus one is precisely the number Lacan posits as the symbol of the subject, making it a concept in Lacan nearly as impossible to fathom as the Real. Woolf's description of Mrs. McNab makes the negative consciousness "positive." In the old woman, Woolf makes consciousness visible in the way of objects in a photographic negative: "she lurched (for she rolled like a ship at sea) and leered (for her eyes fell on nothing directly, but with a sidelong glance that deprecated the scorn and anger of the world—she was witless, she knew it)" (196). As with those garments that once reminded one of subjects before the mirror, so Mrs. McNab brings one back to it. The index of her nearly negative humanity is her inability to face it squarely. "Rubbing the glass of the long looking-glass and leering side ways at her swinging figure a sound issued from her lips—something that . . . was robbed of meaning, was like the voice of witlessness, humour, persistency itself" (196). But since darkness subtends being as the unconscious subtends consciousness, Mrs. McNab accomplishes a small, necessary step upward by her representing a break in the darkness: "there must have been," Woolf writes, "some cleavage of the dark . . . , some channel in the depths of obscurity through which light enough issued to twist her face grinning in the glass" (197). Not much of a start, it is a start nonetheless.

Woolf's description offers a painful burlesque of Lacan's mirror stage, even to the questions asked. The old dance hall tune she mumbles might have given an answer to basic human questions—"What am I," "What is this?" (198)—but listeners would have had to be mystics or visionaries to understand that answer, and even so "they could not say what it was" (198). Despite a social stratification here invidious to this old woman, it nevertheless seems that what Mrs. McNab represents most of all is an absence, precisely the absence of Mrs. Ramsay, who is Woolf's image of the positive, shaping, creating human consciousness. But as the absence of such consciousness, old Mrs. McNab is no less than the human Real, the bare, witless rock on which a more symbolic "Reality" eventually may be built. Though Woolf early on had implied that Mrs. McNab's "dream of a lady"—that is, of Mrs. Ramsay—might not be a force sufficient to withstand the entropic slant of nature, she later suggests otherwise (207). "But there was a force working; something not highly conscious; something that leered, something that lurched; something not inspired to go about its work with dignified ritual or solemn chanting" (209). Consequently, asked to prepare the house, that empty metaphorical potential for consciousness, for their return by one of the daughters, Mrs. McNab (and, now, her own mirror double, Mrs. Bast) does indeed rescue the house "from the pool of Time" (209). The whole process, Woolf suggests, is a sort of "rusty laborious birth" (210), and what, ultimately, is borne out of it is subjectivity itself. Out of the loss of Mrs. Ramsay, mediated by poor witless Mrs. McNab, with her alter ego, Mrs. Bast, comes once more Woolf's image of the new consciousness to replace the primal mother. It is not Mrs. McNab who emerges to represent that new subjectivity; it is another for whom she has prepared the way. The other is the painter, Lily Briscoe. Within Lily Briscoe, who represents Woolf's figure of the artist, there once again sings "the voice of the beauty of the world" (213).[11] As we shall see in the novel's final chapter, "The Lighthouse," the world whose beauty Lily commemorates is not that of the Real. Rather, it is that of the Imaginary "reality" created in the signifiers of art and language—in, that is, the material of the Symbolic.

The Symbolic and "The Lighthouse"

> [T]he process of symbolization, in the sense of engendering, unfolds between two poles, the first of which—the minimum threshold of opening—is the imaginary, and the second of which—the threshold of accomplishment—is the social relation recognized in discourse.
>
> —Anika Lemaire, *Jacques Lacan*

In the aesthetic arrangement of the three sections of *To the Lighthouse* it seems evident that, in the order of human existence, the second passage ("Time Passes") is somehow primal, quite fundamental in its representation of a subject's relation to the world external to consciousness. In Lacan's epistemology, that world—the Real—is "full"; it is marked by a material plenitude, but it is also impossible, ineffable, unincorporable. Since it is outside or beyond language or symbolization, it thus can also, paradoxically, signify the lack that comes to mark the human subject once he or she (in, Lacan says, the mirror stage's recognition of—and relation to—an other not one's self) is separated from the (m)Other and cast into a universe alien to one's self. In this respect, the Real represented in "Time Passes" is also associated with absence of being—with, therefore, death, both the ultimate Real and the incorrigibly alienated. As the generalized "subject" of Woolf's novel moves, then, from the middle passage to the final one, "The Lighthouse," it must reconcile to or internalize the fact of lack, loss, or absence of the object of desire through the work of mourning. Mourning itself is not adequately accomplished in "Time Passes," though subjectivity is restored, nor do all subjects of "The Lighthouse" respond to the object loss in the same ways when mourning is taken up. What we find is that Lily Briscoe quite overtly deals with the loss— that is, the loss of Mrs. Ramsay as the (m)Other—and finds her own symbolic way to internalize it. But each of the Ramsays who stands in for the subject in this passage—Mr. Ramsay, Cam, and James—finds other ways, other necessities for handling the *béance* in existence. For the children, the passage comes to represent castration and the internalization of the Oedipal complex; for the father it represents the final acceptance of the place of the Name-of-the-Father in whose name he speaks. In all instances (for Lily, Cam, James, and Mr. Ramsay), the passage seems to represent a positive movement toward the Symbolic register in the domain of subjectivity. But the movement is only aesthetically fulfilling, for it is the case that the Symbolic does not represent a permanent plateau that, once attained, places the subject beyond the reach of the Imaginary. For "normality," one has to achieve the Symbolic, but it is not a place one can move into and therein live happily ever after.

The Name-of-the-"F(Ather)"

Mrs. Ramsay is the symbol for all characters of the object of desire; as her husband, Mr. Ramsay is the first figure who must deal with the problem of mourning her loss. Woolf represents his accommodation within the first two sections of "The Lighthouse." As is his wont, Ramsay immediately attaches himself to the first woman available to him as a substitute object for his wife. Ramsay's drive is to satisfy a "demand"; demand is a void that once may have been a physiological need (as, for example, a need for sustenance from the mother in her anaclitic role), but that is now a void hollowed out in the space of desire. Need becomes *démande*. "In Seminar Twenty," says Ragland-Sullivan, "Lacan said that demand emanates from the *je* and resides in the substitution of finite and concrete objects for the denied and obscure, infinite object of Desire; these substitutions are just so many metonymous ways to compensate for the split between being and wanting that marked the end of the mirror stage" (*Séminaire* XX 114; *JLPP* 86). When Ramsay fastens his desire on Lily she is manifestly the object substituting for his lack, now more painful (as we saw in "Time Passes") because it is permanent. That lack signifies his (and our) alienation in desire and in the world. Woolf makes all this clear (though she uses both *demand* and *need*) in the moment Lily perceives Ramsay's look: "Suddenly Mr. Ramsay raised his head as he passed and looked straight at her, with his distraught wild gaze which was yet so penetrating . . . ; and she pretended to drink out of her empty coffee cup so as to escape him—to escape his demand on her, to put aside a moment longer that imperious need" (219).

Lacan recognizes that language may serve as well as real objects in satisfying demands of desire and mourning. In their effects, the words become real objects. Lily's first turn from Ramsay's demand on her is indeed toward language. As he strides by her, he mutters two words, "Alone" and "Perished." These two words represent his isolation and loss, but around them might be woven what Lily thinks of as "the truth of things" (219); for Lacan, too, they might *be* the truth of things since they signify alienation and death. "Like everything else this strange morning," Lily perceives, "the words became symbols." They "wrote themselves all over the grey-green walls. If only she could put them together, she felt," if only she could "write them out in some sentence, then she would have got at the truth of things" (219). Desire, in fact, is a truth of things. It is a truth of objects, *objets a,* or, as Lacan says, a metonymy: "Desire is a metonymy" (*Ecrits: A Selection* 175). It is caught up in a syntax of things. In the presence of Ramsay's need, Lily seems actually to recognize that fact, but she has trouble deciding what to do or what to say or on what objects to focus: "she could say nothing; the whole horizon seemed swept bare of objects to talk about" (227). But Ramsay's demand is immense, having to do (Lacan would insist) with his very being since "demand begins with the ideal ego's formation and answers finally to the superego, or the limits intrinsic to a specific *moi*" (*JLPP* 86). Consequently, without her knowing what she does (as if, indeed, she were directed by an Other), Lily does alight upon the one object that will satisfy Ramsay's demand. She is directed to it/them, no doubt by the Other in Ramsay, as he notices that his bootlaces are untied. "Remarkable boots they were too," Lily thought. They are "sculptured; colossal; like everything that Mr. Ramsay wore," Lily notes. "She could see them walking to his room of their own accord, expressive in his absence of pathos, surliness, ill-temper, charm" (228–29). Though she thinks that to praise those boots is frivolous in the face of his demand, when she says, "What beautiful boots!" Ramsay smiles and, remarkably, "his infirmities fell from him" (229). Those boots are his *objet a,* and by her praise, Lily creates in him a moment of joy that can fill his sense of lack: "They had reached," Lily thinks, ironically, "a sunny island where peace dwelt, sanity reigned and the sun for ever shone." It was, she thinks, "the blessed island of good boots" (230).[12]

One may feel that Ramsay's displacement of grief for the death of his wife is too easily accepted here. But, while it has indeed seemed facile, there is no reason to suspect that his pain is neither real nor substantial. He easily displaces the grief because (one must surmise) he has had to deal with it for quite some years, and, in a sense, long practice (of the unconscious, to be sure, not the conscious mind) has made it easier to master in each recurrence. The fact is, if he were not able to control the mourning rather easily by this time in his life we would have to regard him as somehow immature or undeveloped. He *is* an old man, over seventy now, and what has become absolutely incumbent upon him is to take his place in the normal structure of personality and family discourse. To remain caught up in mourning too long is to remain trapped in an unhealthy Imaginary relationship. One has to let go of the desired object, accept the loss or lack or absence of the beloved. One must accept, in short, castration in yet one more form, but that acceptance is part of an ongoing Symbolic process whether it occurs in the mourning of a Real loss as such or merely in the mourning of a lost object in which desire has been momentarily invested (as in Minta's brooch). Conceivably, each one of us in each day of our lives has to reaffirm the acceptance of our own lack, the impossibility of ever achieving satisfaction or a grounding for the phallus as a mark of our lack. Thus, what Ramsay does in his early morning encounter with the psychic fact of mourning (brought on by demands dating back, one is sure, to infancy and to the real mother) is to pass once more through a displaced version of the mirror stage and the Oedipus encounter. Traversed successfully, this passage represents (once again) the passage from Imaginary to Symbolic.

Happily for Ramsay's children Cam and James, his passage is successful (as, again one is sure, it always has been for him), and Ramsay is enabled in the unconscious discourse he constructs with them to move into his proper place. He takes his place in relation to them (they are all, literally and figuratively, in the same boat) where the Name-of-the-Father resides in the Symbolic. He becomes Other to them, not merely antagonistic or narcissistic other in their Imaginary conflicts or projections. After praising those boots, Lily herself notes a change in Ramsay, though she may misunderstand its nature. But the shift in her attitude (from hostility to sympathy) and the appearance of Cam and James at this moment begin to suggest Ramsay's new role. The boy and girl appear something like Adam and Eve at the end of *Paradise Lost:* "They came, lagging, side by side, a serious, melancholy couple" (230).[13] In this context, suddenly, the old man moves over to the place of the Other, of God-the-Father, a figure to be feared and worshipped. Thus Lily becomes angry at the boy and girl: "But why was it like *that* that they came?" she wonders; "they might have come more cheerfully; they might have given him what, now that they were off [to the lighthouse], she would not have the chance of giving him" (230–31). In short order, Ramsay has been transformed within Lily's mind (but, as we shall see, in the domain of the text as well) into the heroic Other. "He had become a very distinguished, elderly man, who had no need of her whatsoever" (231). He becomes yet more heroic to her (though not yet to the children). "He had all the appearance of a leader making ready for an expedition. Then, wheeling about, he led the way with his firm military tread, in those wonderful boots, carrying brown paper parcels, down the path, his children following him" (231). Lily's meditation on Ramsay ranges far in the next few moments, but the end result is precisely to acknowledge his representing Otherness, his withdrawal into "that other final phase which was new to her and had, she owned, made herself ashamed of her own irritability, when it seemed as if he had shed worries and ambitions, and the hope of sympathy and the desire for praise, had entered some other region, was drawn on, as if by curiosity, in dumb colloquy, whether with himself or another, at the head of that little procession out of one's range" (233).

It is from within this "other region"—the place of the Other—and "in dumb colloquy" that Ramsay conducts his discourse with Cam and James hereafter. Representing this discourse, several sections are then devoted largely to the silent discourse of the children with the father. Essentially, their response is to the Law (which is silent) more than it is to the actual father, but, Oedipally, since they prefer to resist, they displace their resistance from the person toward a concept: "they vowed, in silence," we are told, "to stand by each other and to carry out the great compact—to resist tyranny to the death" (243). Ramsay's

power over them thus is more than biological or familial. "Their griev-
ance weighed them down," we are told. "They had been forced; they
had been bidden. He had borne them down once more with his gloom
and his authority, making them do his bidding, on this fine morning,
[making them] come, because he wished it, carrying these parcels, to
the Lighthouse; take part in these rites he went through for his own
pleasure in memory of dead people" (246). In effect, Ramsay has now
been identified with the silent dead, with Prue, Andrew, and Mrs.
Ramsay, and progressively he moves more and more toward silence
on the boat ride as he disappears into the pages of his (and Woolf's)
book: "But what might be written in the book which had rounded its
edges off in his pocket," we are told of Cam, "she did not know. What
he thought they none of them knew. But he was absorbed in it" (283).
Or, through James, he is felt to look "like some old stone lying on
the sand," the stone becoming a figure that also brings him into align-
ment with the lighthouse itself, "a stark tower on a bare rock" (301)
onto which he springs at the arrival at their destination (see 308). In
a variety of ways, then, the text shows that for Cam, James, and Lily
Briscoe, Mr. Ramsay has taken his proper place in the Symbolic. He
takes his place in the Name-of-the-Father, but, portentously, the place
he takes is the place of the dead as well.

Male Castration

Male and female castration are both manifested in the relations of
Mr. Ramsay with his children James and Cam. The theme is focused
of course in the Oedipus complex. James's confrontation with the
Oedipus, as we shall see, is less complicated than Cam's. The imagery
in which it is represented is almost perfect. Since James and Cam are
united in their pact to "fight tyranny to the death," much of what we
learn about the boy's response to his father comes through or in con-
junction with his sister's. It is Cam, for example, who notes that Ramsay
has thrust onto James the task of steering the boat to the lighthouse,
a task that generates the antagonism and permits the reconciliation of
the Oedipus conflict to occur. Cam notes, "James would be forced to
keep his eye all the time on the sail. For if he forgot, then the sail
puckered and shivered, and the boat slackened, and Mr. Ramsay would
say sharply, 'Look out! Look out!' " (244). The boy and girl are united
in their vow to fight the tyrant, but since their father represents that

dominating image of law to them, of him "they were conscious all the time" (245). Steering the boat, however, James on occasion fantasizes escape rather than confrontation: he thinks that "he might escape; he might be quit of it all. They might land somewhere; and be free then" (246–47). With his mother dead, James displaces his feelings regarding the mother toward his sister; thus he suffers moments of anger toward and alienation from Cam when he observes his father's entreaties for sympathy from the girl. His feelings at sixteen are little different from those seen at six. "I shall be left to fight the tyrant alone. The compact would be left to him to carry out. Cam would never resist tyranny to the death, he thought grimly, watching her face, sad, sulky, yielding" (250). The threat of the girl's yielding to his father grows even more grim—incestuously so—when out of his unconscious emerges a very primal memory of the father's coming between the boy and his real mother. The memory comes, naturally enough, in that moment we shall call Cam's secondary castration, in that moment when he identifies her with "woman," with some primal otherness—some castrating "they." "*They* look down he thought, at their knitting or something. Then suddenly *they* look up" (251; my emphasis). What he is remembering here is that scene, when he was six, of Oedipal conflict represented in "The Window" (9). "It must have been his mother, he thought, sitting on a low chair, with his father standing over her" (251), he tall, erect, threatening, "stopped dead, upright, over them" (252).

In this memory, James's consciousness reveals both how the unconscious works as a structure we may call a text and how the text contributes to the already formed unconscious for the reader. James plays upon this primal episode during the remainder of his journey to the lighthouse. It brings out all the latent violence in the boy's imagination. So when imagining the father's reprimands of him for the boat's slowing down, James explicitly recalls that other scene, that scene of the Oedipal other: "once before he had brought his blade down among them on the terrace and she had gone stiff all over, and if there had been an axe handy, a knife, or anything with a sharp point he would have seized it and struck his father through the heart" (277). But in fact James's anger there is as much directed at the mother as at the father who intrudes, for he feels it is the mother who abandons him: "She had gone stiff all over, and then, her arm slackening, so that he felt she listened to him no longer, she had risen somehow and gone away and left him there, impotent, ridiculous, sitting on the floor grasping a pair of scissors" (277–78). The ambivalence of James's anger accounts for the ambiguous role of the mother in castration in the Oedipal conflict. That ambiguity, as Ragland-Sullivan contends, is easily thrust upon "woman" or women. Thus, in James's imagery, as in Lacanian theory, the figures associated with the intrusive "father" may as easily be female as male. "He had always kept this old symbol of taking a knife and striking his father to the heart. Only now, as he grew older, and sat staring at his father in an impotent rage, it was not him, that old man reading, whom he wanted to kill, but it was the thing that descended on him—without his knowing it perhaps: that fierce sudden black-winged harpy, with its talons and its beak all cold and hard, that struck and struck at you" (273).

In this ambivalence toward the androgynous "black-winged harpy" (is it father? mother?) James actually is engaged in a necessary step toward gender maturation.[14] One thing he needs to do to be gendered male is to identify his future as a male with his father; he needs to identify with the symbols and occupations of the father. He does that, strangely enough, even as he contemplates his Oedipal revenge: "Whatever he did—(and he might do anything, he felt, looking at the Lighthouse and the distant shore) whether he was in a business, in a bank, a barrister, a man at the head of some enterprise, that he would fight, that he would track down and stamp out—tyranny, despotism, he called it—making people do what they did not want to do, *cutting off* their right to speak" (274; my emphasis). Thus, even while he cannot yet quite dissociate the *principle* of law or authority from his own father, James can recognize his identificatory link to him: "he had come to feel, quite often lately, when his father said something or did something which surprised the others, [that] there were two pairs of footprints only; his own and his father's. They alone knew each other" (274–75). Feeling such an identification with his father, James thus begins to investigate the basis of the fear of and hostility toward "this terror, this hatred" of the "black-winged harpy." He finds his explanation of the law of denial (castration) in a metaphor of cause and effect. He concludes that an instrument, say, a wagon wheel crushing a foot, is not to be blamed for what it does; the fault lies somewhere else, in some causal agent. But who or what is that agent? James struggles toward an answer in the notion of Law, in abstract principle. It is Law, rather than the mere person who happens to be present, that is to be faulted. His imagery[15] for that principle seems, finally, indeed to evoke castration, the fact of loss and alienation: "It was in this world that the wheel went over the person's foot. Something, he remembered, stayed and darkened over him; would not move; something flourished up in the air, something arid and sharp descended even there, like a blade, a scimitar, smiting through the leaves and flowers even of that happy world and making it shrivel and fall" (276). If James exonerates his father-*as*-father, then he does so in the end at the expense of the mother, for while it must be she who resides behind the black wings of that harpy, the father it seems can withdraw behind the black robes of Law.

As part of James's identification with his father in the process of gender maturation, he begins consequently to mythologize the role of his mother in a different direction. She becomes lost to him as woman in the process, for in accordance with the Oedipus passage she must be desexualized. Thereafter, she reappears, precisely as Ragland-Sullivan suggests of woman in general, in the place of truth or knowledge. "The absence of the signifier *woman*," moreover, "also accounts for the illusion of the infinite," Jacques-Alain Miller has said. "The passion for things symbolic has no other source. Science exists because *woman* does not exist. Knowledge as such substitutes for knowing the other sex" (as quoted in *JLPP* 297). Thus, James searches for both mother and woman and *knowledge* in the dominating presence of the phallic signifier represented by his father. The shift toward knowledge is evidenced in James's investigation of his haunting memory images. What he seems to want to do is to find out where his mother "went" on that day when he was six and his father came between them. The imagery of that discovery is rather explicitly that of the primal scene. "James stealthily, as if he were stealing downstairs on bare feet, afraid of waking a watchdog by a creaking board, went on thinking what was she like, where did she go that day?" (278). In his thoughts (as he steers the boat) James follows "her from room to room" (278). But it is clear that like the father become the Law of the Father (the crushing wheel of what—of fate?), the mother has moved into the Symbolic as a form of the unknowable Other. She has moved into the same Symbolic realm. There, in the Symbolic, "She alone spoke the truth; to her alone could he speak it. That was the source of her everlasting attraction for him, perhaps; she was a person to whom one could say what came into one's head" (278). But even there in the Symbolic the baleful, Oedipal presence of patriarchal authority tends to limit the search for or utterance of a truth displaced from the forbidden woman. "But all the time he thought of her, he was conscious of his father following his thought, surveying it, making it shiver and falter. At last he ceased to think" (278).[16]

The end of the Oedipal journey for James is the arrival at the lighthouse and the Symbolic. There, he comes to terms with his father and the symbol of his own masculinity. Section 12 of "The Lighthouse" develops these themes overtly. First, James perceives his place in a paternal, identificatory lineage, for he sees that his father "looked very old. He looked, James thought, getting his head now against the Lighthouse, now against the waste of waters running away into the open, like some old stone lying on the sand; he looked as if he had become physically . . . that loneliness [the empty place vacated by woman] which was for both of them the truth about things" (301). Then he perceives and internalizes the symbolic power of the lighthouse: "it was a stark tower on a bare rock. It satisfied him. It confirmed some obscure feeling of his about his own character" (301–2). In the starkness of the lighthouse, James sees the alienation of life and of his own identity. Finally, he internalizes[17] the role of the father. He does that by imitation of the words of a father who shares the knowledge that life is bleak, hard: " 'We are driving before a gale—we must sink,' he began saying to himself, half aloud, exactly as his father said it' " (302). And when his father compliments him on a job of steering and navigation done well, through Cam we learn how much the boy has wanted just those words from the father: "There," Cam thinks, "You've got it at last. For she knew that this was what James had been wanting, and she knew that now he had got it he was so pleased that he would not look at her or at his father or at any one. There he sat with his hand on the tiller sitting bolt upright, looking rather sulky and frowning slightly. He was so pleased that he was not going to let anybody share a grain of his pleasure. His father had praised him" (306).

Female Castration

The psychic work that engages both Cam and James in "The Lighthouse" is their internalization of the Law of the Father—their acceptance, that is, of the law of castration revealed in the passage through the Oedipus conflict. "Freud defined the Oedipus complex," says Ragland-Sullivan, "as the organized ensemble of loving and hostile desires felt by the child toward her or his parents. This has been recast by Lacan to account for the evolution that, little by little, substitutes the father for the mother" (*JLPP* 278). The passage to the lighthouse is as much for Cam as for James the passage through the Oedipus complex. The two of them are as insistently oriented toward their father as the boat is oriented toward the lighthouse. For Cam the passage is slightly different from James's passage, because as a female she has a different relation to the phallus and its loss. While, like her brother, Cam has to realize that she cannot *be* the phallus for her mother, she never has to deal with having symbolically to lose the actual phallus possessed in the Real by the male child. Moreover, as a female, Cam seems in a favored relation to her father because she absorbs the values possessed by her mother-as-female. Thus Cam's relation to father and law may be symptomatic of the relatively less traumatic *primary* passage through Oedipus some Lacanians think the female may have. On the other hand, she also represents the greater difficulty the female experiences in what Ragland-Sullivan calls the *secondary* castration—the necessity of being identified *as* woman in a phallocentric, patriarchal Symbolic culture.[18] Cam's image of the difference comes in relation to Macalister's story about the wintry shipwreck; Ramsay "relished the thought of the storm and the dark night and the fishermen striving there. He liked that men should labour and sweat on the windy beach at night; pitting muscle and brain against the waves and the wind; he liked men to work like that." But what he likes of the woman is that she "keep house, and sit beside sleeping children indoors, while men were drowned, out there in a storm" (245). Although the men are given the more dangerous options, at least they are given options outside home and hearth. "Wild" Cam surely will recognize that difference— as it is clear Woolf herself did.

Cam's relation to Ramsay reveals the evolution of the female in the Oedipal passage. The dominant (castration) theme of that relation is difference, alienation, separation. The child is identified in its fusion with the mother's body, but it is further identified in the symbol of its differentiation through its relation to the father. In effect, in the face of the No-of-the-Father the child has also to enunciate its own "No." Cam does that in concert with James in their vow to resist "tyranny," meaning of course the demands of the father that they do this or do that. But try as she might to "resist tyranny to the death" (246), Cam cannot resist the place into which her father thrusts her in his own thoughts. That place insistently is not that of her as child; rather, it is of her as Woman, located in Ramsay's Imaginary, ambiguously, as fulfillment and obstacle to his demands. On the one hand Ramsay can rant inwardly because Cam does not know the points of the compass: "women are always like that; the vagueness of their minds is hopeless" (249). On the other, he feels he must make up to her because he rather liked "this vagueness in women. It was part of their extraordinary charm" (250). So he will try to make her smile by tempting her with an image of something a woman presumably cannot resist. He will tempt her by a "little thing," just another *objet a* that may substitute for the missing phallus: "There was a puppy. They had a puppy. Who was looking after the puppy today?" (250). The old man's surmise is plain: the way to a girl's—or woman's—heart is through the baby or the little object that may stand for one, the *objet* itself always standing in for the phallus.

The validity of Cam's acceptance of primary castration, her recognition of law, is illustrated in her confrontation with her father's Imaginary perception of her. Cam understands clearly that there is a higher authority than her father-as-father. In this scene she identifies that law, ironically, with the son, her brother James. All the while that Cam is trying to "resist [Ramsay's] entreaty—forgive me, care for me" (251), James sits there representing "the lawgiver, with the tablets of eternal wisdom laid open on his knee (his hand on the tiller had become symbolical to her)," he saying, "Resist him. Fight him" (251). Even so, at this very moment James himself is casting Cam into the same realm of secondary castration as had her father. James, too, insists on her definition as woman, but as woman defined in the castrated mother's act of betrayal of the child: "She'll give way, James thought, as he watched a look come upon her face, a look he remembered. They look down he thought, at their knitting or something. Then suddenly they look up. There was a flash of blue, he remembered, and then somebody sitting with him laughed, surrendered, and he was very angry. It must have been his mother" (251). What James is imposing upon Cam here, then, is the "double Castration" referred to by Ragland-Sullivan, and regarded as instrumental in the history of the oppression of women. Ragland-Sullivan describes this oppression as occurring in three steps: First,

> At the Real structural level of primary Castration, both males and females experience loss of the symbiotic attachment to the mother

as a kind of Castration. At the secondary or substantive level, Imaginary representations and social meanings are attributed to the mother and father in an effort to understand or explain the separation drama.

Next:

Secondary Castration inheres in Imaginary and Symbolic efforts to explain a Real effect. The Other(A) is the place of the unconscious and thus is either a dark-faced and absent part of oneself which one must flee or a mysterious force which one renders divine and proceeds to worship.

Finally:

The primordial (m)Other at the mirror-stage, structural base of the ego becomes confused with woman; and women are consequently seen as secretly powerful. The mother within both sexes therefore implies an unseen dominance. This makes woman—as her [the mother's] displacement—someone to be feared, denied, ignored, denigrated, fought, and conquered—or conversely worshipped and enshrined. (*JLPP* 297)

Despite the Imaginary violence done to Cam's identity, however, the girl is able to deal with her father in a proper or normal way. She can resist his Imaginary importunities—she does not play his game of name-the-puppy, for example. But she can accept him—as well as the mother (seen in Cam's frequent references to images of the peaceful, protective island receding behind them)—for what the Symbolic makes of him. That is, he can be both a narcissistic and an anaclitic image for her. Narcissistically: "For no one attracted her more; his hands were beautiful, and his feet, and his voice, and his words, and his haste, and his temper, and his oddity, and his passion, and his saying straight out before every one, we perish, each alone, and his remoteness" (253). Anaclitically, he is an image of the protector-father: "for she was safe, while he sat there; safe, as she felt herself when she crept in from the garden, and took a book down, and the old gentleman, lowering the paper suddenly, said something very brief over the top of it" (283). Similarly, at the arrival at the lighthouse, Cam "felt as she did in the study when the old men were reading *The Times*. Now I can go on thinking whatever I like, and I shan't fall over a precipice or be drowned, for there he is, keeping his eye on me" (304). Most of all she can internalize his image as the Other, that ultimate, arbitrary, silent interlocutor whose place is really in the unconscious: "What was he thinking now? she wondered. What was it he sought, so fixedly, so intently, so silently?" (307). And it is his role as the Other, the one who is supposed to know, that permits him to pose for Cam the two dominant questions of one's being—death and plenitude, loss and fulfillment: "He sat and looked at the island and he might be thinking, We perished, each alone, or he might be thinking, I have reached it. I have found it" (308). But as the silent Other, "he said nothing" (308). Such has Ramsay's identity come to be for Cam (and James) at the moment he lightly springs "on to the rock" of the lighthouse that possesses his Symbolic being. As a young woman, Cam, too, has arrived at her destination—or, more properly, her destiny within, we say redundantly, a patriarchal culture.

The Name-of-the-"M(Other)"

Aesthetically, the most significant of the passages into the Symbolic in "The Lighthouse" is that accomplished by Lily Briscoe. Hers is so expansive in scope that it subsumes all others in its metapsychological sweep. Lily is the substitute in the last movement of the novel for Mrs. Ramsay in that both represent (or come to represent) the novel's metaconsciousness, its over-soul of subjectivity. All the others—Ramsay, James, Cam—are subjects of course, but Lily enfigures the heightened, pervading subjectivity observed in Mrs. Ramsay and characterized by Woolf in the artist. As noted in the discussion of "Time Passes," Lily represents the re-emergence of subjectivity following the loss of it in the dark, mournful passage through the order of the Real. Consequently, Woolf creates the sense that Lily is not entirely a whole consciousness at the start of "The Lighthouse." She has to move toward psychic reintegration. She begins in a state of denial, primarily denial of loss, *béance*, castration. The hole in the Real is still gaping in her consciousness. Woolf makes the point clearly: "What does it mean?" Lily wonders; "she could not, this first morning with the Ramsays, contract her feelings, could only make a phrase resound to cover the blankness of her mind until these vapours had shrunk. For really, what did she feel, come back after all these years and Mrs. Ramsay dead? Nothing, nothing—nothing that she could express at all" (217). Thus

Woolf makes readers feel that Lily has not yet accomplished the work of mourning the loss of Mrs. Ramsay and the others—"Mrs. Ramsay dead; Andrew killed; Prue dead too—repeat it as she might, it roused no feeling in her" (219). What Lily does to reestablish "the link that usually bound things together [and that] had been cut" (219) is to return to her painting, the picture she had abandoned ten years before.

Lily has an ambivalent relation to the painting, however. It obviously represents for her an *objet a;* it is a substitute for the thing desired (always, symbolically, the phallus), an object to fill the gap (always resulting, symbolically, from castration) that she suffers in being. But the painting is also a barrier she wishes to erect between her and the nearest representative of the phallus—Mr. Ramsay. One sees that plainly in her almost frantic efforts to avoid his "penetrating" gaze when he is searching for someone to fill his loss, while, that is, she is trying "to escape his [sexual] demand on her" (219). The painting will fill the place of the phallus, for the construction represented in the work of art (as in the science of which Miller speaks) is a way to get "at the truth of things" (219), though that "truth" be nothing more than the denial of castration in its representation. That truth is also associated with a paternal metaphor, the lighthouse. But the lighthouse is as ambiguous to her as Ramsay's presence and demand. "The extraordinary unreality was frightening; but it was also exciting. Going to the Lighthouse. But what does one send to the Lighthouse?" (220). Since she does not go with the others, what Lily sends there is consciousness, her heightened aesthetic perception. In Lily's mind the lighthouse becomes associated with her painting, for both are signifiers by which she will restore unity to a fragmented existence and fill "the empty places" vacated by woman in the Oedipal passage (220). Seeing in Ramsay's demand a reminder of the loss, the castration, effected in Mrs. Ramsay's death, Lily attempts to escape the work of mourning (and also of love) by plunging into her painting: "It seemed as if the solution had come to her: she knew now what she wanted to do" (221).

But so long as the painting is merely a "barrier, frail, but she hoped sufficiently substantial to ward off Mr. Ramsay" (223), Lily sees that she is only playing at painting, and that her playing is "a kind of blasphemy" (224). Lily's sense of loss and frustration thus turns (in another example of woman's secondary castration) to anger at Mrs. Ramsay: "It was all Mrs. Ramsay's doing. She was dead. Here was

Lily, at forty-four, wasting her time, unable to do a thing, standing there, playing at painting, playing at the one thing one did not play at, and it was all Mrs. Ramsay's fault. She was dead. The step where she used to sit was empty. She was dead" (223–24). The anger is the means by which Lily begins to perceive her loss, and the anger will eventually lead to the effective act of mourning. But at this point she merely questions the need to "repeat this over and over again" (224), this effort "to bring up some feeling she had not got" (224). But the one thing she can do, besides work at her painting, is to accept her role as a substitute for Mrs. Ramsay in meeting Ramsay's need. She might at least accept her maternal role vis à vis the others, though she does not understand it yet. "Surely, she could imitate from recollection the glow, the rhapsody, the self-surrender, she had seen on so many women's faces (on Mrs. Ramsay's, for instance) when on some occasion like this they blazed up—she could remember the look on Mrs. Ramsay's face—into a rapture of sympathy, of delight in the reward they had, which, though the reason of it escaped her, evidently conferred on them the most supreme bliss of which human nature was capable. Here he was, stopped by her side. She would give him what she could" (224–25). To give him what she could is to accept her role in the cultural Symbolic as "a woman" instead of "a peevish, ill-tempered, dried-up old maid" (226). Still, there is a hole where woman was, and Lily will try to fill it both with her painting and with her body.

If Lily's painting links to an *objet a*, the *objet a* emanates from the Other, the subject supposed to know. In this linkage, the painting or the act of painting for her thus represents what she feels about the maternal signifier, Mrs. Ramsay. Consequently the dialogue between Lily and her painting modulates into a dialogue with Mrs. Ramsay and therefore into a dialogue with the insufficiently mourned dead. Lily is like the child in the mirror stage, for she is now a split subject, divided between desire and loss. The split is represented in the relation between Mrs. Ramsay and Ramsay, the one dead and gone, the other simply departed to the lighthouse. "She felt curiously divided, as if one part of her were drawn out there" to the lighthouse, whereas "the other had fixed itself doggedly, solidly, here on the lawn" with her canvas (233–34). At this moment Ramsay is merely Imaginary other; the canvas stands in the place of the Symbolic Other that interrogates her. For her the canvas is "this formidable ancient enemy," "this other thing, this truth, this reality, which suddenly laid hands on her, emerged stark at the back of appearances and commanded her attention" (236). What that Other creates in her is a resistance to the voice from the past of another of her Imaginary others, the one who—as he had to young James—says "no" to her in imitation of the Name-of-the-Father: "she heard some voice saying she couldn't paint, saying she couldn't create, as if she were caught up in one of those habitual currents in which after a certain time experience forms in the mind, so that one repeats words without being aware any longer who originally spoke them" (237). The voice from the past belongs to Charles Tansley, Lily's Imaginary other, her "whipping boy" (293) from across the divide of all the years. What she needs to get on with her painting, the only form of reproduction she has chosen, is this almost sexual stimulation the memory of Tansley provides her. Woolf's language is explicit: it was "as if some juice necessary for the lubrication of her faculties were spontaneously squirted" (237).[19]

In her rememoration of Charles Tansley, Lily reenacts the mirror phase in which she becomes differentiated from the maternal figure at the same time she recognizes the place that that figure has filled in her life. As mirror image or alter ego for Lily, Tansley has the curious function of stimulating Lily to paint (which, judging from Woolf's language, is obviously an erotically charged activity for her), but he also enables her to recognize the loss she has experienced in Mrs. Ramsay's death. Thinking of the time on the beach when she and Tansley were there together, Lily cannot avoid thinking of Mrs. Ramsay, who was also there. "When she thought of herself and Charles throwing ducks and drakes and of the whole scene on the beach, it seemed to depend somehow upon Mrs. Ramsay sitting upon the rock, with a pad on her knee, writing letters. . . . That woman sitting there writing under the rock resolved everything into simplicity; made these angers, irritations fall off like old rags" (239). What Lily sees in Mrs. Ramsay is the principle of art, the ability to bring disparate things together and to preserve them. But that identification—of Mrs. Ramsay and art—leads Lily to a recognition of loss. "Mrs. Ramsay making of the moment something permanent (as in another sphere Lily herself tried to make of the moment something permanent)—this was of the nature of a revelation. In the midst of chaos there was shape; this eternal passing and flowing . . . was struck into stability. Life stand still here, Mrs. Ramsay said. 'Mrs. Ramsay!' she repeated. She owed it all to her" (241).

In this moment, as she begins to get control of her painting, Lily feels that she has been returned to the maternal space. Lily's painting, her link to her *objet a*, evokes in her the memory of another object, the boat or cork or cask she and Mrs. Ramsay had seen on the ocean that long ago day, the bobbing of one on the water's surface permitting Lily to create on the surface of her canvas the *dérive de la jouissance*, the wake of infantile pleasure derived from the appearance of Mrs. Ramsay as what Roy Schafer (*Aspects of Internalization* 117–39) calls a "primary process presence": "And she began to lay on a red, a grey, and she began to model her way into the hollow there. At the same time, she seemed to be sitting beside Mrs. Ramsay on the beach" (255). More than that, Lily, as she works further into her painting, moves into a sort of womb: "And Lily, painting steadily, felt as if a door had opened, and one went in and stood gazing silently about in a high cathedral-like place, very dark, very solemn" (255). What Lily feels she is enabled to capture at this moment is the fullness of being, that plenitude Lacan associates with the phallic signifier; in this moment she has become what Lacan would term the phallus. The setting, the painting, the memories welling up from her unconscious—all enable Lily to capture or to be the phallus, albeit for a moment only. "She rammed a little hole in the sand and covered it up, by way of burying in it the perfection of the moment. It was like a drop of silver in which one dipped and illumined the darkness of the past" (256). If the dip into the past (in memories also of Paul and Minta—the Rayleys) eventually makes Lily recognize her loss once again in the memory of "the dead," it is still not active grief Lily feels even here; instead, Lily feels triumph over a Mrs. Ramsay now dead, "dusty and out of date" (260). Her most intense internalization of loss, grief, castration is yet to come.

Lily's moment of triumph over dead, dusty, out-of-date Mrs. Ramsay is short-lived. Remembering Mrs. Ramsay through the remembered tales told of her by William Bankes, Lily very shortly begins to feel other than triumphant. Using Augustus Carmichael now as if he were the silent Other in relation to her, Lily wants to ask him about everything that he, the subject who knows, "like a creature gorged with existence" (265), might be able to tell her. But she realizes she will be unable to say to him what she feels, for what she feels is "not one thing, but everything" (265). The talking cure will not be sufficient for her. "Little words that broke up the thought and dismembered it said nothing. 'About life, about death; about Mrs. Ramsay.' . . . Words fluttered sideways and struck the object inches too low. . . . For how could one express in words these emotions of the body? express that emptiness there?" (265). Lily, in this realization, is beginning to face the gap, loss, emptiness of being left by the death of the maternal figure. She is facing a repetition of the birth of desire in mourning, the emergence of desire out of a realization that one may not have what one misses. "To want and not to have, sent all up her body a hardness, a hollowness, a strain. And then to want and not to have—to want and want—how that wrung the heart, and wrung it again and again! Oh, Mrs. Ramsay!" (266). Wanting to ask Carmichael what it all means and feeling that "the whole world" has seemed to dissolve into "a deep basin of reality" (266), Lily acknowledges, finally, the profound loss she has suffered in Mrs. Ramsay's death. She recognizes, moreover, that while her painting might substitute in the Symbolic for Mrs. Ramsay, it cannot ever bring her back.

Even so, by persisting in her feeling that Carmichael (as Other) has greater knowledge, that he is a being who sails "serenely through a world which satisfied all his wants" (267), Lily manages to believe that the phallus might be restored. "For one moment she felt that if they both got up, here, now on the lawn, and demanded an explanation, why was it so short, why was it so inexplicable, said it with violence, as two fully equipped human beings from whom nothing should be hid might speak, then, beauty would roll itself up; space would fill; those empty flourishes would form into shape; if they shouted loud enough Mrs. Ramsay would return. 'Mrs. Ramsay!' she said aloud, 'Mrs. Ramsay!' The tears ran down her face" (268). But Lily's moment here is counterpointed in what is perhaps the most blatantly literary symbolic event in the novel, the senseless mutilation of a fish by the Macalister boy on the boat heading to the lighthouse. That act, like the deaths of Mrs. Ramsay, Prue, and Andrew in "Time Passes," is represented as a bracketed hole in the narration. But instead of forming a hole in the Real, the mutilation seems an intrusion here of the brute real into the Symbolic:

> [Macalister's boy took one of the fish and cut a square out of its side to bait his hook with. The mutilated body (it was alive still) was thrown back into the sea.] (268)

Beyond this Symbolic moment, as if from this crucifixion, which is outside her purview, though not that of the text or the textual unconscious, Lily suffers through her most intense pain of mourning, feeling an "anguish [that] could reduce one to such a pitch of imbecility" as to cause her to "step off her strip of board into the waters of annihilation" (269).

But beyond this moment, too, the anguish begins to subside; she has now felt the "sorrow for Mrs. Ramsay" she thought she would never feel (269). Moreover, she takes a renewed interest in completing her painting, for again she feels that primary-process presence, a "mysterious" "sense of some one there, of Mrs. Ramsay, relieved for a moment of the weight that the world had put on her, staying lightly by her side and then ... raising to her forehead a wreath of white flowers with which she went" (269). In this image of the flower-wreathed Mrs. Ramsay, Lily reenacts in memory the earlier scene of mourning that had accompanied the news of Mrs. Ramsay's death. For Lily the scene has to be repeated constantly—it is a "vision [that] must be perpetually remade" (270)—because she has not accepted the ultimacy of symbolic castration, the necessary shift from the fusional Imaginary to the distancing of the Symbolic. At the end of this scene of her imagining Mrs. Ramsay's traversing the "fields of death" (270), Lily finally seems prepared to shift her focus away from the maternal (m)Other to the paternal Other. That shift occurs as the result of another intrusive object, not remembered, but seen now on the ocean's surface; it is "a brown spot in the middle of the bay" (270) that turns out to be Ramsay's boat heading toward the lighthouse. On that boat is the paternal signifier, and it is this signifier that Lily seems finally able to acknowledge and accept. "Where was he, that very old man who had gone past her silently, holding a brown paper parcel under his arm?" (271). Now Lily is faced with achieving "that razor edge of balance between two opposite forces: Mr. Ramsay and the picture" (287). Clearly, the balance of these two represents for Lily the balance between Mr. and Mrs. Ramsay, father and mother, male and female. When Lily, in her extensive rememoration of the past, imagines the marriage of these two, she is prepared to accept the place of the dominant signifier. Thus as Mrs. Ramsay becomes for Lily a "part of ordinary experience" (300), Lily becomes ready to yield to Mr. Ramsay, the father in the Symbolic. "Where was the boat now? And Mr. Ramsay? She wanted him" (300). As Lacan would say, it is he—and what he represents—that Lily "wants," "lacks," "desires."

When Lily surmises that Mr. Ramsay "must have reached" the light-house (308), the psychic fact is that she too has reached it, reached, that is, the phallic signifier, the domain of the Symbolic. The feeling Lily evinces in this moment is rather erotic, as well it might be (see Pratt). For her "the effort of looking at it and the effort of thinking of him landing there, which both seemed to be one and the same effort, had stretched her body and mind to the utmost. Ah, but she was relieved. Whatever she had wanted to give him, when he left her that morning, she had given him at last" (308-9). At this ecstatic moment of submission to the phallic signifier, Lily turns to that other figure of the Other, Carmichael, now "looking like an old pagan god" (309), like one who has the power to offer a benediction or "sancti-fication" (Rosenthal 127) to the passage Lily and the others have made to the lighthouse. "Carmichael stood there as if he were spreading his hands over all the weakness and suffering of mankind; she thought he was surveying, tolerantly and compassionately, their final destiny. Now he has crowned the occasion, she thought, when his hand slowly fell, as if she had seen him let fall from his great height a wreath of violets and asphodels which, fluttering slowly, lay at length upon the earth" (309).

With this blessing from her more immediate Other from the domain of the Symbolic, Lily is enabled to complete her painting. The mark on the canvas that completes the painting is one that commemorates the lighthouse and the phallic signifier at the same time that it is a cut reifying the lesson of the Law (see Fleishman and Harrington for dis-cussions of the "central line"). In effect, Lily's brush becomes the blade in the air that Lily frequently imagines. "With a sudden intensity, as if she saw it clear for a second, she drew a line there, in the centre. It was done; it was finished. Yes, she thought, laying down her brush in extreme fatigue, I have had my vision" (310). Her vision, Lacan might conclude, is precisely to picture the place of the Symbolic amidst the turmoil of the Imaginary in human life.[20] As I have suggested before, the stay against confusion effected by Lily's painting and Woolf's novel is only momentary, as is the momentary triumph of the Symbolic over death and mourning. But it seems likely that Lacan and Woolf—as well as Hawthorne and James—would agree that however momentary those Symbolic, aesthetic stays, they are the only ones we shall get. And they may also be all we shall need.

Notes

1. For excellent readings of *To the Lighthouse*, see Apter, Fleishman, Kelley, Leaska, Naremore, Novak, and Rosenthal. The novel has received some of the finest critical attention given to any modern novel, Joyce's and Faulkner's notwithstanding.

2. For various types of psychological or psychoanalytic interpretations of the novel, see Corsa, Di Battista, Gliserman, Lidoff, Lilienfeld, Minow-Pinkney, and Strouse. In the context of my Lacanian reading, one ought especially to see Abel, who says, "Lily Briscoe is Woolf's vehicle for posing a Kleinian challenge to the Freudian/Lacanian narrative" (47).

3. See De Salvo for an insightful, highly focused assessment of Woolf's relations with her family and others during her formative years, the fifteenth year particularly.

4. The chapter on *To the Lighthouse* in Di Battista covers virtually all its Freudian aspects, as well as many others in the novel.

5. Régis Durand has written on the general relation of the registers of the Symbolic and the Imaginary to fictional and other narratives; referring to the example of Melville's *Moby-Dick,* Durand says that the Symbolic mode "would be the successful achievement of the 'family romance,' a linear and non-contradictory discursive and symbolic mode," but the Imaginary mode, "opposed to linear coherence, emphasizes discontinuity, oscillation, and non-differentiation" (51). Durand points out that the tension found between the two modes in Melville is not particularly unusual. It would appear, however, that narratives in the Symbolic mode are more normal, particularly where conventional realism is concerned; Imaginary narratives are likely to be more experimental, possibly more amenable to "modernism." Although I do not follow Durand's model, it is clearly the case that what I shall show of the first and third sections of *To the Lighthouse* fits his definitions. He provides no modality for the Real.

6. Di Battista, in a section called "The Oedipal Dream," is very good on the Oedipal features of the relations among James, his mother, and his father. Her summation is precise: "The Oedipal origins of *To the Lighthouse* determine not only its subject, but its structure. The form of the novel is contained in the dream of a child" (69).

7. See Jane Gallop's witty, incisive discussion of the problems associated with the concept of *jouissance* in the translations of Roland Barthes and the French feminists; unaccountably, Gallop does not refer to Alan Sheridan's remarks about the term in his "Translator's Note" to *Ecrits: A Selection;* moreover, she works binarily in such a way as to avoid the problem introduced.

8. Lacan's comment on the frustrated desire for unity in human life leads him to his remark about the *dérive:* "life is something which goes, as we say in French, *a la dérive.* Life goes down the river, from time to time touching a bank, staying for a while here and there, without understanding anything. . . . The idea of the unifying unity of the human condition has always had on me the effect of a scandalous lie" (Lacan, "Of Structure as an Inmixing," 190).

9. It may be that the shift involves a shift in tropes—the move from a dominance of metaphor to a dominance of metonymy. Teresa L. Ebert has addressed this sort of tropological move in Woolf's *Mrs. Dalloway*. Ebert argues that the tropic modalities are associated with gender differences: metaphor—in its demand for unity—being identified with the feminine; metonymy—because of its dispersiveness—being identified with the masculine. It is certainly clear, as we shall see, that the metonymical dominates the dispersive space of "Time Passes" during the time consciousness or subjectivity is attempting to reassert itself.

10. For a similar thesis see Minow-Pinkney 101. Susan Dick's edition of the holographs of *To the Lighthouse* shows indeed that Woolf had at one time intended to use Mrs. McNab as the narrative perspective of "Time Passes." Jane Marcus says of the old cleaning women: "What Woolf sees in the charwomen's rhythms and words, tunnelling a channel into the obscure origins of language, is the place where art and work meet, where language follows the rhythms of the body" (12-13). In this context, it is perhaps worth noting Marcus's comment on other images in the novel: " 'Time Passes' in all its several versions is a lament for the dead mother. The figure of the empty house, the questioning of the meaning of life, the horror and chaos of the universe, devastation and meaninglessness, is a portrait of the dead mother's body and the daughter's appalling sense of loss. For women *are* their houses" (6).

11. For an interpretation of the novel that focuses on Lily's role and seems contradictory to mine, see Naremore. Where I see Lily as the metapsychological subject-consciousness emerging in the novel's third section, Naremore sees her as the subject minus consciousness there—a condition I would locate in the novel's middle section. "Indeed the whole point," writes Naremore of Lily's point of view in "The Lighthouse," "is that Lily no longer has a consciousness; the intense, dreamy emotion she feels is rendered through the voice of Virginia Woolf, who, by means of a series of intricate metaphors, tries to communicate not what Lily thought but what her experience felt like" (148). From Naremore's comment, one might surmise that Lily ought instead to have been central to "Time Passes," but the fact is that the workings of metaphor and metonymy within Lily's mind do indicate the workings of "depth psychology" and "the psycho-pathology of everyday life" (Naremore 148).

12. Kelley, too, links Lily's praise of the boots to Ramsay's *imago:* "In praising his boots while recognizing that they bear the imprint of his soul, she is in fact praising him, acknowledging his power and importance to her own vision" (140-41).

13. While I would not claim (or disclaim) an allusion here, the lines at the end of *Paradise Lost* I have in mind are:

> The World was all before them, where to choose
> Thir place of rest, and Providence thir guide:
> They hand in hand with wand'ring steps and slow,
> Through *Eden* took thir solitary way. (12.645-49)

Di Battista, in a discussion of Mrs. Ramsay's reciting of "The Fisherman and His Wife," relates the plot and theme of the novel to the myth of Eden and the tale of the Fall (74–88).

14. See Corsa for a discussion of the relation between mourning and James's maturation; see Lilienfeld on the dual, ambivalent nature of the mother in the novel.

15. Di Battista remarks on this passage in the novel: "The name Oedipus in Greek means swollen foot. In the childhood tragedy James stages in his mind, the crushed foot is linked to paternal tyranny. The Oedipal encounter between father and son does not take place at the crossroads, but in a garden, romantically linked here to the lost world of childhood. The garden, though happy, is not innocent of desire" (71).

16. In passages such as this it becomes easy to see why some Lacanians— MacCannell, for example—are so insistent in their critique of the Symbolic's subjugation of women.

17. See Schafer for a book-length discussion of the basic concepts associated with internalization: introjection, identification, and incorporation. Schafer favors the more general term *internalization* for most purposes of description; the other three terms he suggests ought to be used in very specific ways and contexts. By and large, literary critics misuse the terms; I probably shall also.

18. See MacCannell for a discussion of the ways in which Lacan shows that women suffer in cultures subjugated to the Symbolic, rather than operating freely under the aegis of the Imaginary. Her view of the Imaginary, as it might relate to narrative, seems very similar to Durand's; she, too, emphasizes difference, discontinuity, as Durand does. MacCannell writes: "From the symbolic point of view, the particulars and rich imagery associated with male and female, parent and child, ethnicity and politics must be sacrificed as, literally, indifferent; only the concept matters" (174).

19. See Lacan, "The Mirror Stage as Formative of the Function of the I," for a discussion of the necessity of "mirroring" for sexual behavior in some animal species (*Ecrits: A Selection* 3).

20. Lacanian essays on this novel have already appeared. The ones I have seen—those by Lidoff and Minow-Pinkney (see her chapter 4)—are both interesting and instructive, though their foci are different from mine.

Works Cited

Abel, Elizabeth. *Virginia Woolf and the Fictions of Psychoanalysis*. Chicago: University of Chicago Press, 1989.

Apter, T. E. *Virginia Woolf: A Study of Her Novels*. London: Macmillan, 1979.

Bär, Eugen. "Understanding Lacan." In *Psychoanalysis and Contemporary Science*, vol. 3. Ed. Leo Goldberger and Victor H. Rosen. New York: International Universities Press, 1974, 473–544.

Corsa, Helen Storm. "*To the Lighthouse*: Death, Mourning, and Transfiguration." *Literature and Psychology* 21 (1971): 115–31.

De Salvo, Louise A. "1897: Virginia Woolf at Fifteen." In *Virginia Woolf: A Feminist Slant*. Ed. Jane Marcus. Lincoln: University of Nebraska Press, 1983, 78–108.

Di Battista, Maria. *Virginia Woolf's Major Novels: The Fables of Anon*. New Haven: Yale University Press, 1980.

Dick, Susan, ed. *The Original Holograph Draft of "To the Lighthouse."* Toronto: Hogarth, 1983.

Durand, Régis. " 'The Captive King': The Absent Father in Melville's Text." In *The Fictional Father: Lacanian Readings of the Text*. Ed. Robert Con Davis. Amherst: University of Massachusetts Press, 1981, 48–72.

Ebert, Teresa L. "Metaphor, Metonymy, and Ideology: Language and Perception in *Mrs. Dalloway*." *Language and Style* 18, no. 2 (Spring 1985): 152–64.

Felman, Shoshana. "Turning the Screw of Interpretation." *Yale French Studies* 55–56 (1977): 94–207.

Fleishman, Avrom. *Virginia Woolf: A Critical Reading*. Baltimore: Johns Hopkins University Press, 1975.

Gallop, Jane. "Beyond the *Jouissance* Principle." *Representations* 7 (Summer 1984): 110–15.

Gliserman, Martin. "Virginia Woolf's *To the Lighthouse*: Syntax and the Female Center." *American Imago* 40, no. 1 (1983): 51–101.

Harrington, Henry R. "The Central Line down the Middle of *To the Lighthouse*." *Contemporary Literature* 21, no. 3 (1980): 363–82.

Jameson, Fredric. "Imaginary and Symbolic in Lacan: Marxism, Psychoanalytic Criticism, and the Problem of the Subject." *Yale French Studies* 55–56 (1977): 338–95.

———. *The Political Unconscious: Narrative as a Socially Symbolic Act*. Ithaca: Cornell University Press, 1981.

Johnson, Barbara. *The Critical Difference: Essays in the Contemporary Rhetoric of Reading*. Baltimore: Johns Hopkins University Press, 1981.

Kelley, Alice Van Buren. *The Novels of Virginia Woolf: Fact and Vision*. Chicago: University of Chicago Press, 1973.

Lacan, Jacques. "Desire and the Interpretation of Desire in *Hamlet*." *Yale French Studies* 55–56 (1977): 11–52.

———. *Ecrits: A Selection*. Trans. Alan Sheridan. New York: Norton, 1977.

———. "Of Structure as an Inmixing of an Otherness Prerequisite to Any Subject Whatsoever." In *The Structuralist Controversy: The Languages of Criticism and the Sciences of Man*. Ed. Richard Macksey and Eugenio Donato. Baltimore: Johns Hopkins University Press, 1972, 186–200.

———. *Séminaire I*. Paris: Seuil, 1975.

———. *Séminaire III*. Paris: Seuil, 1981.

———. *Séminaire XX*. Paris: Seuil, 1975.

Leaska, Mitchell A. *The Novels of Virginia Woolf: From Beginning to End*. New York: John Jay Press, 1977.

Lemaire, Anika. *Jacques Lacan*. Trans. David Macey. London: Routledge and Kegan Paul, 1977.

Lidoff, Joan. "Virginia Woolf's Feminine Sentence: The Mother-Daughter World of *To the Lighthouse*." *Literature and Psychology* 32 (1986): 43–59.

Lilienfeld, Jane. " 'The Deceptiveness of Beauty': Mother Love and Mother Hate in *To the Lighthouse*." *Twentieth-Century Literature* 23, no. 3 (1977): 345–76.

MacCannell, Juliet Flower. *Figuring Lacan: Criticism and the Cultural Unconscious*. Lincoln: University of Nebraska Press, 1986.

Marcus, Jane. *Virginia Woolf and the Languages of Patriarchy*. Bloomington: Indiana University Press, 1987.

Minow-Pinkney, Mikiko. *Virginia Woolf and the Problem of the Subject*. Brighton: Harvester Press, 1987.

Muller, John P., and William J. Richardson. *Lacan and Language: A Reader's Guide to "Ecrits."* New York: International Universities Press, 1982.

Naremore, James. *The World without a Self: Virginia Woolf and the Novel*. New Haven: Yale University Press, 1973.

Novak, Jane. *The Razor Edge of Balance: A Study of Virginia Woolf*. Coral Gables: University of Miami Press, 1975.

Pratt, Annis. "Sexual Imagery in *To the Lighthouse*." *Modern Fiction Studies* 18 (1972): 417–31.

Ragland-Sullivan, Ellie. *Jacques Lacan and the Philosophy of Psychoanalysis*. Urbana: University of Illinois Press, 1986.

Rosenthal, Michael. *Virginia Woolf*. New York: Columbia University, 1979.

Schafer, Roy. *Aspects of Internalization*. New York: International Universities Press, 1968.

Strouse, Louise F. "Virginia Woolf—Her Voyage Back." *American Imago* 38, no. 2 (1981): 185–202.

White, Hayden V. *Metahistory: The Historical Imagination in Nineteenth-Century Europe*. Baltimore: Johns Hopkins University Press, 1973.

———. *Tropics of Discourse: Essays in Cultural Criticism*. Baltimore: Johns Hopkins University Press, 1978.

Wilden, Anthony. "Lacan and the Discourse of the Other." In *Speech and Language in Psychoanalysis* by Jacques Lacan. Trans. Anthony Wilden. Baltimore: Johns Hopkins University Press, 1981, 159–311. Orig. pub. as *The Language of the Self: The Function of Language in Psychoanalysis,* 1968.

Woolf, Virginia. *To the Lighthouse*. New York: Harcourt, Brace, and World, 1927.

Using Lacan, Reading Otherwise

To conclude this study of ways of using Lacan in reading works of fiction, I would like to look at several recent studies of Lacan and Lacanian theory that in revealing other dimensions of the man and the work also suggest other uses of Lacan—a reading of Lacan otherwise by readers who are "other" in the theory. All the studies are by women. One of these, Shoshana Felman's *Jacques Lacan and the Adventure of Insight*, looks at the question of Lacan's original contributions to psychoanalysis from a perspective different from the one I took in my introduction. Another, Catherine Clément's *The Lives and Legends of Jacques Lacan*, adds a dimension to that same question, but in addition raises the issue of Lacan and gender that has become so important in current critical theory and practice. A third, Juliet Flower MacCannell's *Figuring Lacan*, takes the issue of gender considerably further in the book's feminist reading of Lacanian theory, particularly as it pertains to Lacan's notions of metaphor and metonymy. Finally, a fourth, Christine van Boheemen's *The Novel as Family Romance*, draws a feminist reading of the genre of the novel toward a Lacanian history of the genre. These four works thus suggest the wide range that Lacanian theory and practice may cover, for it may be employed in analysis of psychoanalysis itself, as in Felman, in analysis of social and political movements, as in Clément, in analysis of general cultural formations, as in MacCannell, and in analysis of literature along both its paradigmatic and syntagmatic axes, as in Boheemen. Moreover, these four works indicate not only that there are other ways of using Lacan, but also that women, despite Lacan's claim that *the* woman does not exist, have found Lacan a particularly useful, albeit always challenging, theorist.

Felman's *Jaques Lacan and the Adventure of Insight* is not as systematic in its extrapolation of Lacanian theory as, say, Ellie Ragland-

Sullivan's *Jacques Lacan and the Philosophy of Psychoanalysis* (1986) or Anika Lemaire's *Jacques Lacan* (1970; trans. 1977), but, then, it is not meant to be that kind of book. It is rather more personal, in many ways, than the usual scholarly book, for the adventure of insight to which Felman refers in her title is her own adventure. The insight pertains to her own view of the world as much as it does her view of Lacan or the Lacanian view itself. Thus, as a book, Felman's belongs to a genre formed by Catherine Clément's *The Lives and Legends of Jacques Lacan* (1983), Stuart Schneiderman's *Jacques Lacan: The Death of an Intellectual Hero* (1983), and Jane Gallop's *Reading Lacan* (1985). These other three, like Felman, offer rather personal "adventures" with Lacanian theory. In three of the cases (Felman, Gallop, and Schneiderman), moreover, the author decided to undergo psychoanalysis, not only as a means to self-awareness, but also as a way to understand Lacan and psychoanalysis better. Thus, when Felman analyzes the specimen story of psychoanalysis, the Oedipus story that forms the core of her work, she gives us yet one more example of what may be viewed as the specimen story of the Lacanians as well.

Whereas in my Introduction my argument for the originality of Lacan for literary analysis lies in his powerful emphasis on language, Felman offers another argument that substantiates my view and, moreover, is interesting in its own right. Though not concerned immediately with Lacan's originality, Felman suggests early on that her fundamental assumption regarding Lacan is that he offers a new way of reading, "a theory of reading that opens up into a rereading of the world as well as into a rereading of psychoanalysis itself" (9). She demonstrates this thesis in chapters 1 and 2, called "Renewing the Practice of Reading, or Freud's Unprecedented Lesson" and "The Case of Poe: Applications/Implications of Psychoanalysis." In the former, where one suspects she does not give enough credit to Freud's "Constructions in Analysis," Felman suggests that what Lacan has added to Freud's theory of reading the unconscious is that "the activity of reading is not just the analyst's, it is also the analysand's: interpreting is what takes place *on both sides* of the analytic situation" (21). In the second chapter, Felman addresses in more detail what it is that Lacan brings to analysis (literary, in this case, since the focus is on Poe's "Purloined Letter"). Here she is more persuasive, for she focuses on the notion of the signifier that does distinguish Lacan from Freud. She assesses such Freudian interpretations of Poe as Joseph Wood Krutch's and Marie

Bonaparte's, as well as Lacan's own. She focuses on the repetition compulsion as it manifests itself in Poe's tale, as well as in the way it is treated by Bonaparte, for example, and Lacan. While Bonaparte emphasizes the concept of identity in repetition, Lacan emphasizes difference. "For Lacan, what is repeated in the text is not the content of a fantasy but the symbolic displacement of a signifier through the insistence of a signifying chain; repetition is not of *sameness* but of *difference*, not of independent terms or of analogous themes but of a structure of differential interrelationships, in which what *returns* is always *other*" (43). But more than this, says Felman, the second repetitive scene in Poe's tale becomes important for Lacan because, as a scene of the repetition of the same with a crucial, analytic difference, that scene is an allegory of analysis itself.

The themes of repetition and difference lead Felman to her main claim regarding Lacan's originality. Oddly enough, she addresses this theme in a chapter whose title asks "What Difference Does Psychoanalysis Make?" and is given the alternative title "The Originality of Freud." "Simply put, the originality of Lacan," says Felman, "lies in his radical understanding of the radicality of Freud's discovery, and in his eagerness to carry the consequences of this discovery to their logical limits. In so doing, Lacan assesses and thinks out not just the significance of psychoanalysis but, specifically, the significance of the difference that it makes, of the difference it has introduced into Western culture. Lacan's originality, in other words, lies in his uncompromising inquiry into the originality of psychoanalysis" (53). But Lacan's originality is also related to repetition for Lacan insists on a return to Freud. Freud stands in relation to Lacan as the origin of a trauma stands to its expression in a symptom. Lacan's relation to Freud is thus defined in terms of *Nächträglichkeit*. "Freud's discovery of the unconscious can thus itself be looked at as a sort of primal scene, a cultural trauma, whose meaning—or originality in cultural history—comes to light only through Lacan's significantly transferential, symptomatic repetition" (54). As to the difference that psychoanalysis makes, Felman suggests that it lies in its focus on a new center of knowledge—the subject, rather than the object. Freud thus introduced a "new and unprecedented *mode of reflexivity*," one that stresses asymmetry rather than symmetry between the "self departed from and the self returned to" (60). But to Freud, Lacan adds a further twist; where Freud focuses on the "revolutionized status of the center and of centrality," Lacan

stresses the "revolutionized conception of the very moment of re-
volving. Freud therefore emphasizes the revolutionized *observed*—the
resulting revolutionized image of the human mind; Lacan brings out the
implication of the revolutionized scientific *status of the observer*"
(65). This shift, to Felman, represents a reorientation of the world.
What Freud introduced was a shift as radical as the shift from a Ptol-
emaic to a Copernican astronomy. The shift from Freud to Lacan is
less radical, but is no less important. Felman suggests that the "orbit"
of knowledge, for Lacan, becomes not circular, but elliptical, a shift
that, appropriately, reflects the difference not between Copernicus and
Ptolemy, but that between Copernicus and Kepler.

Felman pursues Lacan's originality further in a later, much longer
chapter called "Beyond Oedipus: The Specimen Story of Psychoanalysis." Constituting more than a third of the entire book, the chapter
looks at narrative and narrative interpretation from the perspective,
one might say, of the self-reflexive modernist or postmodernist novelist.
Felman begins with the concept of "the key narrative," the story that,
like the tale of Oedipus for Freud, validates both a theory and a practice. For Felman, however, the Oedipus story, like the relation of
Copernicus to Kepler, is also a key to Lacan's relation to Freud. "I
would suggest," writes Felman, "that an exploration . . . of the way in
which the Oedipus mythic reference holds the key to a Lacanian psychoanalytic understanding . . . may hold the key in turn to the crux
of Lacan's innovative insight into what Freud discovered and, consequently, into what psychoanalysis is all about" (102). The crux of
Felman's analysis here lies in her assessment of the difference between
two pairs of works: *Oedipus the King* and *Oedipus at Colonus* on the
one hand, and Freud's *Interpretation of Dreams* and *Beyond the Pleasure Principle* on the other. The way beyond Oedipus, as Felman explains it, lies in the story of Oedipus, blind and dying, in exile at
Colonus. At Colonus, Oedipus faces death and at last becomes the
Other—or assumes the sought-after Other in himself. Felman, in her
story, takes each protagonist—Oedipus, Freud, and Lacan—through the
meaning of Colonus, and in the end takes psychoanalysis through Colonus, as well. As Lacan talks about *Oedipus at Colonus*, she says,
"he is telling and retelling not just Freud's, and his own, psychoanalytic
story but the very story of psychoanalysis, seen from Colonus: the
story of Freud's going beyond Freud, of Oedipus' going beyond Oedipus, the story of psychoanalysis' inherent, radical, and destined self-

expropriation" (148). Beyond the king lies Colonus; beyond Colonus lies death, the Other, the always unknowable end and—perhaps—aim of analysis.

From among that genre of "adventures of insight" comprised of those books by Felman, Clément, Schneiderman, and Gallop, Clément's is the one I want to look at in a bit more detail. Though Gallop, Clément, and Schneiderman all are useful and interesting because of the importance of Lacan to a moment in twentieth-century intellectual history, Clément's is the one that looks at that moment virtually from the inside, not quite from Lacan's perspective, but from very close to it. As I indicated in my introduction, Lacan became one of the more important figures to emerge from the foment of French structuralism and post-structuralism during the past quarter century or so. Now Lacan's career, to be sure, goes back at least to the early 1930s when he was taking his medical degree and writing a thesis in psychiatry. His first book was that thesis *De la psychose paranoïaque dans ses rapports avec la personnalité* (1932), but a portion of it had already been published in *Annales médico-psychologiques* in 1931, and later (1933) its other two essays were also separately published in *Le minotaure*. The three essays forming the medical thesis helped prepare Lacan's thought for his most innovative theory, that of the mirror stage, outlined first in a paper of 1936, revised in a paper of 1949, and eventually published in Lacan's major collection, the *Ecrits* of 1966. Lacan's influence beyond France's borders really started with *Ecrits*, but his fame (or, more to the point, notoriety) began in earnest in 1953 when he was "excommunicated" by the International Psychoanalytic Association, an event followed in 1964 by the formation of his own school, *L'école freudienne*, later to be dissolved by Lacan (in 1980) in an act as controversial as the excommunication itself. Though by the mid-1980s seminars on Lacan at the Modern Language Association convention were drawing standing-room-only crowds, the fact is, however much we may have read—or read about—him, most of us understand Lacan today no better (probably less well) than we understand Barthes, Foucault, Derrida, or Lévi-Strauss. Clément helps us to understand the man as well as the work.

In *The Lives and Legends of Jacques Lacan*, Clément writes on Lacan from the perspective of one who knew him and who sat in on the famed seminars he conducted in the *école freudienne*. Clément tells us of the exciting discovery of Lacan by her and other philosophy students in the 1960s. To these students, Lacan was a "magical" figure. He was not a certified *normalien* or professor in the usual sense, but he certainly had much to profess in his weekly lectures, and he drew an astonishing range of people to (what can only be called) his performances. Those who came included psychoanalysts and regular university students in a variety of disciplines, of course, but also writers, actors, and journalists. "Seldom did we leave the auditorium without some aphorism capable of stimulating an almost indescribable state of meditative euphoria," writes Clément (13). "Little by little, hour by hour, week by week there was woven in us an implacable mesh of language, unconscious but effective, that had the property of rendering all other modes of thought obsolete." Lacan's delivery ranged from the tedious to the brilliant, and his speech was often slow, halting, and no louder than a whisper, but his audience took it in. "We thought about what he had said," Clément remarks, "but even more about the enigma of what he might have meant." His fame and influence were assured when he became not only a man, but a mode of thought. "In the end we forgot Lacan's thought and thought Lacan. We passed him on as the Greek rhetoricians probably passed on their teaching: bit by bit, by means of endless citation." Says Clément, "Anyone who did not immediately walk away in disgust was caught. This is how a dogma is born" (13).

Given the nature of the personal experience, the adventure of insight, Clément records, *dogma,* indeed, is the proper word to describe Lacan's teachings. The man's words drew an almost religious reverence to them, and, what is more, those words came to be written down by others, by disciples, as it were, whose names might have been Matthew, Mark, Luke, and John. Clément in fact uses a mythical figure to organize her picture of Lacan, but the figure is not Jesus: rather, it is the phoenix, the fabled firebird who regenerates itself in a fire fueled by its own fundament. The firebird permits Clément to suggest the self-destructive and regenerative capabilities Lacan manifested in his relations to the International Association of Psychoanalysis and in his quixotic dissolution of his own school. But the figure also allows her to suggest Lacan's ambivalence about his own roles. He seems to alternate between the masks of the public prophet and the private shaman, for he was the dedicated public clinician-teacher who, privately, became the seemingly mad magician, a Prospero who would throw away his book. Clément wants to help us understand not the former, but the elements of the latter in Lacan. To do so she speaks of the shaman. Shamans, she says, are comic, androgynous, possessed of unknown tongues, capable of astonishing tricks upon their own bodies, of therapeutic functions upon the bodies of others, and of containing the language and culture of their people. Lacan, Clément says, was not physically the shaman.

> With him everything was transposed into the key of language. Acrobatics, levitation, poetic stigmata—all these were included in his panoply. A sort of linguistic transvestite, he found in the fantasies of women a passion for language that constantly obsessed him. He identified with their tortures, their anguish. Incorruptible, invulnerable, he gave the impression—he, the 'subject-supposed-to-know'—of being untouchable and always ready to be reborn. A traveler in ancient and foreign linguistic realms, he was the repository of the language and culture of the psychoanalysts, notwithstanding their rejection of him—*meglio ancor*. A therapist, he treated his own language and hence the language of others as well. A comedian, he made people laugh, he was playful. He was strictly abnormal, as any man with the body of a bird and a skeleton of iron would have to be. Lame, awkward of build, he was both heroic and foolish, grandiose and ridiculous with his feathers and his bow-tie. Hopping about from place to place in the hope of avoiding his fate, he was old-fashioned, retrograde, obsolete—and timeless. (49–50)

But illuminating as such flights of metaphor can be, Clément explains more prosaic, but equally valuable things as well. She discusses, for example, some of the social history involving Lacan, the International Psychoanalytic Association, the *école freudienne,* and, later, the 1968 student rebellion in France and the country's move toward the political left. Clément (like Schneiderman) also treats such matters as Lacan's variable short session (as opposed to the traditional "fifty-minute hour") and the matter of the training of psychoanalysts. Although Clément does not pretend to give us a biography of Lacan, she nonetheless manages amid her very personal asides and flights of poetic enfigurations to suggest the life, at least as it can be related through his religious background (Catholic), his education, his marriage (to a Jew), his public crises, and his emerging philosophy of psychoanalysis (to use Ellie Ragland-Sullivan's term). Clément shows just how much Lacan belonged to a culture of psychoanalysis, but she also shows just how French and even Christian were Lacan's ideas in comparison with the distinctly Germanic and Jewish ones of Freud. But like Felman, Clément also shows how Lacan went back to Freud, how he "re-read" Freud and reinterpreted such case studies of Freud's as those of Dora, Judge Schreber, and the dream of the butcher's beautiful wife. Perhaps best and most interesting of all, perhaps because it becomes so personal, is Clément's discussion of Lacan's "ladies' way," for everything, even the clinical basis of the mirror stage, adverts to women and their fantasies, as Clément shows in her discussions of the women subjects— Aimée, Marcelle, and the Papin sisters—of Lacan's psychiatric thesis. Clément's discussion of Lacan and women is part of a massive dialogue that has gone on during the past two decades and more and involves many of the most important figures in Lacanian or post-Freudian scholarship—Juliet Mitchell and Jacqueline Rose, editors of Lacan's *Feminine Sexuality,* and Julia Kristeva and Luce Irigaray, authors of various books with a distinctly Lacanian and feminist slant, and Ellie Ragland-Sullivan, whose final chapter—"Beyond the Phallus?"—to *Jacques Lacan and the Philosophy of Psychoanalysis* offers a very useful critique of Lacanian theory in regard to female identity. It is this essentially feminist interest—the reading otherwise—that I would like now to take up more directly, for it represents one of the most important aspects of Lacan's interest for today's literary and social critics.

Clément's feminist critique of Lacanian theory is radically extended in Juliet Flower MacCannell's *Figuring Lacan.* Though she reveals an apparently more negative view in an earlier book, *The Weary Sons of Freud,* here Clément is finally more affirmative on Lacanian theory from the feminist angle than MacCannell. MacCannell regards Lacan positively, but is distressed by what Lacanian theory posits for the female in Western culture. For MacCannell the issue hangs on the distinction between truth and knowledge. Lacan comes down on the side of truth. As virtually everyone these days perceives, Lacan is more like the literary artist who is to be read, explicated, interpreted for his truth, than the scientist or philosopher whose works of knowledge are thought to be objective, totally transparent, and unneedful of constructive or deconstructive critique. In the face of this traditional dichotomy, these days most intellectuals understand that no works—putatively literary or otherwise—are necessarily beyond what must be termed imaginative interpretation. And more than most, Lacan himself has contributed to the intellectual dilemma that confronts truth by knowledge. In *Figuring Lacan,* MacCannell suggests that Lacan's role, in part, has been in the devaluation of "knowledge" and "the subject who is supposed to know" in favor of a play of discourse that creates "the techniques of the exclusion of truth by means of knowledge" (xix). It is not that Lacan valorizes discourse as truth; it is simply that he recognizes that knowledge in any culture is always a product of discourse. Thus, if one is to be intellectually free, one must always both construct and deconstruct discourses. The frame within which such a seemingly contradictory project might occur, MacCannell argues, is provided for Lacan by a philosophical-literary tradition that includes, among others, Hegel, Rousseau, Stendhal, Pascal, and Joyce. But MacCannell bears out Hayden White's contention that we live in an "absurdist moment," for, paradoxically, read inside this deconstructive frame, Lacan exhibits a system of his own that one may also construct. "I wrote this book because I was convinced, after reading through Lacan," says Mac-Cannell, "that he had a 'system.' I found that, as I read him, I began to be able to predict how he would handle certain themes, certain topics. But I was not at all convinced that his critics and analysts had adequately described that system. I am equally convinced that that system constituted an important new departure for examining, and perhaps beginning to cure, certain of the (unconscious) ills of cultural life" (xix–xx).

Analyzed from within her feminist perspective, the source of the cultural cure is identified in a chapter on metaphor and metonymy at the end of part 1. Why MacCannell focuses on tropes may not be immediately obvious, for though one suspects she would rather regard herself as a "social" or "materialist" or merely "objective" feminist critic, her approach is not tropological in the mode defined by White in works such as *Metahistory* and *Tropics of Discourse.* One of her feminist aims is to show that rather than being phallo- or perhaps phallogo-centric himself in any ideological way, Lacan exposes the method by which the valorization of metaphor in economy, as well as in psychoanalysis, *sub*jects women by making them subordinate to the authority of the male. Her major theme regarding Lacanian theory, therefore, is that Lacan exposes the "gendering" of metaphor and metonymy, the two tropes on which Lacan's structuralism (rooted in

Jakobson et al.) is based. For MacCannell, metaphor is masculine, metonymy is feminine. Such a gendering of tropes means that metaphor dominates metonymy. It also means that the metonymic domain of human life—the family and society, both of which are rooted in the mother—is inevitably placed in a role secondary to the father, a domain including the paternal metaphor, the rule of metaphoric Law, and the metaphor of the regnant Other. *None* of these, MacCannell argues, exists or ever existed in any material sense; they exist only as posited in the structure of metaphor itself (see my Introduction for a discussion of that structure). Thus, in MacCannell's view, it is plain that where metonymy always has a material basis, metaphor neither does nor can. Metaphor is thus tied to philosophical idealism, metonymy to a realistic, not merely nominalistic, materialism.

But MacCannell argues that culture does not have to operate this way. The Symbolic order, which is identified with civilization and the paternal and built on metaphor, is really only an economy, a system of differential values, not a priori essences. MacCannell argues that culture can be changed if these merely differential values are opened to change. She argues that for Lacan civilization is a vast unconscious that can work on us only through its "executive arm"—which is value itself (125). What happens in the executive transactions of culture is that humans substitute hypostatized *values* for material *meanings* (126). Therein—in the merely symbolic value—lies the triumph of the Symbolic, which (like metaphor) is only an ideal realm. MacCannell's attack on the Symbolic thus must inevitably relocate value to the other register, the one Lacan calls the Imaginary. Admittedly, where some Lacanians are concerned, this argument presents certain structural difficulties. But some Lacanians have made the same reversal. MacCannell refers to Anthony Wilden's valorization of the Imaginary over the Symbolic and relates his position to Laura Mulvey's discussion of the cinema's Imaginary ways to break out of the hegemony of the Symbolic. MacCannell suggests, however, that where Wilden sees one's resort to the Imaginary as a negative trap, she would regard it positively as the only way out (133). MacCannell then shows that Lacan himself outlines strategies of resistance to the Symbolic along several lines, one of which—the need to resist "the morality of the Symbolic Order" (138)—provides a focal point for her discussion of "Kant *avec* Sade," one of Lacan's most radical texts.

Lacan's aim, says MacCannell, is to create a society not of laws, but of human beings (149). To do that, one must counter the "drive of the Symbolic to break up 'natural' and conscious relationships" (149). "What we have failed to notice," says MacCannell, "is that that 'principle' has a very particular form, the rhetorical one of metaphor, carried to a higher power, abstracted to the level of values beyond worth, the form of negation-in-the-mode-of-free-choice. And in the new, the economical order, it cannot remain anchored or attached to meaning. It must be content-free, able to move on to symbolise, mediate and render unconscious any social arrangement, any particular economic order" (149-50). In a sense, MacCannell's hope for what she sees as Lacan's new ideology of the *metonymic* is merely to capture the drive of culture (and thus of the Symbolic) and to put it to a better use—not merely to perpetuate itself, but to counter our alienation within a culture subsumed in the Symbolic. What's more, Lacan's work, for her, is a "constant critique of one-ness and individualism—the ideological forms of the 'one' which create the 'Other' " (160). MacCannell thus proposes a turn to a culture of desire, rather than repression, a culture not of metaphor, but of metonymy in order to effect "a retrieval of connection, [and thus] a loss of isolation" (160). Lacan's ultimate aim, she says, would be to reframe "the ideology of love beyond the Law" (172). Toward that end, she would propose that the complex formed by Law/Other/Metaphor must not prevent "natural, necessary and pleasurable combinations" (172) as they are empowered by metonymy.

In the book's final chapter, MacCannell makes her most radical claims built on the distinctions between metaphor and metonymy. She argues that Lacan recognizes not one, but two versions of the unconscious. The first is a "place outside of metaphoric enclosures" that may never have existed. The second, formed by "the fall into alienated desire" (156), is always negative and, alas, provides the basis of our civilization. The first, associated with desire, originates in the *eros* of the family, the site of "the sheer pleasures of association" (156); it must also be regarded as opposed to the *polis,* culture, civilization (158). It is located in a scene of what "*could have been between* human beings" (156) had it not been displaced by the second. The second unconscious is associated with the Symbolic, the civilized scene; it is "the scene of alienation, order and negation—the scene of culture" (157). The first, uncivilized, culturally resistant unconscious is dominated by metonymy, the second by metaphor (158). "Finally," says MacCannell, "what metaphor fathers is only the Other" (161).

MacCannell's claim that the metaphoric is reduced to the visual signifier, the "little letter" that covers over an invisible spirit—all "mere markings become signifiers" (164)—leads her to an analysis of Lacan's notion of the *petit a* and the drive. The "little letter" (the *other* spelled with the lowercase) is "*the* point on which the drive turns, swerving from its 'aim' (satisfaction), toward putting itself on a circular path of the signifier. For Lacan, the conceptual drive is inherent in the signifier" (166). But the drive suffers the same scission from the reality of the sexual as do the other metaphor-dominated terms in Lacan's economy (as MacCannell describes it). The drive, because of the advent of desire, displaces the original *aim* (which is, purely and simply, *satisfaction*) by the *object* that is regarded as the means of satisfaction. With the drive displaced onto the object, the human subject is caught in a never-ending circuit of desire. "The object as pseudo-aim, then, is also the source of the metaphoric drive toward substitutability" (166). The *objet a* is thus, on the one hand, "the by-product or nuclear waste of me-taphoric fission" (166)—"a *metonym*, a rejected connection"; "on the other, as a signifier, an incipient metaphor, it is the *objet a* of which Lacan speaks" (167). MacCannell thus concludes that the *objet a,* which is often misunderstood, is "the switch point . . . for the analytic cure" and "for the power culture has over us" (167). In a densely packed passage, MacCannell explains the process:

> When seen in the field of the Other, the object appears at that point where the alienating process of desire begins (the translation of satisfiable need into the insatiable demand for love), where the split between the ego-ideal and the ideal ego becomes definitive. In this gap, this split, this cut, the object appears not as a means to satisfaction, but as an obstacle to it. A 'good' object from the point of view of alienated desire because it blocks immediate satisfactions and raises the subject to the level of the Other; a 'bad' object from the point of view of the subject because it is not the Other's demanded love, but only one of the 'proofs of love.' It has 'come' from the Other, which also means that it has somehow fallen from the level of the Other, is a signifier of the subject's separation from the other. With the potential for be-coming, nonetheless, a medium of exchange with the other. (167)

Lacan's model of the transference, MacCannell suggests, is "the only counter to the drive of the signifier" (168). To explain how this transference works, MacCannell, in a very difficult passage, focuses on Freud's Dora and Kleist's *Penthesilea*. In her discussion of Freud's case history of Dora, MacCannell seems simply to make the ordinary feminist claim that it was really Freud who revealed his love of Dora, rather than the reverse. "More importantly, what he is also proving—demonstrating with his very being—is the law of the separation of the sexes, the failure of heterosexuality, the law of Oedipus and of civilisation" (169). In this scene, as MacCannell interprets it, Freud might have overthrown the ideology of civilized "love" had, ironically, he not been "too 'civilised' to touch her" (169). Touching her, Freud would have stepped outside the prison of culture and recognized not her desire, but his own demand (beyond the insatiable drive) for connection, a demand for physical satisfaction apart from the ideology of the sexual or genderfication. For MacCannell, Dora represents a case of the almost successful return to metonymy, demand, the sign, the maternal: "The *objet petit a*—the little thing, the penis—is *almost* revalued by this transference, this connection that is *almost* made. The [real] penis is almost retrieved from the [Symbolic] phallic, the metaphoric drive, disrupted by Freud's love for Dora—'outside the limits of the law, where alone it may live' as Lacan put it" (169-70). MacCannell's point here, as I understand it, is that instead of recognizing his own love of Dora, Freud translated her ostensible love of him into just another affirmation of the phallocentric in culture, thereby displacing himself from her as a real person toward a metaphorized relation of her to a Symbolic value—whether phallus, father, or Other. Thus, perhaps inevitably, Freud merely capitulates to the Law of culture and covers over once again the original metonymical (maternal) unconscious by the second—and secondary—unconscious defined by metaphor (and the father).

In MacCannell's view, Lacan—when properly understood—would enable human beings to reframe the ideology of love beyond the constrictions of phallocentric Law. Her argument in the last several pages of the book is very dense, but, again, it can be reduced to her general claim not for oneness or unity, but twoness or multiplicity. *Her* Lacan argues for the latter and against the universalization of the concept; he argues for the revalorization of the concrete, the material, the phenomenological. She shows, for example, how the concept underlying

romantic love—to make *one;* to make the child—"requires the construction of an *ideal* love alternative to narcissistic and familial *eros*"
(173). But this ideal love merely covers over (and thus, by its structure,
metaphorizes) the biological and cultural imperative to produce a child
from the genital union of the sexes. In this negative, romantic love-
ideal, there is nevertheless a retreat or displacement from the concrete
toward the abstract. A "supplementary order appears," and " 'love' is
not simply a set of charming images, logically related so as to produce
a desired end—the child, cultural surplus—but a promise—of something
even more significant, more valuable"—the *concept* of union, unity,
oneness (173). Such a "sacrifice" of the concrete, MacCannell insists,
is precisely what one must resist and what Lacanian theory makes it
possible to resist. The tragedy of culture—the Symbolic, as opposed
to the Imaginary—is captured in MacCannell's final, ironic words of
the last chapter: "*E pluribus unum:* one god, one people. From the
symbolic point of view, the particulars and rich imagery associated
with male and female, parent and child, ethnicity and politics must be
sacrificed as, literally, indifferent: only the concept matters: *'faire un'* "
(174).

Building on these several, largely feminist approaches to the life and
work of Lacan, I want now to turn to a fruitful use of a feminist
Lacanian poetics in the analysis of the genre of fiction, specifically the
novel. In my estimation the most illuminating recent discussion of the
relationship between fiction and Lacanian principles of psychoanalysis
is that by Christine van Boheemen. *The Novel as Family Romance*
makes a clear Lacanian case for what previously I have regarded as
the intertextual relationship between fictions and human psychic identity. Boheemen takes a position not really much different from the
premises underlying the work of Peter Brooks and Ragland-Sullivan I
considered toward the end of my Introduction, though Boheemen gives
no evidence that she relies on either of these. The especial usefulness
of Boheemen to my project lies in the staging of the premises of her
presentation of an essentially Lacanian study of literary history. The
basic premises are outlined in chapter 1, "The Fiction of Identity/The
Identity of Fiction" (13–43). There, she makes several crucial moves.
First, she insists that there is a determinative interaction between literary narratives and our constitution of a self-identity. Second, she
bases this point on the Lacanian premise that language itself is fun-

damental to any subjectivity whatever. Third, she argues that the novel-as-a-genre is built upon three premises essential to Lacanian theory: that the self is unable to establish itself as a subject without language; that the self must inevitably form itself around the structure of differences built into language as a system; and that the identification of the self with the father in the Oedipal passage alienates one irreparably from the mother. Beyond the staging of a Lacanian poetics of the novel, Boheemen takes up other themes of great importance to contemporary theory, including the questions of "realism," the "subject," patriarchy, modernity, and feminist criticism itself. In short, Boheemen sets up a Lacanian poetics and history of the genre of the novel, but she does so with much of the Lacanian theory taken as a presupposition, as an often unstated set of assumptions. She takes the view, in other words, that the assumption of an authority in Lacanian theory is adequate to describe both literary and psychoanalytic texts and to describe as well the intertextual relation between the two forms of discourse.

I shall begin with Boheemen's premises regarding the position of language in relation to identity and textuality. Boheemen is much more willing than Brooks (in "The Idea of a Psychoanalytic Criticism") to admit the intertextual nature of the relationship between the self and the text in the process of reading or interpretation. One reason for her willingness is the grounding of her argument in Lacanian theory regarding language and human subjectivity. The human subject, she says, " 'inscribes' himself or herself in culture through language" (15). But that inscribed relationship is not one we always readily acknowledge. She adverts to two of Lacan's remarks: first, "man speaks, then, but it is because the symbol has made him man"; second, " 'that he sustains [himself] as [a] subject' means that language allows him to regard himself as the scene-shifter, or even the director of the entire imaginary capture of which he would otherwise be nothing more than the living marionette" (*Ecrits: A Selection* 64, 272). But she recognizes that our inscription in/by language is not one we always willingly acknowledge. "Since we seem to believe that our relationship to the medium [of language] is one of perfect mastery rather than dialogic interdependence, we also fail to inquire how and to what extent not merely the idea of subjectivity but its conceptual configuration depends upon identification with the structural patterning of language and culture," that which another would call " 'the secondary modeling' of customs,

models, and roles" (15). Thus, for Boheemen as for Lacan, our identities come to us from somewhere else, from something that exists
prior to us and outside ourselves—from an Other, yes, but from an
Other that exists within language.

The way by which our "identities" come to us, Boheemen argues
more specifically, is through narratives, stories, tales told us, and tales
of ourselves we tell. These stories may express our unique individu-
alities, but the forms of those stories are not unique. They are inherited,
though not through our genes. Rather, those forms are a transmission
of culture through the agency of language. Through them, she suggests,
we learn the models, the laws, of our culture. "The significance of our
stories derives from their relation to the models of signification op-
erative in our society—causality, centrism, linearity, and teleology,"
laws that "are our inescapable unconscious heritage" (13). Her summary on the importance of narrative is unequivocal:

> I suggest that narrative provides an unconscious pattern of cultural
> conditioning, a grammar of structuration, about which we reflect
> as little as about the grammar of our mother tongue. Though it
> usually remains unconscious, its importance is tremendous. From
> infancy, the world and the "self" are mediated through the formal
> and semantic patterns this grammar of structuration imposes. Our
> lives enact these patterns, and our identity is molded and defined
> by the slots, channels, and grids the collective discourse allows.
> (14)

But the basic form of the collective discourse is oriented toward
one parent and one gender more than the other. The view Boheemen
offers here is essentially Lacanian. The realization of identity that results
from all those culturally transmitted narratives is keyed to the father.
The rule she outlines here is strictly Oedipal, though at this point in
her argument she does not specify the conventional psychoanalytic
structure. Her focus, to begin with, is on the family, the positioning
of the child within the structure that later will yield the "romance."
The baby, she says (speaking specifically of Joyce's Stephen Dedalus),
"is part of a family, the most elementary form of social structure. More
specifically, the realization of his own identity coincides with the acknowledgment of the differences from but basic similarity to the father.
This, in turn, positions the child in relationship to his medium, language. It is the father who tells the story [in the Joycean example]. He

is the source of language, authority, and order. He controls and provides the medium for the projection of self-identity" (15). Though Boheemen's remarks here are directed to the example of Joyce's Dedalus, her general theme relates to all subjects, male and female alike, for, as she will insist later, the premises of those engendering narratives belong to a patriarchal culture. The structures of awareness, of knowledge, and of identity will inevitably take on the shapes of that patriarchy, for those stories are "designed" precisely to teach its laws. Thus, says Boheemen, "the transmission of the story from father to son establishes more than the sexual identification of the child. It simultaneously generates, proves, and transmits the authority of the father as the origin of meaning and identity, and it valorizes the transmission of cultural identity in language over the biological reproduction of the species" (16). Her thesis, one that is manifestly Lacanian rather than Freudian, is radically clear:

> First, the self cannot make itself present as self-conscious subject except through language. Second, the language by means of which the self positions itself as self-conscious subject is language that has already undergone a secondary semantic modeling, so that the subject forms itself through identification with a structure of differences. Finally, identification with the story of the father means irremediable alienation from the mother, from a sense of full, symbiotic presence. What we have reached here is a paradox. Without language, there is no subjectivity, no culture, but subjectivity and self-consciousness imply a transcendent alienation from nature, a forgetful repression. We might say that the advent of consciousness, entailing the inescapable lack of full presence, reenacts the biblical Fall in each individual life. (16–17)

From this summation, Boheemen moves to another position that is very significant for literature and literary criticism. She suggests that, more than other genres, the novel, as the dominant narrative form in Western culture, "functions psychologically to cover over the scars left by the separation from nature" (17). She thus grants to the novel, as her paradigm of cultural narrative, a tremendously important role in Western culture. Moreover, her argument for that role is expressly Lacanian, though her initial illustration of how the novel may serve that pervasive psychological function is from Freud's discussion of the *Fort! Da!* game, which she in turn relates to D. W. Winnicott. She

relates the function of the child's bobbin in the game of "here/there"—
or similar games played by or with children such as "peek-a-boo" or
"gone-gone"—to the function of the "transitional object" outlined in
Winnicott. The games or the transitional objects, she suggests, help
the child to master the anxiety caused by the absence of the mother.
This mastery occurs, as Lacan insists, through language, but, she argues
(rightly, I suspect), it is *patterned* language, "language patterned as ritual
play, poetry almost" (17), patterned as one might see (I would suggest)
in the child's "lalling" (Greek: *lalia:* chatter) tendencies, the early echo-
lalia in which the child plays with sounds in repetitive, often—to parents—in maddeningly distracting ways. Boheemen turns to Lacan for
further support. "In other terms," she says, "we might argue that one
of the important functions of patterned language is to heal or dress
the wound of human alienation from self-presence, inflicted by the
realization of dependence on an 'other.'" It is Lacan's surmise that
the child's playing with language allows it to forget what has been lost
and to direct its attention to something both present and fulfilling.
Essentially, this moment represents the initial activation of the Symbolic, as opposed to the Imaginary, register in the child. "Lacan's reading [of the *Fort! Da!* episode] in particular supports this suggestion,"
she says, for Lacan emphasizes "that the repetitiveness of the game
'destroys' the reality of the object and creates a substitute 'reality' that
is imaginary" in its function, but Symbolic in its location. As is typical,
Lacan's comment—"His action thus negatives the field of forces of
desire in order to become its own object to itself" (*Ecrits: A Selection*
103)—is less direct, more abstract, than that of the commentator. For
her part, Boheemen says, "The utterance originally intended as substitute thus becomes its own goal and satisfaction." The child, in short,
"produces its own alternative reality" (18) in its creation of an interface
between the Imaginary and the Symbolic, though the two registers will
not become bound or knotted together until the passage through the
Oedipal stage and the assumption of the Name-of-the-Father.

It is possible for literature generally and fiction in particular to serve
the individual's psychological needs in their turn because of their repeating, in a metaphoric—or allegorical—way, what Lacan calls the
mirror stage. "In order to gain a sense of bodily unity and mastery, of
self-coherence, the individual human subject uses the image of his or
her body in the mirror as a projective gestalt," says Boheemen, sum-
marizing basic Lacanian theory, as well as expressing Ragland-Sullivan's

Lacanian poetics in a slightly different way. "The child's idea of himself or herself as 'self' is mediated by this totalizing reflection in the medium," she adds. More important, from the standpoint of the genre of the novel, she contends that its "psychological function, its synthetic combination of fact and fiction, as well as its role in contemporary culture, are best understood by analogy to these ideas of Lacan" regarding the mirror function of objects. "Through its aesthetically patterned language, the genre [of the novel] provides the transitional substitute for an undifferentiated participation in nature, almost making up for the loss of symbiosis with the mother in the projection of its own cultural reality. As realistic narrative providing a totalizing representation, a fully rounded life story of an individual subject in contemporary history, the novel gives mankind the imago of a distinct, self-present subjectivity" (18). But, Boheemen contends, there is a historical as well as an aesthetic reason why the novel became so useful to subjects in Western culture. That reason has to do with the cultural shift from a theological to a secular or humanist worldview. Just as the mirror image in the mirror stage gives the infant a sense of itself not only as total but also as transcendent (both totality and transcendence illusory, of course), so also did the invention of the novel, by projecting the reader as subject into a transcendent role, provide the subject with a sense of totality and transcendence—as Ragland-Sullivan suggests, a totality and a transcendence that are unconscious elements of the ego contained by the imagined wholeness of the literary text. Says Boheemen, the novel, since its rise in Western culture, has been "the medium that preeminently (more than philosophy, science, history, or latitudinarian theology) constituted and validated the idea of the transcendent subjectivity of human beings" (19).

Besides the mirror stage, Boheemen relates the aesthetics of the novel to the notion of "primal fantasies." Primal fantasies, according to Laplanche and Pontalis (*The Language of Psycho-Analysis*), have to do with the child's speculations about origins, and include the primal scene and scenes of castration and seduction. The focus of the primal scene, for example, is mainly upon the enigma of where the child comes from, how it was made, from one alone or by the union of two, and, if by the latter means, then how? But the novel as a genre does not establish a simple relation to the primal fantasy of origins. Viewed in the anthropological terms of Claude Lévi-Strauss, the mode of origin that the novel establishes falls under the category of "from one, not from two." That mode of origin determines the genre's most conventional plots, precisely those plots exemplified in the novels on which Boheemen focuses in this study: *Tom Jones, Bleak House,* and *Ulysses.* The novel-as-genre, as these exemplary texts suggest, covers over the subject's relation to an origin from the mother to aggrandize the origin from the father. "What makes the novel as [a] form of discourse relating origin and identity unique," says Boheemen, "is its attempt to deny the ineluctable otherness, the presence of absence, the ontological gap that necessitates discourse. Mimetic fiction, in presenting itself not as a mediated, provisional image but as a true reflection, short-circuits the presence of otherness, the lack of full being which inspires and marks human communication in language. The novel represses, or tries to repress, the absence of the mother" (19–20). This repression, moreover, is linked to the very conventions of realism in literature, conventions focused primarily in the novel. Realism itself is little more than a repetition of the concept of the mirror stage. Emphatically, Boheemen says, "the convention of realism—which . . . tautologically mirrors contemporary assumptions about truth, identity, and causality—narcissistically allows humanity to ignore the presence of otherness outside and inside the self. Realism, excluding the different, confirms expectations and affirms self-identity, in turn allowing readers to forget they are dealing with a medium: humanity can take itself for its mirror image" (20).

To this point, Boheemen has been engaged in putting into place a Lacanian poetics, one that is essentially consistent—I would say—with the one derived from Ragland-Sullivan and discussed in my Introduction. What follows, however, is perhaps more critical for our sense of that poetics, for Boheemen answers the question regarding its capacity to become an aesthetics and to deal with literary—or, more generally, cultural—history. Inevitably, since the novel as a genre stands in a subjected relation to culture and its dominating instrument (language), changes that have taken place historically are reflected in the novel's history. Boheemen shows these changes in the course of her analyses of *Tom Jones, Bleak House,* and *Ulysses.* Though there are specific cultural changes reflected in those exemplary fictions by Fielding, Dickens, and Joyce, and, moreover, these range across the whole history of the novel, Boheemen contends—rightly, of course, as other feminist critics have shown—that our culture has not yet overturned the patriarchal, phallogocentric orientations that have marked it for centuries.

Though the potential exists for revolutionary changes, she does not argue that subjects can escape the domination of patriarchy just yet. Boheemen's concern is with the problem that patriarchy and logocentrism represent not just for women, but all those "others" patriarchy posits as standing over against it and helping to define the way the culture thinks.[1] "Patriarchy is the received structure of reason, truth, meaning—in short, of culture as we understand it. Its 'plot' is the exclusion of the presence of the 'other.' The novel as family romance, reductively personifying the complexity of experience as the contrastive pair of father and mother, is both the intensified reflection of the implication of gender in signification and the prime object for studying its history and functioning, especially with regard to the constitution of the subject" (30). Fortunately, for those images of the other such as women and minorities, there is at least the possibility of cultural change, and so there exists the possibility that the relation of these excluded subjects to the hegemonic (that is, the *same* and the *male*) may also change.

Many contemporary critics, especially feminist critics, contend that they see a submersion of patriarchy in specific works through the historical development of the novel, and, more important, that the revolution may be observed in the form now associated with Modernism, especially the Modernist novel. Boheemen is pessimistic on both these points. Works from the past that have been interpreted as overthrowing the hegemony of the patriarchal end up merely reifying it in new ways. Boheemen admits that women writers are placed in a double bind in regard, for example, to works such as Charlotte Brontë's *Jane Eyre*. Indeed, she says that while "*Jane Eyre* would seem to be the living proof that there is an alternative female aesthetic that escapes patriarchal determination" (33), when one looks at this novel's "strategies of articulation," it turns out not to represent a very clean-cut feminist aesthetic at all. At the novel's level of articulation, patriarchy remains triumphant. Boheemen's remarks on the novel show precisely the double-bind in which feminists are caught:

> Jane's reunion with Rochester, the seeming triumph of feminine desire, is brought about at the expense of the exclusion of the otherness of Rochester's legal wife: a man-eating monster, a vampire, "intemperate" and "unchaste," worse than any harlot, a "clothed hyena," with "virile force" (resembling in stature and

type of beauty Jane's rival Blanche Ingram). We may well echo the question of the text: "What crime was this, that lived incarnate in this sequestered mansion, and could neither be expelled nor subdued by its owner?—what mystery, that broke out, now in fire and now in blood, at the deadest hours of night? What creature was it, that, masked in an ordinary woman's face and shape, uttered the voice, now of a mocking demon, and anon of a carrion-seeking bird of prey?" (*Jane Eyre* 239–40). The answer is, of course, a woman, an excluded woman—woman as patriarchy connotes and fears her. (35–36)

But if traditional works such as Brontë's do not escape the toils of patriarchy, what about Modernist experimentalism? Some feminist critics contend that the experimental forms of Modernist fiction such as Joyce's, Woolf's, and Faulkner's offer another way out, even if the conventional novel of realism or romance does not. One reason this opportunity may seem to exist, Boheemen suggests, is related to the epistemological changes that Michel Foucault has analyzed in *The Order of Things*. The most germane changes Foucault is concerned with relate to what we might regard as philosophy of language.[2] Foucault has argued that there has been a movement from language regarded as "representation" (found in the epoch when the novel emerged as a genre) to language regarded as "signification," language as being no more than a "sign" in a differential system of signs for which there is no real origin or any but an arbitrary authority. The very arbitrariness of the sign, Boheemen suggests, might have led to the conclusion that any encoding of gender or even "otherness" would itself be remarked as arbitrary. "Foucault alerts us," she says, "to the tie between the conceptualization of the idea of the mother and the attitude to language. Language, as medium of communication, is defined by its relation to indecidability" (41). She links this to Umberto Eco's notion (which is also Lacan's) that language-as-sign is related to the possibility of lying and so to the authority of paternity. "This possible presence of the lie is what language has in common with woman (who can hide paternity), and just as an ideal patriarchy must repress the possibility of equivocation concerning patrilinear descent, it must fix the referential dispersion of words for absolute self-presence. Thus the history of the inscription of woman in patriarchy is tied to patriarchy's understanding of language and its style of narrative authority" (41).

We would be in error to conclude that such a view of language, which is expressly exhibited in *Ulysses,* suggests that in any sense patriarchy has been overcome at last. True, Joyce gives the feminine a dominant place in this novel, and the novel in turn "flaunts its subversive otherness" in its style, itself "coded feminine" (41). But once again a putatively revolutionary work ends up merely validating in different ways the patriarchal system within which it was created. "Joyce's move is not the opening up to the originary presence of the 'other' but the assimilation of those qualities coded 'other' to what remains the constitutive instrument of patriarchy: discourse, text. The inscription of Molly Bloom—Joyce's creature and muse—remains the obsessed projection of patriarchal ideas of otherness. It still codes the 'other' by means of sexual difference" (41–42). This otherness—Woman—becomes the otherness inscribed most pervasively within the discourse of Modernism.[3] Boheemen calls this epochal style "Modernity," a word—I would suggest—that trails clouds of associations with another term that stands opposite patriarchy: "Maternity." The maternal is *the* text inscribed on/within the mode of the Modern. But that Modernist inscription of maternity, Boheemen contends, does not represent a triumph over patriarchy. "Instead of breaking down the patriarchal project, Modernity provides its most sophisticated expression. Sublating difference, marking everything 'inscription,' it subverts the reality and importance of body, flesh, and matter, which are 'always already' denoted patriarchal text." Boheemen's figure of the eternal female is Eve, and, says Boheemen, "Eve has finally become totally disembodied" (42). Boheemen is not any happier with this result than any other feminist critic, but she does feel that if we will but recognize that gender and otherness are *merely* encoded in an arbitrary and thus changeable system, then change remains possible. "All inscriptions and legitimations are human products, and the future need not be like the present. If that future is to come about—however impossible it may be, at present, to *think* it—we must continue to investigate the complex configurations of woman, origin, and authority in the discourses of our culture" (43).

These four critics—Felman, Clément, MacCannell, and Boheemen—suggest once more that not only is there a viable Lacanian discourse, but also that there is an ongoing Lacanian discourse that takes one into many domains of modern thought. I advert to these four because they broaden my horizons, but the fact remains that *Using Lacan, Reading Fiction* is primarily directed toward just one aspect of that Lacanian discourse, the one devoted to reading fiction. Apart from any conclusions one may draw from my own explanations of Lacan and then the use of Lacan in the reading of specific texts, it seems pretty evident that a Lacanian criticism not only is possible but is being put into very enlightening practice by a large number of readers. Critics such as Jameson, Culler, Brooks, and Ragland-Sullivan—not to mention many others such as Davis, Felman, Wilden, and MacCannell, as well as dozens of participants at the Lacanian conferences held at Kent State University (May of 1988, 1989, and 1990)—certainly ought to have made it clear not only that the necessary elements are in place for a Lacanian criticism of literature, but also what those elements are for a Lacanian—indeed, for any—adequate criticism. First, it must reflect the signifying practices of a culture. Second, it must reflect the self's— the ego's—dependency upon those signifying practices. Third, it must regard those signifying practices as the *subject* of *the* subject—that is, as the desire of the subject. Finally, it must regard those signifying practices and the formations of the subject across the dimension of time; that is, it must show that discursive practices, in Foucault's sense, are historical.

To conclude, it seems especially evident in the work of Boheemen and many others (see the selected bibliography of Lacanian interpretation) that such a criticism is now also being put into practice in ways that go beyond what any of us might have thought possible. Boheemen, for example, does not merely provide extraordinarily fruitful readings of specific works such as *Tom Jones, Bleak House,* and *Ulysses;* she also puts these readings into a needful historical perspective that is as much informed by Lacanian theory as the readings themselves. I believe that what she and others such as Fredric Jameson (see *The Political Unconscious*) have done is possible only within the sort of perspective that Lacan brings to literary analysis. Because Lacan insists upon the letter, insists upon the role of language in the constitution of our culture, and upon language as the heart of the culture that constitutes our "individuality" from the Other, it seems to me that Lacan permits us to read texts both synchronically and diachronically, both as virtual stand-alone objects and as objects conditioned, if not totally determined, by time and history. As Hans Kellner has suggested, the anxiety of most critics today, particularly those influenced by explicitly materialist theories, is that any psychoanalytic "allegory" will deracinate the text and the individual subject from its historical existence. It seems to me that a Lacanian poetics and its attendant aesthetics such as Ragland-Sullivan exposits and many others recognize demonstrates that no uprooting is now necessary. It is possible to see now that a synchronic Lacanian allegory can be historicized, even if it has not always been so handled in the readings—the *uses* of Lacan—we ordinarily see. But history, of course, will change that.

Notes

1. See Frantz Fanon's *Black Skin, White Masks* for a specifically Lacanian analysis of ways in which a dominant culture imposes itself upon the identities of "the other" in a culture, of blacks, for example, within a dominant white culture.

2. For further discussion of Foucault on the changes in philosophy of language from the Renaissance to the modern age, see my *Doing Tropology* and White's "Foucault Decoded," in his *Tropics of Discourse*.

3. See Terry Eagleton's *Literary Theory* (187–91) for a brief discussion of the relations of gender to the Lacanian registers of the Imaginary ("feminine" or maternal) and the Symbolic ("masculine" or paternal) as they are propounded in the work of Julia Kristeva (*Revolution in Poetic Language*). Eagleton, I might add, is very good on psychoanalytic literary theory, though his own persuasion is Marxist, but both he and Kristeva probably represent what will come to be understood as a 1970s understanding of Lacan. The understanding of the 1980s and 1990s no doubt will be that of scholars such as Ragland-Sullivan, Slavoj Zizek, Jacques-Alain Miller, Mark Bracher, and others connected with the annual Lacan conferences begun in 1988 at Kent State University and carried on in the 1990s at other cities around the Americas, Europe, and Australia.

Works Cited

Boheemen, Christine van. *The Novel as Family Romance: Language, Gender, and Authority from Fielding to Joyce.* Ithaca: Cornell University Press, 1987.

Brontë, Charlotte. *Jane Eyre.* Ed. Q. D. Leavis. Harmondsworth: Penguin, 1976.

Brooks, Peter. "The Idea of a Psychoanalytic Criticism." *Critical Inquiry* 13 (Winter 1987): 334-48.

Clément, Catherine. *The Lives and Legends of Jacques Lacan.* Trans. Arthur Goldhammer. New York: Columbia University Press, 1983.

——. *The Weary Sons of Freud.* Trans. Nicole Ball. London: Verso, 1987.
Eagleton, Terry. "Psychoanalysis." Chap. 5 in *Literary Theory: An Introduction.* Oxford: Blackwell, 1983, 151–93.
Fanon, Frantz. *Black Skin, White Masks.* Trans. Charles Lam Markmann. New York: Grove Press, 1967. Orig. pub. as *Peau noire, masques blancs.* Paris: Seuil, 1952.
Felman, Shoshana. *Jacques Lacan and the Adventure of Insight: Psychoanalysis in Contemporary Culture.* Cambridge: Harvard University Press, 1987.
Foucault, Michel. *The Order of Things.* New York: Pantheon, 1970.
Freud, Sigmund. "Constructions in Analysis." In *The Standard Edition of the Complete Psychological Works of Sigmund Freud,* vol 23. Ed. and trans. James Strachey. London: Hogarth, 1964, 255–79.
Gallop, Jane. *Reading Lacan.* Ithaca: Cornell University Press, 1985.
Jameson, Fredric. *The Political Unconscious: Narrative as a Socially Symbolic Act.* Ithaca: Cornell University Press, 1981.
Kellner, Hans. "Triangular Anxieties: The Present State of European Intellectual History." In *Modern European Intellectual History: Reappraisals and New Perspectives.* Ed. Dominick LaCapra and Stephen Kaplan. Ithaca: Cornell University Press, 1982, 111–36.
Kristeva, Julia. *Revolution in Poetic Language.* Trans. Margaret Waller. New York: Columbia University Press, 1984.
Lacan, Jacques. *Ecrits: A Selection.* Trans. Alan Sheridan. New York: Norton, 1977.
Laplanche, Jean, and J.-B Pontalis. *The Language of Psycho-analysis.* Trans. Donald Nicholson-Smith. New York: Norton, 1973.
Lemaire, Anika. *Jacques Lacan.* Trans. David Macey. London: Routledge and Kegan Paul, 1977.
MacCannell, Juliet Flower. *Figuring Lacan: Criticism and the Cultural Unconscious.* Lincoln: University of Nebraska Press, 1986.
Mellard, James. *Doing Tropology: Analysis of Narrative Discourse.* Urbana: University of Illinois Press, 1987.
Ragland-Sullivan, Ellie. *Jacques Lacan and the Philosophy of Psychoanalysis.* Urbana: University of Illinois Press, 1986.
Schneiderman, Stuart. *Jacques Lacan: The Death of an Intellectual Hero.* Cambridge: Harvard University Press, 1983.
Turkle, Sherry. *Psychoanalytic Politics: Freud's French Revolution.* New York: Basic, 1978.
White, Hayden V. *Metahistory: The Historical Imagination in Nineteenth-Century Europe.* Baltimore: Johns Hopkins University Press, 1973.
——. *Tropics of Discourse: Essays in Cultural Criticism.* Baltimore: Johns Hopkins University Press, 1978.
Wilden, Anthony, ed. *System and Structure: Essays in Communication and Exchange.* 2d. ed. New York: Tavistock, 1980.

SELECTED BIBLIOGRAPHY
OF LACANIAN CRITICISM

The items in this bibliography have been selected from two main sources, the annual bibliographies of the Modern Language Association and Michael Clark, *Jacques Lacan: An Annotated Bibliography* (New York: Garland, 1988).

Ahearn, Edward J. " 'Simplifier avec gloire la femme': Syntax, Synecdoche, Subversion in a Mallarmé Sonnet." *French Review* 58, no. 3 (1985): 349–59.

Alcorn, Marshall, Jr. "Conrad and the Narcissistic Metaphysics of Morality." *Conradiana* 16, no. 2 (1984): 103–23.

Ames, Sanford S. "Pynchon and Visible Language: *Ecriture*." *International Fiction Review* 4, no. 2 (1977): 170–73.

Asp, Carolyn. "Subjectivity, Desire, and Female Friendship in *All's Well That Ends Well*." *Literature and Psychology* 32, no. 4 (1986): 48–63.

Beaver, Harold. "Melville and Modernism." *Dutch Quarterly Review of Anglo-American Letters* 13, no. 1 (1983): 1–15.

Bennett, Donna. " 'Naming the Way Home.' " In *A Mazing Space: Writing Canadian Women Writing*. Ed. Shirley Neuman and Smaro Kamboureli. Edmonton: Longspoon, 1986, 228–45.

Benstock, Shari. "Authorizing the Autobiographical." In *The Private Self: Theory and Practice of Women's Autobiographical Writings*. Ed. Shari Benstock. Chapel Hill: University of North Carolina Press, 1988, 10–33.

Bernheimer, Charles. " 'Etre la matière!': Origin and Difference in Flaubert's *La tentation de Saint Antoine*." *Novel* 10, no. 1 (1976): 65–78.

Bishop, P. E. "Brecht, Hegel, Lacan: Brecht's Theory of *Gest* and the Problem of the Subject." *Studies in Twentieth-Century Literature* 10 (1986): 267–88.

Blake, Nancy. "Fiction as Screen Memory." *Delta: Révue du centres d'études et de recherche sur les écrivains du sud aux Etats-Unis* (Montpelier, France) 21 (Oct. 1985): 95–104.

———. " 'Out of Time, Out of Body': An Erotic Map of *The Heart of the Heart of the Country*." *Révue française d'études américaines* 20 (1984): 265–74.

Bleikasten, André. "Fathers in Faulkner." In Davis, ed., *The Fictional Father*, 115–46.

———. "Writing on the Flesh: Tattoos and Taboos in 'Parker's Back.' " *Southern Literary Journal* 14, no. 2 (1982): 8–18.

Bogue, Ronald L. "Meaning and Ideology in Robbe-Grillet's *Topologie d'une cité fantôme*." *Modern Language Studies* 14, no. 1 (1984): 33–46.

Boheemen, Christine van. "Chaucer's *Knight's Tale* and the Structure of Myth." *Dutch Quarterly Review of Anglo-American Letters* 9, no. 3 (1979): 176–90.

———. *The Novel as Family Romance: Language, Gender, and Authority from Fielding to Joyce.* Ithaca: Cornell University Press, 1987.

———. " 'The Universe Makes an Indifferent Parent': *Bleak House* and the Victorian Family Romance." In *Interpreting Lacan.* Ed. Joseph H. Smith and William Kerrigan. Psychiatry and the Humanities, vol. 6. New Haven: Yale University Press, 1983, 225–57. Also in Boheemen, *The Novel as Family Romance*, 101–31.

Brenkman, John. "The Other and the One: Psychoanalysis, Reading, and *The Symposium*." *Yale French Studies* 55–56 (1977): 396–456.

Broca, Roland. "La fonction de l'écrit dans la psychose." In *Littérature et psychanalyse: Une clinique de l'écriture.* Nantes: Department of Psychology, University of Nantes, 1986, 102–33.

Brooks, Peter. "Godlike Science/Unhallowed Arts: Language and Monstrosity in *Frankenstein*." *New Literary History* 9 (1978): 591–605.

Brown, Homer Obed. "The Errant Letter and the Whispering Gallery." *Genre* 10, no. 4 (1977): 573–99.

Buckley, Jerome. "The Persistence of Tennyson." In *Victorian Experience: The Poets.* Ed. Richard Levine. Athens: Ohio University Press, 1982, 1–22.

Burk, Robert Eugene. "Reading Shepard and Lacan: A Dramaturgy of the Subject." *Dissertation Abstracts International* 47, no. 2 (June 1987): 4236A.

Burkman, Katherine H. "Pinter's *Betrayal*: Life before Death—and After." *Theatre Journal* 34 (1982): 505–18.

Calderwood, James L. "Appalling Property in *Othello*." *University of Toronto Quarterly* 57 (Spring 1988): 353–75.

Carey, Douglas M. "*Lazarillo de Tormes* and the Quest for Authority." *PMLA* 94 (1979): 36–46.

Carmichael, Virginia. "In Search of Beein': *Nom/Non du pere* in *David Copperfield*." *ELH* 54 (Fall 1987): 653–67.

Carpenter, Mary Wilson. " 'A Bit of Her Flesh': Circumcision and 'The Signification of the Phallus' in *Daniel Deronda*." *Genders* 1 (Mar. 1988): 1–23.

Carroll, David. "For Example: Psychoanalysis and Fiction or the Conflict of Generation(s)." *Sub-Stance* 21 (1978): 49–67.

Casillo, Robert. "Antisemitism, Castration, and Usury in Ezra Pound." *Criticism* 25, no. 3 (1983): 239–65.

Cassell, Anthony K. "The Letter of Envy, *Purgatorio* XIII-XIV." *Stanford Italian Review* 4 (1984): 5–22.

Champagne, Roland A. "The Architectural Pattern of a Literary Artifact: A Lacanian Reading of Balzac's 'Jesus Christ en Flandre.' " *Studies in Short Fiction* 15 (1978): 49–54.

Charney, Hannah. "Lacan, Don Juan, and the French Detective." *L'esprit créateur* 26, no. 2 (Summer 1986): 15–25.

Chase, Cynthia. "The Accidents of Disfiguration: Limits to Literal and Rhetorical Reading in Book V of *The Prelude.*" *Studies in Romanticism* 18 (1979): 547–65.

———. "Oedipal Textuality: Reading Freud's Reading of *Oedipus.*" *Diacritics* 9, no. 1 (1979): 54–68.

Cixous, Hélène. "Introduction to Lewis Carroll's *Through the Looking Glass* and *The Hunting of the Snark.*" Trans. Marie Maclean. *New Literary History* 13 (1982): 231–51.

Claridge, Laura P. "Discourse of Desire: The Paradox of Romantic Poetry (Vols. I and II)." *Dissertations Abstract International* 47, no. 4 (Oct. 1986): 1330A.

Clark, Michael. "Imaging the Real: Jameson's Use of Lacan." *New Orleans Review* 11, no. 1 (1984): 67–72.

———. "The Lure of the Text; or Uncle Toby's Revenge." In *Murray Krieger and Contemporary Critical Theory.* Ed. Bruce Henricksen. New York: Columbia University Press, 1986, 135–56.

Clark, Nate. "Joyce and Lacan: Re-reverberating Discourses." In *James Joyce: The Augmented Ninth.* Ed. Bernard Benstock. Syracuse: Syracuse University Press, 1988, 188–94.

Cook, Carol June. "Imagining the Other: Reading Gender Differences in Shakespeare." *Dissertation Abstracts International* 47, no. 7 (Jan. 1987): 2592A.

Cousineau, Thomas J. "Descartes, Lacan, and *Murphy.*" *College Literature* 11 (1984): 223–32.

———. "*Molloy* and the Paternal Metaphor." *Modern Fiction Studies* 29, no. 1 (1983): 81–91.

———. "The Significance of Repetition in Beckett's *Embers.*" *Southern Humanities Review* 19, no. 4 (Fall 1985): 313–21.

———. " 'Watt': Language as Interdiction and Consolation." *Journal of Beckett Studies* 4 (1979): 1–13.

Cummings, Katherine. "Clarissa's 'Life with Father.' " *Literature and Psychology* 32, no. 4 (1986): 30–36.

Dauber, Kenneth. "The Problem of Poe." *Georgia Review* 32, no. 3 (1978): 645–57.

Davis, Robert Con. "Lacan, Poe, and Narrative Repression." In Davis, ed., *Lacan and Narration*, 983–1005.

———. "Post-modern Paternity: Donald Barthelme's *The Dead Father.*" In Davis, ed., *The Fictional Father*, 169–82.

———, ed. *The Fictional Father: Lacanian Readings of the Text.* Amherst: University of Massachusetts Press, 1981.

———, ed. *Lacan and Narration: The Psychoanalytic Difference in Narrative Theory.* Baltimore: Johns Hopkins University Press, 1983.

Detweiler, Robert H. "Updike's *A Month of Sundays* and the Language of the Unconscious." *Journal of the American Academy of Religion* 47 (1979): 609–25.

Diamond, Elin. "Refusing the Romanticism of Identity: Narrative Interventions in Churchill, Benmussa, Duras." *Theater Journal* 37, no. 3 (Oct. 1985): 273–86.

Dolis, John. "Hawthorne's Morphology of Alienation: The Psychosomatic Phenomenon." *American Imago* 41, no. 1 (1984): 47–62.

Durand, Régis. "Aphanisis: A Note on the Dramaturgy of the Subject in Narrative Analysis." In Davis, ed., *Lacan and Narration*, 860–70.

———. "On the Pertinaciousness of the Father, the Son, and the Subject: The Case of Donald Barthelme." In *Critical Angles: European Views of Contemporary American Literature*. Ed. Marc Chenetier. Carbondale: Southern Illinois University Press, 1986, 153–63.

———. " 'The Captive King': The Absent Father in Melville's Text." In Davis, ed., *The Fictional Father*, 48–72.

Eagleton, Terry. *The Rape of Clarissa: Writing, Sexuality, and Class Struggle in Samuel Richardson*. Oxford: Basil Blackwood, 1982.

Earl, James W. "Eve's Narcissism." *Milton Quarterly* 19, no. 1 (Mar. 1985): 13–16.

Ebbatson, Roger. "The Opening of *The Rainbow*." In *D. H. Lawrence 1885–1930: A Celebration*. Ed. Andrew Cooper. Nottingshire: D. H. Lawrence Society, 1987, 72–76.

Ellmann, Maud. "Floating the Pound: The Circulation of the Subject of *The Cantos*." *Oxford Literary Review* 3, no. 3 (1979): 16–27.

———. "Spacing Out: A Double Entendre on Mallarmé." *Oxford Literary Review* 3, no. 2 (1978): 22–31.

Felman, Shoshana. "Turning the Screw of Interpretation." *Yale French Studies* 55–56 (1977): 94–207.

Ferguson, Margaret W. "*Hamlet*: Letters and Spirits." In *Shakespeare and the Question of Theory*. Ed. Patricia Parker and Geoffrey Hartman. New York: Methuen, 1985, 292–309.

———. "Sidney's *A Defence of Poetry*: A Retrial." *Boundary 2* 7, no. 2 (1979): 61–95.

Ferrar, Peter. "Why Molly Menstruates: The Language of Desire." *Sub-Stance* 4 (1972): 51–62.

Ferry, Anne. *The 'Inward Language': Sonnets of Wyatt, Sidney, Shakespeare, Donne*. Chicago: University of Chicago Press, 1983.

Fineman, Joel. "Fratricide and Cuckoldry: Shakespeare's Doubles." *The Psychoanalytic Review* 64 (1977): 409–53.

———. *Shakespeare's Perjured Eye: The Invention of Poetic Subjectivity in the Sonnets*. Berkeley: University of California Press, 1985.

———. "The Structure of Allegorical Desire." In *Allegory and Representation*. Ed. Stephen Greenblatt, Jr. Baltimore: Johns Hopkins University Press, 1981, 26–60.

Flieger, Jerry Aline. "Trial and Error: The Case of the Textual Unconscious." *Diacritics* 11, no. 1 (1981): 56–67.

Foshay, Toby. "The Desire of Writing and the Writing of Desire in *Ulysses*." *Dalhousie Review* 62 (1982): 87–104.

Freccero, Carla. "The 'Instance' of the Letter: Woman in the Text of Rabelais." *Literature and Psychology* 32, no. 4 (1986): 18–29.

George, Diana Hume. "Who Is the Double Ghost Whose Head Is Smoke? Women Poets on Aging." In Woodward and Schwartz, eds., *Memory and Desire*, 134–53.

Godin, Jean Guy. "Sur le Sinthome." In *James Joyce: The Augmented Ninth*. Ed. Bernard Benstock. Syracuse: Syracuse University Press, 1988, 210–14.

Goldberg, Jonathan. *Voice Terminal Echo: Postmodernism and English Renaissance Texts*. New York: Methuen, 1986.

Gould, Eric. *Mythical Intentions in Modern Literature*. Princeton: Princeton University Press, 1981.

Green, André. "The Unbinding Process." Trans. Lionel Ouisit. *New Literary History* 12 (1980): 11–39.

———. *Un oeil en trop: Le complexe d'Oedipe dans la tragédie*. Paris: Editions du Minuit, 1969.

Grossman, Marshall. "Milton's Dialectical Visions." *Modern Philology* 82, no. 1 (1984): 23–39.

Halpern, Richard. "The Great Instauration: Imaginary Narratives in Milton's 'Nativity Ode.' " In *Re-membering Milton: Essays on the Texts and Traditions*. Ed. Mary Nyquist and Margaret W. Ferguson. New York: Methuen, 1987, 3–24.

Hanzo, Thomas A. "Paternity and the Subject in *Bleak House*." In Davis, ed., *The Fictional Father*, 27–47.

Harasym, S. D. "Ideology and the Self: A Theoretical Discussion of the 'Self' in Mary Wollstonecraft's Fiction." *English Studies in Canada* 12, no. 2 (June 1986): 163–77.

Hengen, Shannon. " 'Your Father the Thunder, Your Mother the Rain': Lacan and Atwood." *Literature and Psychology* 32, no. 3 (1986): 36–42.

Hirsh, Elizabeth A. " 'New Eyes': H. D., Modernism, and the Psychoanalysis of Seeing." *Literature and Psychology* 32, no. 3 (1986): 1–10.

Hobson, Irmagard W. "Goethe's Iphigénie: A Lacanian Reading." *Goethe Yearbook* 2 (1984): 51–67.

Hogan, Patrick Colm. "James Joyce/Jacques Lacan: Introduction." In *James Joyce: The Augmented Ninth*. Ed. Bernard Benstock. Syracuse: Syracuse University Press, 1988, 181–83.

———. "*King Lear*: Splitting and Its Epistemic Agon." *American Imago* 36 (1979): 32–44.

———. "*Macbeth*: Authority and Progenitorship." *American Imago* 40 (1983): 385–95.

Hogan, Patrick Colm, and Lalita Pandit, eds. *Criticism and Lacan: Essays and Dialogue on Language, Structure, and the Unconscious*. Athens: University of Georgia Press, 1990.

Irwin, John T. "The Dead Father in Faulkner." In Davis, ed., *The Fictional Father*, 147–68.

Jacobus, Mary. "Wordsworth and the Language of the Dream." *ELH* 46 (1979): 618–44.

Jameson, Fredric. "Imaginary and Symbolic in *La rabouilleuse*." *Social Science Information* 16, no. 1 (1977): 59–81.

Kahane, Claire. "The Nuptials of Metaphor: Self and Other in Virginia Woolf." *Literature and Psychology* 30 (1980): 72–82.

Kauffman, Linda. "Devious Channels of Decorous Ordering: A Lover's Discourse in *Absalom, Absalom!*" *Modern Fiction Studies* 29 (1983): 183–200.

Kerrigan, William. "Psychoanalysis Unbound." *New Literary History* 12, no. 1 (1980): 199–206.

———. "Ritual Man: On the Outside of Herbert's Poetry." *Psychiatry* 48, no. 1 (1985): 68–82.

Kitch, Sally L. "Gender and Language: Dialect, Silence, and the Disruption of Discourse." *Women's Studies* 14 (1987): 66–78.

Kneale, J. Douglas. "Wordsworth's Images of Language: Voice and Letter in *The Prelude*." *PMLA* 101 (1986): 351–61.

Lernout, Geert. "Joyce or Lacan." Trans. Albert Sonnenfeld. In *James Joyce: The Augmented Ninth*. Ed. Bernard Benstock. Syracuse: Syracuse University Press, 1988, 195–203.

Liu, Alan. "Toward a Theory of Common Sense: Beckford's *Vathek* and Johnson's *Rasselas*." *Texas Studies in Literature and Language* 26, no. 2 (1984): 183–217.

———. "Wordsworth, the History in 'Imagination.' " *ELH* 51 (1984): 505–48.

Logan, Marie-Rose. "Rhetorical Analysis: Towards a Tropology of Reading." *New Literary History* 9 (1978): 619–25.

Lukacher, Ned. "K(Ch)ronosology." *Sub-Stance* 25 (1979): 55–73.

MacCannell, Juliet Flower. "Oedipus Wrecks: Lacan, Stendhal, and the Narrative Form of the Real." In Davis, ed., *Lacan and Narration*, 910–40.

———. "Nature and Self-love: A Reinterpretation of Rousseau's 'Passion Primitive.' " *PMLA* 92 (1977): 890–902.

Macksey, Richard. " 'Alas, Poor Yorick': Sterne Thoughts." In Davis, *Lacan and Narration*, 1006–20.

Marquis, Claudia. "The Power of Speech: Life in *The Secret Garden*." *Journal of the Australasian Universities Language and Literature Association* 68 (Nov. 1987): 163–87.

Mellard, James M. "The Disappearing Subject: A Lacanian Reading of *The Catcher in the Rye*." In *Essays on J. D. Salinger*. Ed. Joel Salzberg. Boston: G. K. Hall, 1989, 197–214.

———. "Faulkner's Miss Emily and Blake's 'Sick Rose': 'Invisible Worm,' *Nachträglichkeit*, and Retrospective Gothic." *The Faulkner Journal* 2, no. 1 (Fall 1986): 37–45.

———. "Flannery O'Connor's *Others*: Freud, Lacan, and the Unconscious." *American Literature* 61, no. 4 (Dec. 1989): 625–43.

———. "Lacan and Faulkner: A Post-Freudian Analysis of Humor in the Fiction." In *Faulkner and Humor*. Ed. Ann Abadie and Doreen Fowler. Jackson: University Press of Mississippi, 1986, 195–215.

——. "Pearl and Hester: A Lacanian Reading." In *Critical Essays on "The Scarlet Letter."* Ed. David Kesterson. Boston: G. K. Hall, 1988, 193–211.

——. "The 'Perverse Economy' of Malamud's Art: A Lacanian Reading of *Dubin's Lives.*" In *Critical Essays on Bernard Malamud.* Ed. Joel Salzberg. Boston: G. K. Hall, 1987, 186–203.

——. "*Something Happened:* The Imaginary, the Symbolic, and the Discourse of the Family." In *Critical Essays on Joseph Heller.* Ed. James Nagel. Boston: G. K. Hall, 1984, 138–55. Also in James Mellard. *Doing Tropology: Analysis of Narrative Discourse.* Urbana: University of Illinois Press, 1987.

Merrill, Cynthia. "Mirrored Image: Gertrude Stein and Autobiography." *Pacific Coast Philology* 20, nos. 1-2 (Nov. 1985): 11–17.

Miller, David Lee. "Spenser's Poetics: The Poem's Two Bodies." *PMLA* 101 (1986): 170–85.

Millot, Catherine. "On Epiphanies." In *James Joyce: The Augmented Ninth.* Ed. Bernard Benstock. Syracuse: Syracuse University Press, 1988, 207–9.

Moore, Kevin Z. "The Beauty and the Beast: Presence/Absence and the Vicissitudes of the Sphinx in Sophocles' *Oedipus Tyrannus* and *Oedipus at Colonus.*" *Boundary 2* 8, no. 3 (1980): 1–42.

Morgan, Veronica. "Reading Hart Crane by Metonymy." *Dissertation Abstracts International* 47, no. 6 (1986): 2160A.

Morris, Wesley. "The Irrepressible Real: Jacques Lacan and Poststructuralism." In *American Criticism in the Poststructuralist Age.* Ed. Ira Konigsberg. Michigan Studies in the Humanities. Ann Arbor: University of Michigan, 1981, 116–34.

Mottram, Eric. "Power and Law in Hawthorne's Fictions." In *Nathaniel Hawthorne: New Critical Essays.* Ed. A. Robert Lee. Totowa: Barnes and Noble, 1982, 187–228.

Muller, John P. "Light and the Wisdom of the Dark: Aging and the Language of Desire in the Texts of Louise Bogan." In Woodward and Schwartz, eds., *Memory and Desire,* 76–96.

——. "Psychosis and Mourning in Lacan's *Hamlet.*" *New Literary History* 12 (1980): 147–65.

Muller, John P., and William J. Richardson. *The Purloined Poe: Lacan, Derrida, and Post-structuralist Reading.* Baltimore: Johns Hopkins University Press, 1988.

Nasio, Juan-David. *Les yeux de Laure: le concept d'objet a dans la théorie de J. Lacan.* Paris: Aubier, 1987.

Neuman, Shirley. "Importing Difference." In *A Mazing Space: Writing Canadian Women Writing.* Ed. Shirley Neuman and Smaro Kamboureli. Edmonton: Longspoon, 1986, 392–405.

Nevo, Ruth. *Shakespeare's Other Language.* New York: Methuen, 1987.

Norris, Christopher D. "Barth and Lacan: The World of the Moebius Strip." *Critique: Studies in Modern Fiction* 17, no. 1 (1975): 69–77.

Norris, Margot. "Narration under a Blindfold: Reading Joyce's 'Clay.' " *PMLA* 102 (1987): 206–15.

Nyquist, Mary. "The Father's Word/Satan's Wrath." *PMLA* 100, no. 2 (Mar. 1985): 187–202.

Oxenhandler, Neal. "The Horizons of Psychocriticism." *New Literary History* 14 (1982): 89–103.

Paccaud, Josiane. "The Name-of-the-Father in Conrad's *Under Western Eyes*." *Conradiana* 18, no. 3 (1986): 204–18.

Pahl, Dennis. "Recovering Byron: Poe's 'The Assignation.'" *Criticism* 26, no. 3 (1984): 211–29.

Patterson, David. "Dostoevsky's *Dvoinik* per Lacan's *Parole*." *Essays in Literature* 10, no. 2 (1983): 299–307.

Pensom, Roger. "Rhetoric and Psychology in Thomas's 'Tristan.'" *Modern Language Review* 78, no. 2 (1983): 285–97.

Perkins, M. L. "The Psychoanalysis *Merveilleux:* Suspense in Sade's *Florville et Courval*." *Sub-Stance* 13 (1976): 107–19.

Perry, Ruth. "Words for Sex: The Verbal-Sexual Continuum in *Tristram Shandy*." *Studies in the Novel* 20 (Spring 1988): 27–42.

Porter, Dennis. "Of Poets, Politicians, Policemen, and the Power of Analysis." *New Literary History* 19 (Spring 1988): 501–19.

Porter, Laurence M. "Mourning and Melancholia in Nerval's *Aurelia*." *Studies in Romanticism* 15 (1976): 289–306.

Prieto, René. "The Two Narrative Voices in Mario Vargas Llosa's *Aunt Julia and the Scriptwriter*." *Latin-American Literary Review* 11, no. 22 (1983): 15–25.

Punter, David. "Angela Carter: Supersessions of the Masculine." *Critique* 25, no. 4 (1984): 209–22.

——. *The Hidden Script: Writing and the Unconscious*. London: Routledge, 1985.

Rabaté, Jean-Michel. "A Clown's Inquest into Paternity: Fathers, Dead or Alive, in *Ulysses* and *Finnegans Wake*." In Davis, ed., *The Fictional Father*, 73–114.

Racevskis, Karlis. "Re(dis)covering Structuralism." *Diacritics* 14, no. 4 (1984): 37–46.

Ragland-Sullivan, Ellie. "Jacques Lacan, Literary Theory, and *The Maids* of Jean Genet." In *Psychological Perspectives on Literature: Freudian Dissidents and Non-Freudians*. Ed. Joseph Natoli. Hamden: Archon, 1984, 100–119.

——. "Lacan, Language, and Literary Criticism." *The Literary Review* 24, no. 4 (1981): 562–77.

——. "The Magnetism between Reader and Text: Prolegomena to a Lacanian Poetics." *Poetics* 13 (1984): 381–406.

——. "The Phenomenon of Aging in Oscar Wilde's *Picture of Dorian Gray:* A Lacanian View." In Woodward and Schwartz, eds., *Memory and Desire*, 114–33.

——. "The Psychology of Narcissism in Jean Genet's *The Maids*." *Gradiva* 2, no. 1 (1979): 19–40.

Ragland-Sullivan, Ellie, and R. B. Kershner. "More French Connections." *James Joyce Quarterly* 26 (Fall 1988): 115–27.

Ragland-Sullivan, Mary Eloise [Ellie]. "Julien's Quest for 'Self': *Qui sui-je?*" *Nineteenth-Century French Studies* 8, nos. 1–2 (1979–80): 1–13.

Rajan, Gita. "A Feminist Rereading of Poe's 'The Tell-Tale Heart.'" *Papers on Language and Literature* 24 (Summer 1988): 283–300.

Rajchman, John. "Foucault, or the Ends of Modernism." *October* 24 (1983): 37–62.

Rapaport, Herman. "Geoffrey Hartman and the Spell of Sounds." *Genre* 17, nos. 1–2 (1984): 159–77.

Reed, Gail S. "Toward a Methodology for Applying Psychoanalysis to Literature." *Psychoanalytic Quarterly* 51, no. 1 (1982): 19–42.

Renner, Charlotte. "The Self-multiplying Narrators of *Molloy, Malone Dies,* and *The Unnameable.*" *Journal of Narrative Technique* 11, no. 1 (1981): 12–32.

Richardson, William J. "Psychoanalysis and the God-Question." *Thought* 61 (1986): 68–83.

Ricoeur, Paul. "The Question of Proof in Freud's Psychoanalytic Writings." *Journal of the American Psychoanalytic Association* 25 (1977): 835–71.

Rimmon, Shlomith. "Problems of Voice in Vladimir Nabokov's *The Real Life of Sebastian Knight.*" *PTL* 1 (1976): 489–512.

Rimmon-Kenan, Shlomith. "Ambiguity and Narrative Levels." *Poetics Today* 3, no. 1 (1982): 21–32.

———. "Doubles and Counterparts: Patterns of Interchangeability in Borges' 'The Garden of the Forking Paths.'" *Critical Inquiry* 6, no. 4 (1980): 639–47.

———. "The Paradoxical Status of Repetition." *Poetics Today* 1, no. 4 (1980): 151–59.

Rosenblum, Dolores. "Face to Face: Elizabeth Barret Browning's *Aurora Leigh* and Nineteenth-Century Poetry." *Victorian Studies* 26 (1983): 321–38.

Ross, Daniel W. "Celie in the Looking Glass: The Desire for Selfhood in *The Color Purple.*" *Modern Fiction Studies* 34 (Spring 1988): 69–84.

Roudiez, Leon S. "*La Condition Humaine:* An Awareness of the Other." *Twentieth Century Literature* 24 (1978): 303–13.

Rowe, John Carlos. "Deconstructing America: Recent Approaches to Nineteenth-Century Literature and Culture." *Emerson Society Quarterly* 31 (1985): 49–63.

Rudnytsky, Peter L. "The Purloined Handkerchief in *Othello.*" In *The Psychoanalytic Study of Literature.* Ed. Joseph Reppen and Maurice Charney. Hillsdale: Analytic Press, 1985, 169–90.

Ryan, Michael. "Narcissus Autobiographer: *Marius the Epicurean.*" *ELH* 43 (1976): 184–208.

———. "Self-deconstruction." *Diacritics* 6, no. 1 (1976): 34–41.

Rzepka, Charles J. "Christabel's 'Wandering Mother' and the Discourse of the Self: A Lacanian Reading of Repressed Narration." *Romanticism Past and Present* 10, no. 1 (Winter 1986): 17–43.

Sadoff, Dianne F. "The Dead Father: *Barnaby Rudge, David Copperfield,* and *Great Expectations.*" *Papers on Language and Literature* 18 (1982): 36–57.

———. "Storytelling and the Figure of the Father in *Little Dorrit.*" *PMLA* 95 (1980): 234–45.

Saldivar, R. "*Jude the Obscure:* Reading and the Spirit of the Law." *ELH* 50 (1983): 607–25.

Scally, Thomas. "Origin and Authority: An Analysis of the Relation between Anonymity and Authorship in Kesey's *One Flew over the Cuckoo's Nest.*" *Dalhousie Review* 62 (1982): 355–73.

Schleifer, Ronald. "Faulkner's Storied Novel: *Go Down, Moses* and the Translation of Time." *Modern Fiction Studies* 28 (1982): 109–27.

———. "The Trap of the Imagination: The Gothic Tradition, Fiction, and 'The Turn of the Screw.' " *Criticism* 22 (1980): 297–319.

Schneiderman, Stuart. "The Saying of Hamlet." *Sub-Stance* 8 (1974): 77–88.

Schwab, Gabriele. "On the Dialectic of Closing and Opening in Samuel Beckett's *End-Game.*" *Yale French Studies* 67 (1984): 191–202.

———. "Reader-Response and the Aesthetic Experience of Otherness." *Stanford Literature Review* 3, no. 1 (1986): 107–36.

Schwartz, M. M., and David Willbern. "Literature and Psychology." In *Interrelations of Literature.* Ed. Jean-Pierre Barricelli and Joseph Gibaldi. New York: MLA, 1982, 215–16.

Schwartz, Nina. "Lovers' Discourse in *The Sun Also Rises:* A Cock and Bull Story." *Criticism* 26, no. 1 (1984): 49–69.

Sedgwick, Eve Kosofsky. "The Character in the Veil: Imagery of the Surface in the Gothic Novel." *PMLA* 96 (1981): 255–70.

Shands, Harley C. "Malinowski's Mirror: Emily Dickinson as Narcissus." *Contemporary Psychoanalysis* 12 (1976): 300–334.

Shapiro, Marianne. "The Status of Irony." *Stanford Literature Review* 2 (1985): 5–26.

Silverman, Hugh J. "Cézanne's Mirror Stage." *Journal of Aesthetics and Art Criticism* 40 (1982): 369–79.

———. "For a Hermeneutic Semiology of the Self." *Philosophy Today* 23, nos. 3–4 (1979): 199–204.

———. "Sartre and the Structuralists." *International Philosophy Quarterly* 18 (1978): 341–58.

Silverman, Kaja. "Histoire d'O: The Construction of a Female Subject." In *Pleasure and Danger: Exploring Female Sexuality.* Ed. Carole S. Vance. Boston: Routledge, 1984, 320–49.

———. "History, Figuration, and Female Subjectivity in *Tess of the d'Urbervilles.*" *Novel* 18 (1984): 5–28.

Simpson, David. "Keats's Lady, Metaphor, and the Rhetoric of Neurosis." *Studies in Romanticism* 15 (1976): 265–88.

Sitterson, Joseph C., Jr. "Psychoanalytic Models and Literary Theory." *University of Toronto Quarterly* 51 (1981): 78–92.

Skoller, Eleanor Honig. "Threads in Three Sections: A Reading of *The Note-books of Malte Laurids Brigge*." *Sub-Stance* 32 (1981): 15–25.

Skulsky, Harold. "The Psychoanalytical Reading of Literature." *Neophilologus* 67 (1983): 321–40.

Snider, Alvin. "The Self-mirroring Mind in Milton and Traherne." *University of Toronto Quarterly* 55, no. 4 (Summer 1986): 313–27.

Soloman, Philip H. "The View from a Rump: America as Journey and Land-scape of Desire in Céline's *Voyage au bout de la nuit*." *Yale French Studies* 57 (1979): 5–22.

Sonne, Harly, and Bent Rosenbaum. "Psychosis, Psychiatry, and the Science of the Text." *Journal of Pragmatics* 5, nos. 2–3 (1981): 205–22.

Sonnenfeld, Albert. "Desire and Fantasm in Joyce/Lacan." In *James Joyce: The Augmented Ninth*. Ed. Bernard Benstock. Syracuse: Syracuse University Press, 184–85.

Spector, Stephen J. "Wordsworth's Mirror Imagery and the Picturesque Tradition." *ELH* 44 (1977): 85–107.

Spivak, Gayatri Chakravorty. "Finding Feminist Readings: Dante-Yeats." *Social Text* 3 (1980): 73–87.

———. "French Feminism in an International Frame." *Yale French Studies* 62 (1981): 154–84.

———. "The Letter as Cutting Edge." *Yale French Studies* 55–56 (1977): 208–26.

———. "Love Me, Love My Ombre, Elle." *Diacritics* 14, no. 4 (1984): 19–36.

Splitter, Randolph. "Proust, Joyce, and the Theory of Metaphor." *Literature and Psychology* 29 (1979): 4–18.

———. "Proust's *Combray*: The Structures of Animistic Projection." *American Imago* 36, no. 2 (1979): 154–79.

———. "Proust's Myth of Artistic Creation." *American Imago* 37 (1980): 386–412.

Spurr, David. "*The Waste Land*: Mourning, Writing, Disappearance." *Yeats Eliot Review* 9 (Summer-Fall 1988): 161–64.

Stamelman, Richard. "The Shroud of Allegory: Death, Mourning, and Melancholy in Baudelaire's Work." *Texas Studies in Literature and Language* 25 (1983): 390–409.

Stoltzfus, Ben. "Camus's *L'Etranger*: A Lacanian Reading." *Texas Studies in Literature and Language* 31, no. 4 (Winter 1989): 514–35.

Tiefenbrun, Susan W. "The State of Literary Semiotics: 1983." *Semiotica* 51, nos. 1–3 (1984): 7–44.

Vergote, Antoine. "Phenomenology and Psychoanalysis: Reflections in Reference to the Book of Alphonse de Waelhens, *Schizophrenia*." *Journal of Phenomenological Psychology* 15, no. 1 (1984): 1–19.

Vivan, Itala. "The Scare in the Letter: An Eye into the Occult in Hawthorne's Text." *Social Science Information* 23, no. 1 (1984): 155–93.

Wasserman, Renata, and R. Mautner. "The Self, the Mirror, the Other: 'The Fall of the House of Usher.'" *Poe Studies* 10, no. 2 (1977): 33–35.

Watson, Robert N. "Who Bids for Tristero: The Conversion of Pynchon's Oedipa Maas." *Southern Humanities Review* 17, no. 1 (1983): 59–75.

Wilden, Anthony. "Death, Desire, and Repetition in Svevo's *Zeno*." *MLN* 84 (1969): 98–119.

———. "Pars divers moyens on arrive a pareille fin: A Reading of Montaigne." *MLN* 83 (1968): 577–97.

Wilson, William. "Behind the Veil, Forbidden: Truth, Beauty, and Swinburne's Aesthetic Strain." *Victorian Poetry* 22 (1984): 427–37.

Wittenberg, Judith Bryant. "Early Hardy Novels and the Fictional Eye." *Novel* 16 (1983): 150–64.

Woodward, Kathleen, and Murray Schwartz, eds. *Memory and Desire: Aging, Literature, Psychoanalysis*. Bloomington: Indiana University Press, 1986.

Wordsworth, Ann. "Household Words: Alterity, the Unconscious and the Text." *Oxford Literary Review* 5, nos. 1–2 (1982): 80–96.

Wright, Elizabeth. "Modern Psychoanalytic Criticism." In *Modern Literary Theory*. Ed. Ann Jefferson and David Robey. Totowa: Barnes and Noble, 1982, 126–32.

———. "The New Psychoanalysis and Literary Criticism: A Reading of Hawthorne and Melville." *Poetics Today* 3, no. 2 (1982): 89–105.

Yaeger, Patricia S. "The Case of the Dangling Signifier: Phallic Imagery in Eudora Welty's 'Moon Lake.'" *Twentieth Century Literature* 28 (1982): 431–52.

Young, Robert. "The Eye and Progress of His Sons: A Lacanian Reading of the *Prelude*." *Oxford Literary Review* 3, no. 3 (1979): 78–98.

———. "Post-structuralism: The End of Theory." *Oxford Literary Review* 5, nos. 1–2 (1982): 3–20.

Zimmerman, Shari A. "Milton's *Paradise Lost*: Eve's Struggle for Identity." *American Imago* 38, no. 3 (1981): 247–67.

INDEX

Abel, Elizabeth, 190n2
Abrahamsen, David: on David Berkowitz ("Son of Sam"), 105n8
Abrams, M. H., 34, 35, 37; his "compass of perspectives," 34-35, 37-38, 61n7
Adams, Michael Vannoy, 103n1
"Agency of the Letter in the Unconscious or Reason since Freud," 7, 23
Aggressiveness, narcissistic: in *The Scarlet Letter*, 75
"Aggressivity in Psychoanalysis," 11, 104n4
Alcorn, Marshall W., Jr., 43, 62n9
Algorithm: Lacan's, 5, 10, 13-14, 23, 24, 49, 51, 82; and formula of repression and metaphor, 52; as monad or synecdoche, 11, 20; Saussure's, 24
Alienation: and castration, 118; desire and, in "The Beast in the Jungle," 117; and language in *The Scarlet Letter*, 76; in mirror stage, 161; onset of, in *The Scarlet Letter*, 77; and scopic drive, 118; and *vel* of, 10, 14, 161
Allegory: anxiety of, in interpretation, 50; and interpretation, 52-53, 55; language and textuality in relation to, 52-53; and sign, 52; and structure of metaphor, 51
Alter ego: see Ideal ego
American Dream, The, 48
Anaclitic: father and, 181; in *To the Lighthouse*, 154
Anal: in *To the Lighthouse*, 154. See also Drives, the
Analyst: Roger Chillingworth as, in *The Scarlet Letter*, 94-103
Annales médico-psychologiques, 199
Aphanisis (or "fading of the subject"), 22, 25, 61n7, 109; and constitution of subject, 116; in *The Scarlet Letter*, 77
Apter, T. E., 167, 190n1
Archetypal criticism, 35
Authority of the Other: foreclosure of, in *The Scarlet Letter*, 88-89; patriarchal, 177

Bakhtin, Mikhail: dialogic, 41

Bal, Mieke, 33
Baltimore: as metaphor of unconscious, 1, 11
Bannet, Eve Tavor, 10
Bär, Eugen: on Heidegger and the Real, 157, 158; "The Language of the Unconscious according to Jacques Lacan," 2; "Understanding Lacan," 2, 59n1, 77, 78-79, 94, 95
Barthes, Roland, 1, 38, 190n7, 199
"Beast in the Jungle, The," 48, 49, 53, 57, 70; and constitution of the subject, 107-36; discussed, 107-39
Beck, Ronald, 137n3
Beckett, Samuel, 38
Bell, Millicent, 103n1
Bellemin-Nöel, Jean, 54
Bentham, Jeremy: "panopticon," 104n7
Benveniste, Emile, 6, 8; Lacan's relation to, 59n2
Benvenuto, Bice, and Roger Kennedy, 58n1
Berkowitz, David: as psychotic "Son of Sam," 101, 105n8
Beyond the Pleasure Principle: discussed by Felman, 198
"Birthmark, The," 101
Boheemen, Christine van, 195, 217, 218; discussion of *Novel as Family Romance* as feminist history of the novel, 208-17; on Freud's *Fort! Da!* and Winnicott's "transitional object," 211-12; on interaction between narrative and constitution of identity, 208-9, 210, 211-13; on *Jane Eyre*, 215-16; on Joyce's Stephen Dedalus, 211; on a Lacanian poetics, 214; on mirror stage and literature, 212-13; on modernism in the novel, 216; on Name-of-the-Father, 212; on the novel as dominant narrative form in Western culture, 211; on the novel as "family romance," 215-16; on patriarchy and the novel, 215-16; on primal fantasies and the novel, 213-14; on realism, 214; on realism in the novel, 209; on registers of

Note on the Author

In addition to many articles on Lacan, James M. Mellard has also written *Doing Tropology: Analysis of Narrative Discourse* and *The Exploded Form: The Modernist Novel in America*. He is professor of English at Northern Illinois University.